NEARLY
FAMOUS

Adventures of an
After-Dinner Speaker

Bob 'The Cat' Bevan

This edition published in Great Britain in 2004 by
Virgin Books
Thames Wharf Studios
Rainville Road
London W6 9HA

First published in 2003 by Virgin Books Ltd

A catalogue record for the book is available from the British Library.

ISBN 0 7535 0906 7

Typeset by TW Typesetting, Plymouth, Devon
Printed and bound in Great Britain by
Mackays of Chatham plc, Chatham, Kent

CONTENTS

DEDICATION

It had crossed my mind to dedicate this book to my friend Brian
Robinson. The fact that you have never heard of him is due entirely
to the self-effacing character of one of the best inventive comic brains
I have ever come across. But more of him later.

Rather more obviously, I had also thought of Laura, my partner, my
fiancée for over ten years and the love of my life. She is also known
as 'Petal' on the basis that she drops off a lot. She does love her sleep.

But no, I'm going to dedicate this book to my father, because he
died while I was writing it. He was 87, so he had a good innings, but
the end was fairly sudden. He had looked after himself until eleven
days before he died. In fact, two days before that we were having lunch
in a pub. So it was a bit of a shock. My mother had died twenty years
earlier and I was much closer to her. I promised Mum, as I was their
only child, that I would look after him. Although we both agreed we
could never live together again, we both made an effort and decided
we quite liked each other most of the time. And, as a friend pointed
out, I had known him for twenty years longer than my mother.

It still has not quite sunk in. From time to time I think of telling
him about my latest bit of news, showing him a photograph or boring
him with our current holiday video. Then I realise he's not there any
more. Once I even had my mobile in my hand to ring him, and at that
point I decided it would be better to take him off the memory. I was
horrified to see him disappear into a Vodafone dustbin. During dark
moments such as this I think of the Noel Coward quotation above.
Although I'm not yet 75, my father mentioned, rather more often than
I would have wished, how much he was looking forward to watching
me draw my pension. He was never slow to hit you with a little black
humour or something that came rather too close to the bull's-eye
of your sensitivities.

He was only little, but he was tough and brave. He was lying on a trolley in the Kent and East Sussex Hospital Accident and Emergency Department ten days before he died. He was just starting to recover from the shock of his heart attack, and of lying on the floor of his flat for several hours, when his humour kicked in again. 'I'm not sure about getting that telegram from the Queen,' he remarked. He had an ambition to be the oldest living resident in his sheltered housing estate. 'In fact, I'm not making any plans for my ninetieth at the moment.'

I was lucky to have a parent last through a longer than average part of my life. A parent who didn't make any demands of me. Who was lucid and competent throughout his days. Who, I was to learn only after he died, was very proud of what I've achieved.

Although I struggled to deliver the words, I felt that as I had spoken at several other funerals I could hardly chicken out for my father. But I still had my cousin Roger standing by, and he was half out of his seat a few times when I choked up as I said these words:

Thanks to you all for coming, and for all the letters and messages that have overwhelmed me in the last week or so. They all speak of my father always having a smile on his face. Of course, I said it was wind.

After my mother died twenty years ago this month he came to many functions with me. At the first he met his big hero Henry Cooper, whom he subsequently met on several more occasions. Among his other heroes was just about anyone from *Dad's Army*. When he met Clive Dunn in Portugal he got uncharacteristically excited. We had to pull him back into the car.

It was cricketer Bob Willis, who always gives people nicknames, who decided that as he was the Cat's dad he should be called Tom. Somehow the name has stuck for nearly twenty years. It stuck so well that on that Lord's Taverners trip to Portugal he was shown on the group passenger list as Mr T. Cat, causing considerable confusion at Portuguese immigration. So although he was christened Eric, many of you also know him as Tom or Tom Eric.

He was born in 1915 into a family which had fled anti-Semitism in eastern Europe. He had two brothers and a sister, Aunt Phil, who's here today. [A few months after my father died a cousin produced a family tree from which I discovered that he had had a third brother, Sidney, who had died as a baby. For some reason my father never told me.] My father's mother and one brother, Gerald, died before the war. They are buried in Bromley along with my mother, and my father's ashes will be laid there soon.

He went to Wilson's Grammar School in Camberwell along with his younger brother, Lionel. They became friendly with one Bob Caden. My father met Bob's sister Iris, they got married, I turned up and, eventually, became the fourth family member to go to Wilson's. It was a proud night for me, when I became President of the Old Boys, to take my father and uncle to the annual dinner. Sadly, my Uncle Lionel had passed away by then.

When my father left school he went into the family business selling rubber soles and heels. He was called up during the war and, much to his own father's surprise, rose to become a Warrant Officer Class 1. He was posted to India before I was born and was responsible for getting stores up to the front. Only when he read Churchill's memoirs in the 1960s did he realise he was a lot closer to the Japs than he had been led to believe.

On his return he found an eighteen-month-old baby waiting for him – jokes about tall milkmen have been banned in the family – but, soon after, his father died and the family firm closed down. He eventually found employment at American Express, and later at Barclays. He never earned a great deal, but I certainly never wanted for anything.

He didn't have the greatest luck in life. He got married the day war broke out so they came back from the church to the sound of air-raid sirens, with no reception or honeymoon. It took us 40 years to put that right at their ruby wedding.

When he retired, he spent the first two years nursing my mother through terminal cancer. I never once saw him cry or heard him complain. He just got on with it. He had toughness and courage, as instanced by his five-hour attempt to reach the cord in his flat when he had the heart attack, and as instanced by his attitude in hospital at the end. He fought all the way.

In small things, though, he was a worrier. When he started going on holiday on his own, no hotel ever passed the Tom Eric quality control test, as he would tell me in great detail. Consequently I cannot now go into a hotel bedroom without checking the kettle for a rusty element. You'll all be doing that now too.

Nor was he totally tactful, especially with my other half, Laura. In the early days he called her 'a middle-aged working bird'. I still don't know how he got away with that. And when she cooked him a meal his highest compliment would be 'saves cooking'. Still, she was wonderful to him, especially at the end. When he wouldn't eat we took him the one thing he said he missed in hospital – a piece of toast cooked by Laura. He would see the irony in it being the last thing he ate.

Whenever I asked him, perhaps rather too often, if he was in pain, he would say, 'Don't go on.' That was virtually the last thing he said to me, and I expect he's thinking the same now, so I'd better stop.

Whenever I dropped him off at home and said goodbye to him, he always said the same thing to me, which I now say to him, 'Thanks for everything.'

So this is for you, Dad, even though you won't be able to read it. Or perhaps you will? In which case it's for Mum as well.

As for you, Robbo, you can have the next one ... but then, what about Laura? Oh sod it. Let's get on with the book.

INTRODUCTION

'It seems entertainer Bob "the Cat" Bevan knows more about Hong Kong than people know about him.'

South China Morning Post, 1990

Unless you believe in reincarnation – and in my more wistful moments I do think how nice it would be if that great spotted woodpecker who brings her young to my bird table might just be my mum – I made my first appearance, just after nine p.m. on Monday, 26 February 1945, in a nursing home in Thurlow Park Road, Dulwich, in south London. There is definitely no blue plaque on the wall there. In fact, I'm not sure now if there's even a wall. I was actually a good-looking baby, and it is not true, as my friend Mick O'Connor often says, that I was so ugly they had to tie a lamb chop round my neck so the dog would play with me. We didn't have a dog.

This book is all about what happened in my life after that birthday. There's a lot of comedy and football, because they have been my major passions. But there's also plenty of cricket and show business, not to mention journalism, public relations, travel, hotels, car ferries and other ships. You will even find, if you look closely, building materials, cattle, Kleen-e-zee brushes and a marquess. Most of all, there is loads of name-dropping – another passion, so my friends tell me.

If you don't enjoy what follows, Virgin Books do, of course, operate a money-back-if-not-delighted guarantee. Now that is a joke.

1. THE WARM-UP

'Mr Chairman, honoured guests, ladies, gentlemen, brother athletes . . .'
Bob 'the Cat' Bevan

This may not be the most famous quotation used in this book, but it is all mine. So if you hear anyone else using it, go and tell them they've nicked it. It is, of course, said with heavy irony. I have always been aware of my sporting limitations and my many failures. But today they have become my fortune.

Of the many things that have happened to me and sent me in a new direction, nothing has been more important than the day I went in goal in an emergency. It prolonged my playing career and brought forth a whole new area of humour for me and many others. It also gave me my nickname, 'the Cat', which, being a commercially minded public relations man, I kept as my gimmick. Many people would not necessarily remember Bob Bevan, but they all recall 'some bloke who calls himself "the Cat"'. Irony is also at the heart of this name. 'The Cat' is a name given to a really good goalkeeper. Remarkably slim and lithe, amazingly agile, and with astonishing cat-like reactions. I am called 'the Cat' because I give my defence kittens.

Terry Neill, former Arsenal and Northern Ireland centre-half and captain, once said to me at a dinner, 'I don't mean to be rude, but do you know what makes your opening line so funny?' He didn't wait for an answer. It can be hard to get a word in when he's talking anyway. 'You don't look like you could run round this table, let alone a football pitch.' Terry went on to manage Hull, Arsenal and – here's another irony – their deadly rivals Tottenham.

British humour is heavy with irony and mickey-taking. It's the sort of humour bred in sports dressing rooms and in any team situation. We are the opposite of our transatlantic cousins. Americans generally don't do irony. They don't understand it. If you make fun of an American he's quite likely to deck you. They take themselves very seriously, and because they don't understand where you're coming from they can quickly take offence. This makes it all the more extraordinary that in *Cheers*, *Friends* and *Frasier* they have produced three of the funniest television programmes ever, the latter being especially sharp. The characters in this show verbally rip one another to shreds.

Clearly, the irony of my opening line has also been lost on Tommy Docherty and my all-time hero Jimmy Greaves. They often use it, but they have missed the point totally. They may not beat me round the table now, but they *were* athletes. So when they say it they don't get a laugh. They were great players. Well, Tommy, who played for Preston, Arsenal and Scotland, was a good player. Maybe a very good player. Jimmy was just legendary. One of the greatest goalscorers of all time. I actually forsook Crystal Palace and even broke my golden rule – of never watching if I had a chance of playing – to go and watch him at Tottenham a few times.

One of the ground rules of using other people's material is to remember where you heard it, and certainly not to do it when the bloke is sitting there. Still, they're professional footballers rather than entertainers, so they can't be expected to know the rules of every game.

There is actually a perverse assumption that because you can do one thing well (i.e. speak at dinners) you are equally adept at everything else. Let me illustrate this for you with a short tale. I remember playing in a midweek game for the Old Wilsonians 6th XI against Centymca 5th XI in the Southern Olympian League ... Minor Section ... Division H. You've got the drift of the level of my footballing ability by now, I think. Let me also advise you that the name Centymca represents the club of the Central London Young Men's Christian Association, ironically one of the dirtiest teams we played against. The game in question took place a few days after my appearance at the Professional Footballers' Association awards dinner in 1981. In those days highlights were broadcast later on ITV across the land, and I had my first 90 seconds of national TV coverage. At half-time it was the home goalkeeper's duty to deliver the small plastic bag of orange quarters to the opposition. On doing so I was recognised by one of the opposition who had clearly not got too close to me during the first half. I heard him ask one of our players, ' 'Ere, is that Bob "the Cat" Bevan who was on telly last Sunday?' On being told that it was indeed me, he was suitably impressed. 'Cor,' he said, 'he must be a flipping [I've cleaned that up] good player!' This was a remarkable assumption, especially given the fact that he had just spent 45 minutes watching me fumble around the goal and probably (I can't remember the score) let in a few soft ones.

Ironic, or what?

At a pre-dinner reception at a function in Cardiff one footballer introduced me to someone in very flattering terms. 'This is Bob "the Cat" Bevan, the funniest after-dinner speaker I've ever, ever, ever heard.'

I blushed prettily at this remark and allowed him to continue, 'I love that story of yours about the ball hitting the bar. I've started using it about a game I played in. I use it all the time and it gets a big laugh.'

I managed to keep a fixed smile on my face while I thought of a suitable reply. Eventually, I managed one.

'Well, I'm very pleased for you, but don't use it tonight [he was on before me]. It's one of my top gags.'

'Oh you'll be all right. You boys have got plenty of material.'

'No, I'd really rather you didn't . . .' but he had wandered off to talk to someone else.

He then actually used it at the dinner with me sitting there.

Former Football Association chief executive Graham Kelly was a goalkeeper in his younger days, and several people started calling me to say he was using a routine I had written about all the goals I had conceded and how they went in. Scriptwriter Alan Simpson, who along with Ray Galton wrote *Hancock's Half Hour* and *Steptoe and Son*, says it's the best football routine he's ever heard. A compliment I'm especially proud of in view of the source. Unfortunately for Graham everyone in football knew it was my routine.

Another rule of the game is that although most people slip another comic's one-liner in the pocket, you never, ever steal a whole routine. Nor do you use it on television. I know I've used a few other people's material in this book but I have given them credit.

After I had appeared with Jeffrey, now Lord Archer, a couple of times I turned up for another engagement to find that he was speaking. As I sat there I found some of my act coming back at me. Jeffrey might simply have forgotten where he had heard it.

Almost as annoying as having your original material nicked is to hear it being wasted.

Veteran comic and after-dinner speaker Stan Taylor has a routine about a submarine during the war. On its own it is a good gag, but only Stan can deliver it with the naval hat and the noises. It is an absolute classic. Everyone in show business knows it and nobody cares how often they hear it. He delivers it brilliantly. One night at a Variety Club dinner in Newcastle, an after-dinner speaker, probably not knowing the origin and history of the material, told the gag when he was on the same bill as Stan. Stan was beside himself, but the audience took over and demanded that he do it before he sat down. To our delight, he relented, did the routine and still brought the house down. As Frank Carson says, it really is the way you tell 'em.

But you will be thinking I am paranoid about this. Actually, I'm not. In most cases my material is wheeled out only to a relatively small group of people who I may never come across again. By the way, if you think I'm going to do the hitting the bar joke or the goals conceded routine in this book, think again. Buy a ticket for my next dinner and I'll personalise and autograph this copy for you. I'll even give you a valid receipt.

TIME OUT

The Association of Football Statisticians, of which I am a fully paid up and anoraked member, amazingly could not tell me how many stoppages there are throughout each football match. However, Sky Sports came up trumps: apparently, there were, unbelievably, on average, 134 stoppages per Premiership game during the 2002/03 season – injuries, offsides, handballs, fouls, red cards, yellow cards, goal kicks, corners, free-kicks, substitutions, fans on the pitch etc. So, just to lighten things up, in case I get too serious, I shall throw in (geddit?) the odd diversionary stoppage of my own.

Meanwhile, as the warm-up has ended and I haven't even pulled a muscle yet (or much else lately), we must be getting near kick-off.

2. BUILDING UP TO KICK-OFF

*'The Low Self-Esteem Support Group will meet Thursday at seven p.m.
Please use back door.'*

St Peter's Church parish magazine, St Leonards, Sussex

When I was seven, I had an Egyptian teacher at Dulwich Hamlet
Primary School in south London. Miss Sofia, or something like that.
She was an odd woman and nobody liked her. Not that she was
particularly into corporal punishment. Although she did once smack
the top of the thighs of a girl called Margaret Rose and we all caught
a glimpse of green knickers. But as it was pre-puberty my only interest
at the time lay in wondering if young Margaret was a Plymouth Argyle
supporter. (If you're not into football, I should explain that Plymouth
were the only League team to play in green – until Yeovil got
promoted.) We went red and giggled, but the girls were outraged. One
said, 'She's going to bring her mum up to the school,' to which one
of the boys, with repartee well beyond his years, replied, 'Why? Does
she want her legs smacked too?'

At the end of the school year Miss Sofia wrote on my report that I
was not a good mixer. My mother initially went ballistic, then lapsed
into being deeply hurt. Looking back, she might have been right. I was
a weedy kid. Very thin. In fact, I was still only ten stone ten pounds
when I was 24 and six feet and half an inch tall (don't forget the half
inch). I was bullied at school. I was useless at sport, even though I
already loved football. For some reason I hated my name (the family
always call me Robert), and generally I had low self-esteem.

At home, though, it was different. I was an only child and we lived
with my maternal grandmother. At one point the family were well off,
but my maternal grandfather, who was big in the fur trade, died
prematurely probably as a result of being gassed during the First
World War. My grandmother never got over it emotionally, and with
less sophisticated insurances available the money was soon fading
away. I lived upstairs with my parents and my grandmother, and my
mother's brother and sister lived downstairs. When my paternal
grandfather died I was about three, and my father lost his job in the

family rubber soles and heels business. Another financial blow that was to sentence him to a life of low earnings, a life eased only by the almost mind-blowing financial management skills of my mother. As I said, I don't remember wanting for anything, and I look back in amazement and gratitude.

So I was largely in the company of adults throughout my early years, and was probably old for my age and therefore not too popular with the other kids in the road. Their parents, on the other hand, loved me. 'Such a polite and well-spoken little boy!'

Apart from football, I had also become hooked on the wireless, especially the comedy programmes. Variety was still alive, so you would get a rather dull bandleader saying, 'Good evening. This is [special emphasis on the "is", as though he were a world-class superstar] Henry Hall, and tonight is my guest night.' Then you would have Jack Watson, an average comic but later to be hailed as a very fine actor, who would say, 'Come where the stars are shining bright. Begone, dull care. It's Blackpool Night!' What a mecca of entertainment the Lancashire resort conjured up in my mind! Now I think of it as a dump with poor train connections.

YELLOW CARD

A little boy said to his granddad, 'Can you make a noise like a frog?'
'Why?' asked Granddad.
'Because Dad says when you croak we can all go on a good holiday.'

But these shows were only halfway up the league. Everything stopped for *Take It From Here* with Jimmy Edwards and *Hancock's Half Hour*. The nation huddled round their radios. For some reason, I once heard a Charlie Chester show so often (repeats happened then, too) that I memorised it. At my primary school a year before Miss Sofia, we had a period under our teacher Mrs Tanner during which we had to entertain the other kids. In the days before my brain had switched on to the fear of performing, I went out to the front and started to reel off the whole of this Charlie Chester show. After a while – and I can see her now – Mrs T leant over and twisted the large round knob on the peg holding the blackboard on its easel and said, quite kindly, 'I think we'll turn the radio off now, Robert.'

My first death. But not my last.

Hard to believe that some 40 years on I would come to know Charlie and, eventually, to sit next to him at the St George's Day lunch at the Grosvenor House Hotel in London. It was a memorable lunch for more reasons than that. It ran very late. So late, in fact, that I was starting to wonder if I would make a dinner I was due at in Woking. On my other side was hotel supremo Rocco Forte, with whom I got on very well. He said he would really have liked to hear me but he had a meeting at 3.30 and would I forgive him if he left. I replied that so long as he didn't go in the middle of my turn I would completely understand. He actually left about 90 minutes before I stood up.

I can't remember who else spoke, but that lunch did drag on. On the other side of Charlie was scriptwriter Jimmy Perry of *Dad's Army* fame, among others. They didn't get to hear me either. They and most of the rest of the top table had had to leave before I went on. In fact, I think there were only two left on the head table when I eventually stood up to speak at about 4.30. After me there was a singsong and a marching band. The staff were going mental as they had another function to set up for that evening. Quite how it was resolved I'm not sure. As soon as I finished my stint I was on my way to Woking.

Equally strange was my only meeting with Jimmy Edwards in 1990. We were at a celebration of the Lord's Taverners 40th anniversary at the Comedy Theatre off the Haymarket. It was celebrities only, plus me, and after a few drinks we were turfed out into the street. As far as I can recall there were eight of us: Jimmy, Willie Rushton, Tim Brooke-Taylor, four others and me. At the time the troubles in Lebanon were at their height, and opposite the theatre entrance was an empty Lebanese restaurant. They had not one customer in the place and the staff were having a smoke outside. As we came out of the theatre they recognised at least three of us, and we were invited in for a meal and drinks. Everything was on the house.

By this time I had read that Jimmy, as former England fast bowler Bob Willis would have it, 'bowled round the wicket'. He had been 'outed' by the *News of the World* amid stories of young men and black silk pyjamas. I still found it hard to believe. After all, he had been married, had loved all the hunting, shooting and fishing, had been a fighter pilot and had played the male chauvinist Mr Glum in *Take It From Here*. Let me give you an example of the script. Catching Ron and Eth on the sofa, his opening line always sent my father into convulsions: ''Allo, 'allo, 'allo. What's going on 'ere, then? Break clean!' Then he would follow in with a reference to his wife – a woman who was never actually seen or heard. Rather like Mrs Mainwaring in *Dad's Army*. 'I'm sorry to bother you, Ron, but have you seen the secateurs? Mrs Glum wants to do her toenails.' In short, I'd always thought of Jimmy as a man's man though, certainly, behind that very manly set of whiskers I recall him being quite camp. But I don't remember much else, especially once the Lebanese liqueurs came out.

Back in my youth I also felt I could do a reasonable impersonation of a comedian called Robert Moreton. Like most comics in those days he ended with a signing-off catchphrase. His was 'Get in there, Moreton.' I have no idea what it meant, and even the encyclopaedic show business memories of the Grand Order of Water Rats struggle to remember him, let alone his catchphrase. Still, it amused my father.

My self-esteem was to rise in the year following Miss Sofia. Now we were in a class with one Mrs Ward, a nice, gentle lady who was deeply hurt if any of her class misbehaved, as I did, for some reason, for much of the year. I can't remember all that I did to be naughty, except for ringing the bell of the school caretaker and running away. These days they call it Parcelforce. On this occasion I didn't run fast enough, and he spotted me through his window.

It was one year before the dreaded eleven-plus exam that would determine whether we went to a grammar school, a central school or, horror of horrors, a secondary modern with all the roughnecks. We had some quite bright kids in our class. Some would do very well the next year and be selected for scholarships at Christ's Hospital School near Horsham, Sussex. That achievement was rather like winning an Olympic gold medal. It was certainly not something in my sights.

It was a Friday afternoon, about 2.45 p.m. Just before we were to have our afternoon break and another game of playground football. Mrs Ward said that she had the end-of-term exam results back. She said we had all done quite well, although she had not been happy with some of our behaviour during the year. She didn't specify, but I think she had been especially disappointed with me. The exam had been no big deal for me. I remembered doing it and finding it quite easy going, but all I wanted to know was where the next game of football was coming from.

THROW-IN

Someone said to a friend, 'I've half a mind to become a footballer.'
His mate replied, 'That's all you'll need.'

Mrs Ward then asked who we thought had come first. We all had
a go. There was a tall girl called Pat, destined for Christ's Hospital in
twelve months' time. No, it wasn't her. About ten names were shouted
out, one or two of them getting a bit of a laugh. These were the names
too ridiculous to contemplate, such as Alan Dollery. A nice little lad,
good footballer, but not the sharpest knife in the drawer. And Derek
Curtis, who was especially unpopular. It didn't help him that he had
a German mother. Not good news for him in the early 1950s.

YELLOW CARD

I wrote this gag for Kevin Keegan. 'When I was in Germany, playing for
SV Hamburg, it was a nightmare getting a seat in the dressing room. All
the German players used to get in early and put their towels down.' I
don't think he ever used it. I wonder why?

Then somebody called my name out, and another laugh started. It
soon stalled when they saw the look on Mrs Ward's face. I can see it
now. Her head slowly turned towards me. I froze. She was still looking
rather sad. Definitely not smiling. I was half expecting another rather
sad bollocking, but I couldn't remember what I'd done.

'Top of the class,' she announced, still with no smile, 'is Robert
Bevan.'

That smile never did break. I think she was hoping to be able to say
that my behaviour had led me to fail miserably. But she was prepared to
play the game. Of ten prizes, the much-sought-after poster paints would
go to the art winner, but I could choose from the rest. I picked some tins
of watercolour paints. God knows why, as my mother said later. I was
definitely not artistic. I should have picked a book, but I was only a
dumb kid. Hang on. No I wasn't. I was top of the class. My prize was all
that counted. But I would never use it. I would just look at it. It's in the
cabinet behind me now as I write. 'Robert Bevan, Dulwich Hamlet
School, for Excellent Progress, July 15th 1955' is the inscription.

I've only just noticed, today, 47 years on, that, while the education
officer, John Brown, has signed it, the headmistress, Mrs Ponds, has

failed to do so. Against her title is a blank. They've got back at me after all these years. I knew they weren't happy about me winning.

Everyone remained in shock until the break. Me included. We played football, then headed back to class when the handbell was rung. We were walking back in a group when little Alan Dollery said, 'Well done.' Then everyone around said, 'Yeah, well done.' It was a touching moment. Suddenly I had a bit of celebrity status. The lad who came from nowhere to be top of the class. My confidence did not totally soar, but it received a serious injection. From then on I started telling jokes and generally mucking about. Who knew then where it would lead?

3. LEAVING THE DRESSING ROOM

'In the land of the blind the one-eyed man is king.'

Anon. (to me at any rate)

These days a new baby is submitted to loads of tests to check that all his or her bits are in working order, but that was not always so in the 1940s. I was already in infant school when I told my mum that I couldn't see properly out of my left eye. I had never been able to, but I didn't think to mention it until I was about six. All hell broke loose, although I can't say I remember much about what followed except for sitting in front of a man and a woman in white coats. I assume they were doctors or specialists of some sort.

In later years I was told that the eye had not developed properly. Although I do have a little vision in it, there is not enough to recognise you, however close you stand (and assuming I know you). The specialist I see annually to check the other one says the duff one is huge. I think he enjoys looking at it and chuckling 'What a monster!'. I was told at one point that if I lost the other one the bad one would come back, but have since been informed that that is not true. Quite why I left it for six years to tell anyone I can't explain. I just thought it was normal. Indeed, as far as I can tell the only thing it has stopped me from doing is looking through red and green lenses simultaneously to see 3D pictures and movies. On the positive side, it has given me plenty of excuses for the thousands of goals I have conceded, and I save 50 per cent on contact lenses. The good one is now so short-sighted I actually wear a lens under the glasses to avoid giving daily impersonations of Benny Hill's famous Fred Scuttle character. I suppose you could say I'm sort of double-glazed.

Back in my infancy, I just about recall the female specialist saying that I should be kept away from all sports and other dangerous activities. The man disagreed. 'Let him lead a normal life,' he said. Thank goodness my parents allowed his view to prevail. Without that decision I would not have gone on to play just about 500 games for the Old Wilsonians Football Club.

Did you hear about the bloke who thought email was something a Yorkshireman said when the post arrived?

That figure is somewhat disputed by the club statistician; I have the feeling he likes me only because of the fame I have brought to the club. When I drew his attention to the fact that on the club website he had left three or four years of my career out of my all-time appearances (452 was the figure that was quoted) he sent me an email with the subject heading MOANS. That led me to pen an article for the Old Wilsonians magazine which I entitled 'All My Yesterdays, or Keeping up Appearances'. After that the appearances list was removed from the website, so don't waste your time looking for it on the net.

It was March 1987 when I finally retired from competitive Saturday football. The time was obviously right because I can't say I've ever missed it. Not that type of football anyway. This despite playing most Saturdays for 25 years. We had gone to west London from Hayes in Kent – not a great journey – with a very young team, some of whom were playing dreadful music on my car stereo. Our 7th XI were playing Great Western Railway 5th XI, and we were awful. We never looked like scoring, and as their eighth goal went in I thought 'I'm not going to do this any more', and I haven't. I didn't even finish the season.

By this time we had the club statistician. It bugged me when I first saw 452 appearances and 39 goals against my name. For years I felt that the figure was wrong, although he wouldn't have it. I can't tell you why it bothered me. It was just a feeling that 25 years of playing OW football must have produced at least an average of twenty games a season. I almost returned for two years to get in my 500th appearance. My old school friend Terry Adams has now passed 1,000 – an amazing achievement in this level of football. Then, a couple of years ago, I saw the OW website and knew, after all those years, that I was right. I was shown as never having played before 1964. That was wrong, and I could prove it.

From time to time you get to speak with various football superstars. Not long ago I spoke with former Liverpool and Republic of Ireland striker John Aldridge. I had forgotten that he used to play for Oxford United and was in the team when they won the Football League Cup. It has had many sponsors, but when they won it, in 1986, it was the Milk Cup. So I was pleased to hand him an old gag which was out of date for me but which he could still use: 'As the holders of the Milk Cup we did, of course, receive free milk for a year. All the players said they were glad we hadn't won the FA Cup.'

I left Wilson's Grammar School, Camberwell, in 1961. Earlier that year my mother had met the football club secretary George Croucher, who was vaguely known to the family. He had asked if I was going to join the Old Boys and I had responded that I would not be joining those old fogeys.

A few weeks before I left, everyone in my year was invited to the OW sports ground at Hayes in Kent for a leavers' supper, and my friends persuaded me to go along, adding that free beer was provided. In those days school uniform was everything and you were actually beaten if found not wearing your cap in the street. Fortunately, I found out before the evening that school uniforms were not worn to this event. I still go cold at the thought of the stick I would have got had I arrived wearing my school blazer. But there were problems. This was the only jacket I owned, so I had to borrow a tie from my father and a sports jacket from my Uncle Jack. My father was a good six inches shorter than me even then. It was rather a jolly evening. A little round man called Dennis Newson showed us around, and he seemed a good chap. I also had a drink for the first time. I slipped a few brown ales down. I was drinking them because it was what my father drank. He was still drinking them until a fortnight before he died. I stopped after a week.

That first year of membership was free, so I signed up. I can't say that the OWs were keen on me for my sporting achievements. They wanted numbers. Much as I loved football, I could hardly get a game at school. I made the house first team only a couple of times and played what few games I got in the house B team with all the goofy and uncoordinated lads who didn't want to play anyway. I actually got more cricket in than football, and even played a couple of times for the school seconds.

Looking back, I was not totally without ability, but there was little or no encouragement unless you were obviously naturally gifted. It was the assistant school groundsman, Ike, who actually produced the only bit of useful motivation I can remember in my school life. I had always hung around at the back of the five-mile cross-country run with the sort of blokes who only got in the house B team – those who walked, or hid in the bushes for a fag, or took a short cut and rejoined the middle of the pack for the run home. Then, one day, Ike said he would give me a bar of chocolate if I went round without stopping. What a dumb kid I was – how would he know? Or maybe I was an honourable chap? Either way, I did run round without stopping. I even kept going against the painful stitch I developed, and found to my surprise that if you run through it, it disappears. I came in well up the field and a week later was presented with my bar of chocolate. After that I always ran round without stopping, and I gradually worked my way up to be the best in my year in my house. In my last year in the annual senior race against a field two thirds of whom were either one or two years older than me, I finished in the top twenty out of about 150. I have to say, though, that I was built for stamina rather than speed, as witnessed in the school athletics championship when I collapsed from fatigue during the half mile, much to everyone's amusement.

Nonetheless, by the time I left I regarded myself as a razor-sharp athlete and decided I should attend pre-season football training. So, with my friend Malcolm Grant, I actually cycled about ten miles from Dulwich to Hayes one evening, trained, then cycled home. I've had a couple of cars since that couldn't manage that. Clearly, such keenness caught the eye of the selectors, and we were picked for the first game of the season.

In those days the OWs had four sides in the league – in fact, the 4th XI had only been formed the previous season. We were selected to play in a 5th XI friendly. We played against Thos Cook, and I remember it was played on the top pitch at Wickham Park FC, the ground next door to ours. I played right-half (remember them?) behind Malcolm, who was a fast, raiding winger. I'm happy to say we won 9–0. I scored on my debut, and there was an own goal. Malcolm got the other seven. Not surprisingly, he went straight into the seconds. I was destined never to play in the same team as him again until we were in the veterans together over twenty years later.

Choosing to play right-half was not a sharp move. Firstly, I was thin and weedy. Secondly, the 4th XI right-half was their captain, Brian McAlister. Consequently, I made the 4th XI on only two or three occasions that year, although I do remember scoring against City of London College but still getting dropped again the next week. That season I can only have played a dozen or so games, largely friendlies in the 5th XI, which we put out when we could.

DIRECT FREE-KICK

Bill Shankly at one point managed Workington Town when they were still in the Football League. One day, when he had become a legend at Liverpool, he went back to go to a funeral of a former colleague. On his way into the church he went past the gravediggers preparing his friend's last resting place. He stopped to speak to them.

'I want a really good job done here, lads,' he said. 'He was a good friend and a good man.'

The diggers confirmed that they had got the message. 'Certainly, Mr Shankly,' they said.

After the service, Bill went back to the graveside for the burial. As the mourners left he approached the diggers.

'Ye've done a really good job, lads,' he said.

'Thank you, Mr Shankly,' they replied.

'Do ye take a drink?'

'We certainly do, Mr Shankly,' they said, lightening up.

'Well,' said Shanks, pointing to his friend, now lying in the grave, 'let that be a lesson to ye.' And he walked away.

As the 4th XI won their league and got promotion, it was decided that we would enter a fifth side in the league for the first time in the club's history. At the age of seventeen I was elected captain, and attended my first selection meeting at club secretary George Croucher's office in Peckham High Street. George was an undertaker of the traditional type. He was always immaculate in striped trousers and black tails, though it is hard to imagine that he travelled like that on the bus from Catford to the foot of Rye Lane, Peckham – *Only Fools and Horses* country – every morning without attracting large quantities of stick. His office had a wooden sliding door with a large glass panel, and the room was barely big enough for the eight or so who regularly attended the meetings. On the walls were shelves on which stood various miniature coffins in different varieties of wood.

From time to time we would pick up one of George's trade magazines and treat ourselves to large helpings of black humour. Although George was a very straight sort of chap, he was always quite happy to join in with this. Sometimes he would halt our debate by asking us to keep quiet while he answered the bell. A black-shrouded figure would slip silently past the glass panel to look their last on a loved one in the room behind us, then disappear back into the night, whereupon all hell broke loose again about the 4th XI centre-half, or whatever.

One of George's less endearing habits on the departure of a skipper attending his first meeting was to creep up behind him and give him a healthy squirt of embalming fluid. Nothing would get the smell out of my mac, which I had to dump. And I nearly got picked up on the bus home.

What a man George was. Secretary for 45 years, assistant secretary for five years before that. I often wonder who did his funeral and got him back at last with that fluid gun. And I can still hear him say, when asked how his business was going, 'Not too good at the moment. What we need is a nice cold snap.'

YELLOW CARD

What would I like said about me at my funeral? I'd like someone to say, 'Look! He's moving!'

Anyway, back to the appearances. I must have played in most of the 22 league games and two cup-ties in 1962/63 because we finished bottom. I know this because, as an anorak, I've kept all the old handbooks. My debut as captain in 1962 was away to Edgware Rovers thirds. I remember the day well. It was played at the notorious Welsh Harp. In case that is not a venue known to the whole football world, I should explain that the Welsh Harp is a large reservoir on the North Circular. One of our team, Ron Meadows, entered OW legend by once swimming out, in full kit, to retrieve the ball. No wonder he retired to start the OW Sailing Club.

I pause here to regale you with an incident that occurred about twenty years later, in 1983. I received a telephone call from one Bob Stewart asking if I would speak at a dinner in north London on 30 December. It was a somewhat unusual day on which to get a booking, but I said I was free (or 'very reasonable') and for £500 agreed to speak at what he described as a family party. Had I known the background, I would have asked for a good deal more.

At that time I was in a relationship with a pretty young blonde girl called Gaby who was sixteen years younger than me. She was quite shy in some ways and was not overly impressed with my newly acquired famous show business and sporting friends. In fact, she would go out of her way to be under-impressed, and she certainly had no wish to trail across London with me to Enfield town hall on a cold and dark December night.

After the letter of confirmation I heard no more until the night before the event, when Bob rang again. 'Are you still OK for tomorrow evening?' I confirmed that I was. 'Well, I couldn't tell you before for all sorts of reasons, and I would ask you not to say anything now or at least until after the event,' he began.

I started to feel nervous. I had already been at several dinners where Stan Flashman, the notorious black-market ticket dealer who later became chairman of Barnet FC, had turned up to do the auction surrounded by a load of heavies. What had I let myself in for?

'My brother,' Bob continued, 'is Rod Stewart. In fact, there's seven of us. It's my dad's eightieth birthday party. Rod has paid for it and he's flying all the relatives down from Scotland and elsewhere. We saw you at the Variety Club Golfing Society stag night and thought your football stuff would be ideal for us.'

Somewhat gobsmacked, I returned to tell Gaby. Suddenly she decided that perhaps, after all, she might come with me.

It was a strange evening. There, in this very ordinary barn of a room, were a load of working-class and not hugely wealthy people. The men were dressed in what looked like their only suit while the women seemed to have raided the local C&A. Right in the middle of them was this spiky-haired guy in a sparkly blue jacket that must have cost thousands of pounds, dripping with gold chains and bracelets. Beside him was a gorgeous, tanned, blonde woman – at that time it was Kelly Emberg – in a stunning gold trouser suit.

Despite being a world superstar, Rod had a normal family like everyone else, and one not without its problems. Right in the middle of the top table was Rod's dad, a little bald man with glasses, also called Bob. Next to him was Rod's mum, in a wheelchair. Apparently she had been unable to walk for some time and old Bob had looked after her over a long period.

After the finest meal Enfield town hall could offer the night before New Year's Eve, most of which Kelly and Rod left, I rose to speak and went down quite well with most of them. I had just made a long-playing record of football jokes, and at the end I produced a wrapped present. 'Bob,' I said, 'you must have some crap LPs in your house so here's one you will enjoy.' Everyone liked that gag.

Rod took all this well, and he struck me as a good bloke. After listening to my stuff about the OWs' lower sides, he told me that his dad used to run a team in which he and his brothers played. Apparently the Welsh Harp was their home ground. It still seems rather bizarre that I should have had an in-depth discussion with this world-famous superstar about the perils of playing on this pitch while this amazing-looking woman stared blankly into the distance. Gaby stood by during all of this. I introduced her to Rod and Kelly but she just froze and, after a nervous hello, never said a word to them.

Let me now return to that game against Edgware Rovers 3rd XI. It is etched into my memory because it was the first time I met Nick Carter. In those days most players didn't carry on much beyond 30. Nick was different. He was still going at 54 – more than three times the age of his captain – and was probably our best player. He recalled that day too. Some years later in the weekly newsletter, he claimed that on this very heavy pitch (thanks to the proximity of the Welsh Harp) 'we defended stoutly for twenty minutes before conceding the first goal, only for the young captain [me] to wander back from inside-forward, without a speck on him, to say, "Come on, defence, you'll have to tighten up."'

We lost 8–3.

CORNER

One ground I don't miss playing on is at Old Bromleians. Badly drained, it was next to a pig farm, so not only was it a mudbath, it had a terrible smell as well. At their annual dinner one year their captain, the late Robin Gonzales, came out with the memorable line, 'When Catford Wanderers [not the most popular of clubs at that time] played here we had 84 complaints from the pigs.'

Back to that second season, 1962/63, I also recall we lost heavily in both cup-ties. But not as heavily as we did in a league game away to Inland Revenue thirds. We went down 18–3. No, I wasn't in goal. That privilege went to Tony Hawker, a non-OW who was making up the numbers. There is this immediate assumption that a heavy defeat is the fault of the keeper. In Tony's case this was not so; it was the rest of us who were crap. I remember him playing for us against Edgware Rovers a year later when we arrived with only nine men and beat their eleven by a goal to nil. Tony had a blinder. And a week after that 18–3 defeat we had to face the same Inland Revenue side on their ground. Amazingly, we won 3–1, but still finished bottom of the table.

In 1963/64 we had thirteen sides in our league and again I played in most of the 24 league games and two cup-ties. Again we finished last.

All this means that I must have played another 50 or so games and notched up another dozen or so goals to add to my 'official' figures – not least because, as captain, I appointed myself to take the penalties. You'll be amazed to hear that I didn't miss one of at least six I recall taking during that time. It was nerve-racking for the rest of the team, because almost without exception they were poorly taken, but somehow they went in. All of which meant, to their continuing irritation, that I would be taking the next one.

It was years later when I finally missed one. It was in a friendly against Unilever which we won 8–2; having never scored more than twice in any game previously, not even a house match at school, I scored six! The game was played at Unilever on what is now Charlton's training ground. I wander down there occasionally just to revive the memory. I also remember that we had a colour clash and, having forgotten the weekly newsletter instruction 'Always pack a white shirt with your kit', I had to get a faded Manchester City-type pale blue shirt out of lost property. I have to tell you I did not return it after the game. It's the only thing I have ever stolen, apart from some hotel soap. I've still got it.

It was a weird game. We led 1–0 at half-time when I nipped in between two defenders, got my foot to the ball as they brought me down, and as I fell looked up to see it powering into the top corner. Nothing beats a good toe-punt, which has now been coached out of the game. Then I missed the penalty. But in the second half every time

I shot it seemed to go in, and the lads carried me from the field. They wouldn't try that now.

I heard that, at a subsequent committee meeting, there was some dispute over whether this game should be wiped from the records as it was only a friendly. I'm pleased to say that that didn't happen.

YELLOW CARD

Joke I told at the Footballer of the Year dinner in 1980. Did you hear about the Irishman who scored a penalty on *Match of the Day* and then missed in the replay? It wasn't all his fault. The keeper sent him the wrong way.

As you can imagine, after that I was desperate to play again, but another week on was the last week of that season. As the 5th XI was in danger of relegation and not all our sides had a game, we rather disgracefully 'packed' the team. It was the only time I've been called a 'ringer'. We played a team called Witan, the sports club of the old Greater London Council. We needed to win to stay up. Five strikers had been picked and everyone wanted to play in the middle. Nobody wanted to play on the left wing, so guess who ended up playing there? And guess who got the coveted centre-forward berth? None other than the club statistician. He was a regular 3rd XI player and a prolific goalscorer.

Having not played much on the left wing it had never occurred to me until that afternoon that a right-footer playing on the left can seriously trouble the right-footed right-back marking him. In our first attack I came inside him, shot weakly across the goal and watched it roll into the far corner. Three minutes later a cross eluded everyone as it came across the goal and I tapped in from a yard out. Statto was beside himself that I'd scored and he hadn't, and although Witan pulled one back he bustled his way to a goal and we led 3–1 at half-time.

In the second half we got a penalty, and there was some pressure to let me take it, but the captain, Les Wilks, gave it instead to our left-back, Charlie Holder. He had a powerful left foot but not much breath, not helped by the fags he smoked during the kick-in and the half-time interval. He missed it. Witan scored again, but Statto netted twice to complete his hat-trick and relaxed a little. Then we got another penalty. I pleaded to take it, but again it went to Charlie. He missed a second time.

Now I was pissed off, but next time I got the ball I cut inside the full-back again and shot across the goal. This time it was a much better strike and it flew low inside the far post. I had another hat-trick. Amazingly, I never again scored more than two in a match, including my penultimate game playing on the left wing for Lloyds Bank Golden Oldies against Cuaco in 1997. I notched up two in five minutes that day in a 3–0 win. Having been between the sticks for so long by that time, I had forgotten how orgasmic it is to score a goal.

BOUNCE-UP

One of the more memorable remarks in old boys football came from Les Nelson, an Old Bromleian veteran who played into his sixties. He played for Bromley when they won the Isthmian League, Dulwich Hamlet, and alongside me for the Lloyds Bank Golden Oldies. After one Veterans cup-tie on the very heavy Bromleians pitch, I heard over the partition in the dressing room next door one of his team-mates utter the cliché, 'I thought the pitch was a great leveller.' Les replied, 'Pity the groundsman isn't.'

After my retirement and a switch to Veterans football I was still destined to play one more OW game on a Saturday. In 1994 I noticed that the OWs had started an 8th XI. Wishing to add this side to my appearances and anticipating that no other player would have achieved playing for all eight sides – by then I had played for each of the other seven – I announced my availability for a local game if they were ever short. It took just 24 hours for the phone to ring, and I set off to Danson Park in Bexley to play in a friendly against Old Sedcopians 4th XI.

They were a strong side, and this mismatch was not helped when four of our players arrived just before the interval, by which time our seven were seriously under the cosh. I won't dwell on the game, but we lost 12–0. Afterwards we learnt that these errant four had arrived at a ground, asked the park keeper if this was the Old Sedcopians pitch and, on being told it was, had got changed and headed out to the game. Halfway there they realised they were heading towards the 2nd XI game at the wrong ground. They got back in the car and

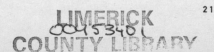

21

eventually found us. In the bar that evening a sixteen-year-old team-mate, whom I had never previously met, came up to me. 'Do you know when we first realised we were heading for the wrong pitch?' he asked. I confessed that I did not. Looking me straight in the good eye, he said, 'When we saw our keeper make a save.'

Later that week I heard that someone else had already got the record of having played in all eight OW sides. So even my last Saturday game brought forth a good story. And a true one. There were many more to come, and many more places where my love of football would lead.

4. WAITING IN THE TUNNEL

'We use every stumbling block as a stepping stone.'
Sam Hammam, when he was chairman of Wimbledon FC

After a dinner, or often during it, the first question most people ask is, 'How did you get into this?'

You do get bored answering the same old questions, and with people who come up and tell you jokes. You've nearly always heard them, and I normally put them out of their misery if I recognise it. Unfortunately, that doesn't always stop them. Some people still insist on carrying on to the end. On the other hand, it is flattering. It means they've enjoyed you and want to know more about you. Unless you've died a death. In which case they look embarrassed and slip quietly away, leaving you sitting on your own.

The seeds were sown after I, a shy lad, had come top of that class at Dulwich Hamlet Primary School a year before the eleven-plus, at which point I acquired a more extrovert personality. This was to be to the detriment of my schoolwork but to my advantage in later life. My mother had really wanted me to go to Alleyns in Dulwich – a sort of minor public school – but my eleven-plus pass was not quite good enough so I opted for Wilson's Grammar School in Camberwell, with Strand Grammar School as my second choice.

Wilson's are not blessed with many famous old boys. The best known is actor Sir Michael Caine, who attended some twelve years before me under his real name Maurice Micklewhite. We did have a dean of St Paul's Cathedral once, and a director of the Tate Gallery, so we're not all plebs you see. Then there was Sir Alan Cobham, who invented in-flight refuelling. Not a lot of people know that, Maurice. And Harry Golombeck who was a world chess champion. And Laurie Pignon, a famous tennis journalist. But that's about it.

There is another OW you may just have heard of – Brian Masters. He is an author, and is often described as a leading criminologist and I do know he has written several books about serial killers. He was head boy at school, and I always found him a bit odd. When he edited the school magazine, he managed to get an interview with Gilbert

Harding. Gilbert, who bowled round the wicket in the manner of Jimmy Edwards, was a famous person then, though it's hard to pinpoint his talent. As Sir Jimmy Savile once said about himself, 'I can't tell jokes, act, dance or sing.' Neither could Gilbert. But he kept popping up on panel games, and in those days *What's My Line?* was the most popular show on TV, attracting some fifteen million viewers every week. Hard to believe, isn't it?

Gilbert, with his glasses, moustache and heavily Brylcreemed hair, looked a grumpy man, and he was. Irascible would be the word. The audience would wait with bated breath for him to lose his temper with some dimwit contestant, rather like a motor racing crowd hoping for a crash. Nor was this an act. He really was a miserable git.

He also became famous for an appearance on a programme with interviewer John Freeman called *Face to Face*. This was groundbreaking TV with serious close-ups on the interviewee's face as he was asked probing personal questions. It had never been done before. When John got into a heavy discussion about Gilbert's mother, it made him cry. In those days men did not blub, and it was front-page news the next day.

YELLOW CARD

Jazz musician George Melly once recalled a piece of graffiti which said 'my mother made me a homosexual'. Someone had written underneath it: 'If I bought the wool, would she make one for me?'

Anyway, young Brian struck up a friendship with Gilbert. I have since been told that the friendship was the subject of serious gossip at school in the 1960s. As usual, I was the last to hear it. In fact, I only just have.

This despite the fact that I appeared in plays with him. He was normally the lead while I had a bit part. At school I was one of the chorus in *Oedipus Rex*. I wasn't entrusted with many lines, but for three nights I had to get made up with grey whiskers and a wig and stand on the stage throughout the play. Then I was in *Murder in the Cathedral* as an attendant, and in *Hamlet* in the Old Boys Dramatic Society. I played a gravedigger and an English ambassador. With bodies all over the stage I had to come on and say, 'The sight is dismal [bit bloody obvious – who wrote that stuff?], and our affairs from England come too late. The ears are senseless that should give us hearing . . . Rosencrantz and Guildenstern are dead . . .' Brian played one of those two, I can't remember which. But I do still remember the words. I've just typed them from memory. Spooky, isn't it?

Famous though Brian and I are – well, I'm nearly famous – both of us have to admit that Michael Caine (sorry, Sir Michael, or Maurice – what should we call him now?) is well in the lead when it comes to Old Wilsonian actors. I know people who were at school with him. On chat shows he has always come over to me as a good bloke, but his schoolmates say he was not popular as he was not into sport, which all seems a bit unfair. Of course he wasn't happy at the school either, but he hasn't endeared himself to OWs by often criticising the place and saying he was beaten by the headmaster. This chap, Gerry Lee, was the same one who interviewed me in 1961. He admitted me, even though I was so nervous I answered every question he put to me wrongly, to the horror of my mother who sat there aghast and gave me a right bollocking when we left. It may be that the world-famous actor is mistaken and did fall foul of a man called 'Min' Matthews, who was a sadist. He may have been the reason why Micklewhite became Caine. Gerry Lee was a very gentle old man who never beat anyone to my knowledge, and was in fact so weak that the school went backwards under his stewardship and only started to turn the corner two years later when Norman Friskney arrived.

Friskney and I did not always get on, even when I left school, as I used to give him some stick when, for several years, I hosted the OW dinners. People used to look forward each year to see how I was going to get under his skin. I'm not sure he really enjoyed any of this until one night he lay in wait for me. Having been given the usual irreverent introduction, he rose to say, rather coldly, 'I would like to thank Mr Bevan for his introduction. I was thinking of Mr Bevan only this morning as I was leafing through Woodworkers Gazette, where it stated that a thin veneer is easily removed by the application of alcohol.' I think it is one of the best put-downs I have ever heard, and since that night we have been good friends.

Norman was a bit of a flogger until it became politically incorrect. I managed to keep out of the way of all of this, even though I was called up once for bad work and threatened with a beating if I made a second appearance. The fear of this probably pushed me towards my one O level. This was in English Language, although my editor at

Virgin Books has found it hard to believe and actually asked to see the certificate.

Yes, I know you want to hear how my entertaining career started. I am coming to the point.

DOG ON THE PITCH

One of the nicest people it has ever been my pleasure to meet was Eric Massey, also known as Fred. He was the maths master at Wilson's, and later deputy headmaster. Absolutely everyone liked him no matter what their age. He and his wife Muriel transcended every generation. They lived in Sutton, and if one of our sides was playing locally Eric would always come, no matter if it was the 1st or 7th XI. He also had a long-haired black and white Jack Russell terrier that followed him everywhere, including the loo. One Saturday our 6th XI had an away friendly with Old Suttonians and the referee didn't show up. Eric, an adequate referee at school, was asked if he would take the whistle. He said he would, but he refused to tie the dog up. We had no choice but to play the game with Eric and the dog strolling around the pitch. The dog didn't seem to enjoy the experience much, especially when one of my mishit drop-kicks nearly took its head off. At that point it was certainly the fastest thing on the pitch. It was one of the funniest afternoons I have ever had on a football pitch, but maybe you had to be there?

My lack of scholastic endeavour meant that had I been a football team I would certainly have been fighting to avoid relegation. But you can't get relegated from a grammar school, unless you set fire to the school sports pavilion, which someone actually did the year before I went there. This all meant that I never got to Speech Day. You had to have been awarded a prize to get there. But I did get there twice after I left. In 1963 I went back to receive the Leavers Cup, a kind of Most Promising Old Boy award, which was handed to me by William Penney, a famous atomic scientist. Although I was looking forward to getting my hands on the silverware, my first ever trophy, I can't say I was looking forward to listening to a speech on atomic science. In fact, it was riveting. I learnt that night that a really clever man, as William, later to be Lord Penney, was, can make anyone understand his subject.

My second visit was not until 1995 when I was the Old Wilsonians Association president, presenter of BBC Radio 5's Six O Six programme and a frequent guest on Terry Wogan's *Auntie's Sporting Bloomers* on

BBC television. I was asked to become William Penney and present the prizes. Quite amazing for a bloke who was not even going to join the Old Boys over 30 years earlier. By then the headmaster was a young man (they're all young to me now) who rejoiced in the name of Chris Tarrant. There the similarity between the two Tarrants ended, but he was a pleasant enough guy.

A few weeks before the event I went up to the school for lunch to discuss my address. Tarrant offered me a sherry in his study, and I wondered why headmasters always have sherry, and only sherry, in their drinks cabinets. Chris didn't know either, and neither of us had one. We discussed the evening, and I stated that I would simply take the mickey out of him as I did at the Old Boys dinner, suggesting that he had a drink problem, an affair with the school cleaner, etc. He went white at the thought. 'God, no!' he cried. 'All the parents will be there. And I don't want you banging on about only getting one O level.' He paused to summon up a little more gravitas. 'This is supposed to be a centre of excellence now.'

As I drove away, I realised I had to give this some more thought. I would need to get some serious points across. Something I'm not so comfortable with. Eventually, it came to me. I would recount the full details of my visit to the headmaster.

On the evening, as I started I could see Tarrant looking very anxious. He would have put his head in his hands if it could have gone unnoticed. But soon I put him out of his misery and began to talk about the university of life, how much I wished I'd studied more at school, etc. I got plenty of laughs in, and when I spotted the old headmaster, Norman Friskney, sitting in the front row I slipped in his *Woodworkers Gazette* put-down, much to everyone's delight, not least old Norman's. It all went very well, and a relieved Chris Tarrant pumped my hand in the reception afterwards and started to ask me who I could get for him the following year.

As it happened, I managed to get a friend of mine called Peter Mead. Peter, who was at the school three or four years before me, has made a fortune in advertising, largely through a company called Abbott, Mead, Vickers. A couple of years ago he sold the group for a massive amount – a few hundred million.

'I hope you got ten per cent,' I said when we had lunch soon afterwards.

'Unfortunately not,' he replied, 'but maybe two or three.'

After Peter had agreed to speak, I found that I would not be able to attend; we met for lunch again so that I could fill him in. I gave him a copy of what I'd said the year before and it turned out that he had left with only one O level too. He told me a lovely story, which he used on the night. He said that when he was about to leave school he was called to the careers master to discuss what profession he felt like following. Peter had just got his first record player, and he had a Frank Sinatra record he loved to play. As he had no idea what he wanted to do, he said that he fancied looking after pop stars and people like that.

'Do you mean advertising?' asked the master.

Not knowing any better, and anxious to get out of this rather boring meeting, Peter said, 'Yes.'

A few days later the careers master said that he had fixed two interviews: one with the country's top agency, J. Walter Thompson, and the other with a company called Bensons. In those days people in the advertising business spoke in frightfully posh accents, and a rather pompous woman at JWT offered Peter a job as an office boy for a few pounds a week. 'There is a staff canteen. But,' she continued, adopting a rather superior yet pitying manner, 'I'm afraid you won't be able to eat there on your salary. However, you can take your sandwiches into Grosvenor Square and eat them there.' Peter thought to himself 'Bollocks to that' and joined Bensons. A few years ago, when Abbott, Mead, Vickers overtook JWT as the United Kingdom's largest advertising agency, Peter took a small Tupperware box of sandwiches into Grosvenor Square, sat down and ate them. Good lad.

We both agreed that even if our old school hadn't fired our scholastic embers, it had given us a good start in life as reasonably rounded individuals. It might have been a grammar school, but it was in a rough area and its pupils were largely the brighter kids of working-class families. During a eulogy to the OWs' former honorary solicitor Jack Robinson, his son, Nick, said that his father had always felt that Wilson's education had given him the ability to mix with princes and paupers. A prophetic remark in my case, since I have been lucky enough to mix with both, even though I still feel I have more in common with the paupers. So does the aforementioned Nick Robinson. He is the secretary of the Ryman League – or, as I prefer it, the Isthmian League – whose clubs have made paupers out of many a non-league chairman.

It was from this background that I sallied forth into the life I now have (you knew I'd get to the point eventually). I took with me from my Alma Mater all the laughter and piss-taking, and the ability to write. It wasn't long before they got me to do the Old Wilsonians Football Club newsletter. And it wasn't too much longer before I came up with a brainwave. In those days of trusted postal deliveries and long before email each player was sent a selection notice (hard to believe now, isn't it?). I suggested that if we were going to post this out, why not incorporate a weekly newsletter with the selection notice? For the next three years I produced this each Sunday, Roneoed it off and took it to the Monday night meetings. My old school friend Mike Pike took it on soon afterwards and is still doing it to this day. The 1,500th edition will be out soon. Most of us get ours by email on a Sunday now.

KID ON THE PITCH

A clean sheet (no goals conceded, for the uninitiated) was always a rare and memorable afternoon for me, but this particular day was unforgettable for another reason. I was playing for the 5th XI away to Fulham Compton Old Boys – not the cleanest of sides. When we met we were one short. One of the ten, Nigel Golley, had brought his little brother along to watch. Mark was twelve, but looked younger and smaller. When we got to the ground we asked Fulham if they minded him playing. They said that they didn't and, to be fair to them, although they kicked the rest of us up in the air as usual, they left little Mark alone as he hung around out on the right wing.

At half-time it was 0–0. In the second half the ball ran loose across their goal following a corner and little Mark tapped it in. Still they left him alone. Ten minutes later we got another corner from which Mark again scored, this time with an overhead kick. After that they tried to kick him as well, except they couldn't catch him. What they didn't know – and neither did the rest of us – was that he was on Crystal Palace's books, where he was already regarded as a bit of a star. We won 2–0.

Mark went on to play semi-professionally and scored one of the goals for Sutton United when they knocked First Division Coventry City out of the FA Cup in 1989.

Needless to say, plenty of stick flew around in the newsletter copy under my editorship, and some of the older guys suggested that I ought to speak at the association dinner. I was, at one and the same time, delighted and terrified. It hung over me for weeks. I ran it through my mind again and again. I struggled to concentrate on my work. It filled my every waking hour. Just occasionally it still does, if I have a really big job coming up or if I'm trying something new, like a specially written poem that will be used only once. I am aware of and ready for these emotions now, but back then I certainly wasn't. I really couldn't work out was happening to me.

I was told I would be proposing the toast to the school, and would go first. One of the last times that would happen. Then the school captain would respond. Someone else would propose the guests and that would be replied to by Mickey Stewart, the England and Surrey opening bat who also played amateur football for Corinthian Casuals and England before turning professional with Charlton Athletic and the now defunct Guildford City of the Southern League. Mickey, who went on to become manager of the England cricket team, is now best known because of his remarkable 40-year-old son Alec, who became a kind of cricketing Cliff Richard until he retired in 2003.

Mickey and I have been friends ever since, and when I did a dinner with him again in 2002 I thought it would be fun to go into my scrapbook and dig out the menu from the original. I've kept all the menus from the dinners at which I've spoken, except when I've been too pissed to remember, so there are more than a few gaps. To my amazement, not only did I find the menu, but my speech notes were clipped to it. I took them along too, and Mickey couldn't believe it. I said to him, 'I can't believe how I've made a career out of this. On reading the notes I can hardly see a laugh in it.' One that did work concerned my old French master Dickie Delvin, a very broad Scotsman. 'The school has not been too helpful with my education,' I said. 'For example, I was taught French by Dickie Delvin. Consequently I am now not only unable to speak French, but no one in Scotland understands me either.'

Even though it was a stag dinner, bad language was not considered acceptable; certainly any use of a four-letter word would have been regarded as scandalous. I agonised for several weeks over whether or not to recite a poem called 'The Robin', the origin of which I cannot recall. I drove people mad asking their advice, and most of what I got back was not helpful. In the end I went for it, and delivered this:

As I woke this morning,
When all sweet things are born,
A robin perched upon my sill
To hail a happy morn.

He was so young and fragile
And sweetly did he sing,
And thoughts of joy and happiness
Into my heart did spring.

I smiled so sweetly to myself
As I paused beside my bed.
I slowly brought the window down
And smashed his bleedin' head.

Yes, I was agonising over whether or not to say 'bleedin''. How life has changed.

At the end of the evening one of many people who came up to congratulate me was Jeff Bellamy. He was two or three years older than me and had been my house captain. He was a fine actor at school and had started a highly successful OW Drama Club when he left. So successful that they used to win top prizes at festivals before they folded. I had played the odd bit part in a production and had done the same at school, but not with any success. So it was with not an inconsiderable amount of amazement in his voice that he came up to me to say, 'You've got good timing.' The strong inference being that I had certainly not shown any when I had appeared with him. At that stage I didn't really know what he was talking about, but I thanked him profusely.

Needless to say, I know what he means now.

As I once heard Dennis Lillee say about fast bowling, if you are blessed with a natural, God-given talent, you can hone it. If you haven't got that natural ability, go and do something else.

And that was how it all started. I told you we'd get there in the end.

It's one thing to get a laugh among your mates at a bar, another entirely to get up and perform in front of 150 people, many of whom don't know you, and get them all chuckling. It's a feeling that's hard to convey. If you've been feeling tired or unwell, that feeling disappears when you perform. It must be the adrenalin rush. And the better you go, the longer the feeling stays afterwards.

All this time I had been waiting in the tunnel, but now I was heading out into the sunlight. The kick-off was getting nearer.

LOOK AGAIN, SIR BOB!

'If there was a contest to find the world's biggest loser, I'd win. Unless there was a prize.'

Stan Bowles

I don't know where he got the number from, but not long after my life-changing performance at the 1980 Footballer of the Year dinner – which is coming up – Bobby Charlton called me at home. He said he was running a dinner to pay tribute to Cliff Lloyd, the retiring secretary of the Professional Footballers' Association. He added that he'd already booked Jerry Stevens (the then other half of the Lennie [Bennett] and Jerry double act on the BBC), and would I also speak? He could offer me some expenses. I said I would be delighted. He told me he would meet me off the train and take me to my hotel, then collect me and take me to the dinner at Old Trafford. I had never been to Old Trafford so I was really looking forward to it.

Sure enough, when I arrived at Manchester Piccadilly Station, there was Bobby. He took me to his Mercedes and we set off through the evening traffic. I thought, 'I'll wake up in a minute.' I'd hardly been in a Merc before, let alone been driven through Manchester in one by Bobby Charlton.

Where are my mates? I want them all to see this!

Later he came back to the hotel to collect me and we went off to the dinner. One of Old Trafford's huge banqueting suites was packed with several hundred people. At least a third were instantly recognisable football people. All the Manchester United and City greats were there: Denis Law, Paddy Crerand, Francis Lee, Mike Summerbee, Colin Bell . . . The list went on and on, but none of them got on the top table with me. On my first ever visit to Old Trafford I was seated between Bobby Charlton and Sir Matt Busby.

Where are my mates? I *wish* they could see this.

During the evening, as we chatted, it became clear how much Bobby loved the game and loved to play it. Even though he was retired he couldn't resist any charity game or even a kick-about. He played most weekends in a Manchester United veterans side and was, apparently, quite put out if he didn't score.

Later on he remarked how nice it was of me to come. I had just been thinking I would have paid *him* any amount just to be there when he added, 'If ever I can do you a favour . . .'

'Well,' I said, 'it's funny you should mention it . . .'

I told him that my Old Wilsonians Football Club needed some improved training lights and wondered if he would come and play in a fund-raising game. He was instantly up for it. He even started to plan it for me. 'A lot of the lads come down the night before the Footballer of the Year dinner [traditionally held the Thursday before the FA Cup final],' he said, and suggested we hold the game on the Wednesday night and call some of the locals to save on expenses. So I phoned Bobby Moore and Geoff Hurst, and they both said they would play. Then I thought 'World Cup '66!' and got hold of all the rest. Only Nobby Stiles and Alan Ball turned it down as they were abroad, and I replaced one of them with Jimmy Greaves. Suddenly we had a big event on our hands. Crystal Palace chairman Ron Noades let me have Selhurst Park free of charge. A newly arrived North American finance house, HFC Trust, sponsored it. The opposing side wasn't too shabby either. It included Alex Stepney, Mike Summerbee, Francis Lee, Ian St John, Terry Neill, Frank McLintock, Derek Dougan, Ron Harris and Alan Mullery.

It was an amazing night and, as not one of these players failed to show, unlike the Old Wilsonians 6th XI, it was hard to believe that you weren't in the middle of a dream. My top memory from the night was Jack Charlton. He caught the train to Norwood Junction with the fans, then strolled to the ground carrying his boots in a Safeway supermarket plastic bag. We had some 4,500 in the ground, and as Bobby Moore led the team out in those famous red shirts we borrowed from the FA, I had such a lump in my throat I thought I was going to cry.

RED CARD

We held another game the next year – Bobby Charlton's Northern Internationals against Jimmy Greaves' Southern Internationals, with an equally impressive line-up. The late John Charles even came down. People were actually calling me for a game. One was former Palace favourite Mel Blyth. I really had too many people by then, but I let him come in. People like Francis Lee, Mike Summerbee, Colin Bell, David Sadler and others all drove down from Manchester and went straight back again afterwards. I offered them expenses but they all refused. Just as I was leaving, Mel, who lived only a few miles down the road, came up and asked for some petrol money! I couldn't believe it. I dropped my left shoulder and sent him the wrong way. Not a new experience for Mel.

During the second half I was put under a lot of pressure to get on the pitch, but, believe it or not, I felt I shouldn't be out there with people of that quality. I was persuaded eventually, and got changed. Twenty minutes from the end I wandered round behind Alex Stepney's goal and we quietly swapped. We didn't bother to go through the normal channels, like telling FA Cup final referee the sadly late Ron Challis. I just quietly slipped on and Alex wandered back to the tunnel. Only our back line – Terry Neill, Alan Mullery and Frank McLintock – spotted this initially and they collectively agreed that the next time Bobby Charlton got the ball they would back off and let him get in range.

Soon, the opportunity arrived. Bobby let fly with a shot of similar power to the one he scored against Mexico in 1966. It flew into the top corner, Bobby wheeled away, and the crowd invaded the pitch.

While the stewards cleared them, Bobby said to Martin Peters, 'I'll give Alex some stick about that tonight.'

Martin said, 'Bobby, look again.'

Suddenly, he realised it was me in goal. It was the proudest moment of my life. For just a few seconds, Bobby Charlton couldn't tell me from Alex Stepney.

After the game we repaired to the bars and lounges, all of which had sold out with premium prices, which included food, meeting the players, etc. Palace was very much in the doldrums at the time and were drawing not many more than the crowd we had that night. Ron Noades put his arm round my shoulder at some point and said what a good night it was. 'I think I'll drop out of the Football League and have one of these each week,' he added.

ILLEGAL COACHING

Fred Eyre is a really good after-dinner speaker who majors on the fact that, although he played for many professional clubs, he only ever played in one Football League game. He came and played in a game we held the following year between Northern and Southern Internationals, and in 1998 there was an article on him in the *Telegraph*. He said, 'They had some great players like Greaves and Charlton, and I played in the back four shoulder to shoulder with John Charles. After the game, when we were sitting side by side in the dressing room, he put his hand on my knee – and remember, he'd played with the very best: Sivori, Boniperti, the very best – and said, "You know what, Fred? You must be the worst f***ing player I've ever played with in my f***ing life."'

This story has a sad postscript. By the time that game took place George Croucher, Old Wilsonians FC secretary for 45 years and assistant secretary for five years before that, had retired from both undertaking and his football club duties. It goes without saying that we made him Life President. He still came to the club from time to time, but he suffered from angina. Nonetheless, he made sure he always came to the club dinner where he was without fail given a genuine and sincere standing ovation.

Although George always gave me the impression that he didn't really approve of professional footballers, he was nonetheless starry-eyed that night at Selhurst Park. During the evening he came up and squeezed my arm. He had tears in his eyes as he said, 'Who would have ever thought that we would have Bobby Charlton playing for the Old Wilsonians?' His doctor, however, had told him not to get too excited, and that as the OWFC dinner was just two days after this game it would be sensible if he went to only one. He told me this two days later at the dinner and said he had told him he couldn't possibly miss either evening.

After his usual standing ovation, we got on with our dinner and then the speeches. I was the penultimate speaker, proposing the guests before Chris Hare of Old Westminster Citizens FC replied. When I finished, George slipped into the dressing room for a wee. He never came back.

We didn't realise he was missing until Chris finished speaking, but then one of our lads found him. His daughter was called, and she came up to the ground. Although naturally upset, she said straight away that this was where he would have wanted to go. After he was taken away we had a minute's silence for him, then carried on with the evening, as he would have wished.

He was a wonderful man, and I learnt a lot from him. He never tried to interfere in team selection, nor did there ever seem to be any politics or controversy while he was secretary. One saying of his which has stuck with me throughout all my own 'good works' was, 'I am a servant of the members.' That conversation with George gave me a strong belief in democracy and an abhorrence of those who operate on charity committees for their own ends rather than the good of the membership. Sadly, I could name quite a few.

5. DELAYED KICK-OFF

'Everyone can do something really well – and some of us find out what it is.'

Bob 'the Cat' Bevan

It was towards the end of 1976 and I was having lunch in the famous old Wig and Pen Club, the only building in the Strand to survive the Great Fire of London. I had invited my friend Marshall Stewart. It was meant to be a business lunch – at least as far as the company accountant at European Ferries plc was concerned. By this time I was head of public relations for the group, and Marshall was an important contact.

He had started as a journalist on the *Coventry Evening Telegraph*, then gone on to edit the BBC's *South-East News* (crucial to us and our ferries from the south coast). After that he became editor of the BBC Radio 4 flagship *Today* programme. Are you old enough to remember Jack de Manio, the much-loved but bumbling presenter who could never get the time right? Well, Marshall's the man who let him go. At the time it caused as much of a public stir as the departure from Radio 2 of Sir Jimmy Young, the difference being that when he went Sir Jim was still brilliant at his job. Then Marshall took over LBC, the then new London commercial news station. It had started appallingly, but once Marshall got hold of it, taking with him one or two stars from the *Today* programme such as Douglas Cameron, it never looked back. Later he was to become head of communications for the BBC and then Central TV.

You will gather that he was something of a high-flyer, and I was therefore always interested in his advice. In fact, I regarded him as a bit of a guru. We also had plenty in common. He liked football and was a lifelong Coventry City supporter. He also liked a joke and obviously understood people who performed.

From this distance, I can't exactly remember how the conversation started. I would guess I was telling him I was getting a little unsettled at European Ferries, where I had held a senior position since a young age – maybe too young. 'Look,' he said, 'you are now at the height of your powers. You've got your own house, you're single with no ties, you've got a good job, enormous experience, lots of contacts, and between now and the next ten or so years, when you reach your forties, you will have as much energy as you are ever going to have.' His words struck a very loud chord with me, but not as much as his next sentences. 'So forget about what you'd like to do, or be able to do. Work out what you really do well and go and do it.'

I went back to my office. My head was spinning. Not, for once, with the Wig and Pen's fine claret, but with the thoughts he had released in my brain. What did I do really well? I wasn't a bad journalist. I could write competently. I was a pretty good PR man and got on well with the press. But it was clear that I was not going to join the fat-cat main board directors who had given themselves the odd villa in the newly acquired golf complex at La Manga in Spain. I was forever going to be stuck one level below on a reasonable but not special salary.

What I really did well was speaking at dinners, and I liked to make people laugh.

A few days later I called Marshall and told him how much I'd been thinking about what he said. He told me of an agent called Dabber Davis. Once a year, according to Marshall, this guy hired a room in a big London hotel. The Women's Institute and similar organisations would come down and meet various minor celebrities and speakers and book them for their regular meetings. This seemed to be my route in, so I called Dabber, who was fairly off-hand. He didn't really want to know me, but after I had pressed the point he suggested I should send him a tape.

CORNER
Which end of a rope do you throw to a drowning agent? Both of them. And if you meet an agent who says, 'My word is my bond,' take his bond.

For one reason or another, probably being very busy at work, I let things slip for a few months, although Marshall's words were now fixed in my mind for ever. Then, in early 1977, I got a telephone call from a guy called Mike Sweeney, who was secretary of Lloyds Bank FC in the Southern Amateur League. At that time the OWs were pushing to get into what was then the most prestigious of amateur leagues and I had offered my services as an after-dinner speaker to the member clubs in order to push our case. Ironically, Old Wilsonians will join the SAL from 2004/5.

'Ah, Bevan?' said this loud, pompous-sounding Welsh voice down the line.

'Speaking.'

'I believe you're available to speak at dinners?'

I confirmed that I was.

'Well, I thought you'd like to speak at the Lloyds Football Club dinner on Saturday March twenty-first,' he said, the pomposity oozing from every syllable.

It was not how I might have put it, but we were keen to get in the SAL so I decided to go along with it. I confirmed that I would be able to speak and then started to ask a few questions: starting time, dress code, who I would be toasting, all the usual information.

He answered the first two questions, and then said, 'You will be toasting the club.'

'Well, that's fine,' I replied, 'but I usually reply on behalf of the guests because most people [I was trying to appear modest here, and really wanted to say "the other speakers" instead of "most people"] like me to go last.'

He gave a hearty Welsh chuckle. 'Oh, no,' he said, 'you won't be going last. We always have a professional [and here he heavily emphasised the word "professional"] to do that.'

As I put the telephone down, I thought, 'What a stuck-up Welsh git.' He is actually a friend of mine these days. Still a stuck-up Welsh git, but a good friend nonetheless.

I decided that I would base my whole speech on this telephone call. At that time I hadn't considered who the professional might be, or the effect such an approach might have on him. He turned out to be Major Bob Gray. I had seen him at one or two stag nights at the Old Wilsonians about ten years earlier. These were interesting affairs which seem to have faded now. Throughout the evening a whole string of blue comics and strippers would come and go from the club, all of them doing three, four, maybe five gigs in the area that evening. It was, of course, highly possible that comics would start telling a joke that had been told earlier, but it was surprising how infrequently that happened.

It was a lesson for me later at a dinner in Kent when I went for a wee before going on and, on my return, found Jimmy Hill on his feet having already started to introduce me. When, after about twenty minutes, I started the 'deaf and dumb dinner/dance' gag I was surprised that it was not hitting the target. Nobody stopped me, so I finished it and moved on. Only afterwards did Jimmy tell me that he had told it while I was having a wee. The audience was too polite to tell me. That certainly wasn't the case with the stag nights. But now I never leave if someone is likely to get to their feet.

Major Bob didn't have the greatest act. If I tell you that he used to produce a packet of soap powder, which, he said, contained the magic ingredients 'FU2', you will get the drift. It seemed funnier then, although, to be fair, not much funnier. By the time he arrived at Lloyds Bank FC he was on the way down, if he'd ever been up. My constant references to his 'professional' status took away whatever chance he might have had. People walked out, which was sad to see, for he was a nice old boy. Afterwards he said some complimentary things about me and suggested I could earn some money doing it. I thanked him, then unwittingly insulted him. I told him that I had a good job and that my Saturday nights were rather precious to me. Certainly not worth giving up for a tenner or so. He said something along the lines of 'please yourself' and cleared off.

Downstairs in the bar, Sweeney bought me a pint. 'That was very good,' he said, and apologised for Major Bob. I said it was not a problem for me; I had actually felt sorry for the old boy. 'Even so,' Sweeney continued, 'I feel bad about it. I think I should give you the sixty quid.' Sixty quid? At the time I was earning about £8,000 a year plus car and some generous expenses, but £60 here and there wouldn't go amiss. Perhaps Saturday nights were not so important after all.

Later that year I started to contact Dabber Davis again. He was not all that interested, so early in 1978 I recorded myself at the Bank of England FC dinner and sent him a tape. Still there was no response. After several reminder letters I called him. 'Have you got my tape?' He said he had. He had listened to it but felt it was just a collection of old gags. That might be true now, but then I felt it was ridiculous. Much of my material was original and based on my failure as a goalkeeper.

It was to become a point of principle between us. From time to time, as I broke through, I would send him a press cutting. When I made an LP of football gags in 1982, I sent him a copy but still got no response.

Years later, I was sitting having a drink in Fred Trueman's lounge when the phone went. It was Dabber. Fred had his usual animated conversation with him.

'Yes, Dabber, just let me check the book. No, Dabber, I can't manage that. No, I'm in the north-east, Dabber. Sorry, Dabber . . .'

'Tell him I can do it,' I cut in. I didn't even know what the date was but I was trying to score a point.

'Oh, hang on, Dabber. I've got Bob "the Cat" Bevan here, Dabber, and he says he can do it. Oh, right. Oh, I see, Dabber. Right, Dabber. OK, Dabber. Bye, Dabber.'

'What did he say?' I asked as Fred put the phone down.

'He said he wanted a sportsman,' Fred replied.

I finally met Dabber when he was a guest at the Benedictine After-Dinner Speaker Awards in 1990, which I won. He was very pleasant, and said at the end of the evening, 'I suppose I had better get you a job now!' I never heard from him again. But I might send him a copy of this book – with an invoice.

YOU COMIN' OR WOT?

'All marriages are happy. It's the living together afterwards that causes all the trouble.'

Anon

It was mid-summer in 1991 and I was skippering the Lord's Taverners side at Milton Keynes when I first noticed her. She had a very pretty face and a good figure with plenty of curves in the right places. She was wearing a white trouser suit and, as she walked away, I asked my friend, Lennie Lawrence, who she was. What I actually said was, ' 'Ere, Cocker [one of Lennie's nicknames], that's a bit fit.'] He told me she was Laura Collins and that she was at the games quite often. I was sure that she had never been at the games in which I had played but, after that, I noticed her at one or two other Taverner events.

Laura had been born in Croydon and had a wonderful childhood. She was very close to her parents, as she remains to this day. Her father was a jazz musician and she travelled the country with them, having very happy memories of summer seasons at the seaside and of staying up late and dancing to the music almost as soon as she could stand.

Later she went to Italia Conti Drama School and had a varied career in show business. Perhaps the most notable achievement was as a member of the famous dance group, Pan's People. Though she was not part of the team that appeared on *Top of the Pops*, she was involved later on in shows with Les Dawson and Jim Davidson.

She appeared in many pantomimes, repertory and TV shows. She played a barmaid in a series called *Potter* with Arthur Lowe and Robin Bailey and, to my great envy, was also on several Tommy Cooper shows. Outside of comedy she was in many drama productions, some of them live. Not long ago she received a cheque for 50p from the Performing Rights Society. One of her early plays must have been shown in Botswana, or somewhere, Her father, now an agent for dwarfs (yes, really) said that it would cost 75p to cash it and what about his commission? I said we should frame it.

Late in the season I played at Sittingbourne and Laura came up to speak to me. She was on the Lady Taverners Ball Committee and she had been nominated to ask me if I would be the master of ceremonies for the evening. Despite the fact that she is always sun-tanned I felt sure that she was blushing. She denies it but her mother, who was also there, agrees with me.

I was unattached at the time and was enjoying the experience so, when a single ticket arrived, I sensed that I was being lined up with her. I asked a girl friend, Georgina Sullivan, who was PR at the Sheraton in Knightsbridge and one of my clients, to come with me as protection. Like most women, on hearing the story about why, Georgina couldn't wait to come and spent much of the night watching Laura. My PR company was doing well at the time and the girls who worked for me were also always on the lookout to set me up with someone or seeking out the latest news on any date I might have had.

THROW-IN

It is said, and I accept it may not be true, that Jack Charlton never buys a drink in Ireland where he achieved wonders managing their football team. In a bar he allegedly always pays by cheque and the owner is so knocked out at having him in the place that they frame it rather than cash it. I do hope it is true.

A week later I was picked to play for the Taverners in Florida – more for my cabaret appearance than my cricketing ability. Just before I went I had a job at the England versus Germany football match at Wembley and my colleague John Norris drove me up there. To my amazement, in the hotel bar we met Laura who had been given some tickets and, although she doesn't like football, decided to take her parents.

When she saw me she came over and gave me a show business kiss, much to John's delight – he was already planning how he would deliver the news in the office the next morning. Laura then followed this up by saying to John, 'Bob and I are off to Florida together next week.' John almost died of happiness on the spot.

I had had no idea that Laura was in the party going to Florida but there was little point in trying to convince John of that. What I was unaware of was that, in addition to the players, people were paying

£700 a head to come with us. Laura had had a traumatic year: her marriage had folded almost before it started and, after a five-year wait, her divorce had come through; her father had also just recovered from a heart attack. She wanted to get away but not on her own and this trip, with many of her friends, seemed an ideal opportunity.

It sounds spooky but, when we got to the airport, our luggage matched. We did not sit together on the plane although I did notice her from time to time. She was always asleep (hence her nickname of 'Petal' as she drops off a lot).

At Miami, when I boarded the coach I had to choose between sitting next to former Hampshire and England fast bowler Butch White or Laura. I chose the pretty one. Don't even go there. Of course it was Laura. We chatted away for a bit and then she asked, 'Do you mind if I put my head on your shoulder?'

'What? I queried.

'Do you mind if I put my head on your shoulder?'

What else could I do but agree? Although I did think that here was a forward young woman. She now says she was bored by my chatter but I know that sleeping is her favourite pastime.

On our first morning I went shopping with my friend Derek Ufton, Judith Chalmers and former Somerset and Northamptonshire cricketer, Roy Virgin and their better halves. When we got back they invited me to join them for lunch on the coast. I went back to my free room by the pool (as opposed to Laura's £700 room which, rather disgracefully, she was having to share with a courier). As I went by I saw her by the pool and asked if she wanted to make up the numbers for lunch. She was clearly interested but said it was rather awkward as someone had just bought her a drink. I went on to my room and when I came back I uttered the immortal pulling line 'You comin' or wot?'

She came and I treated her to an eight quid lunch. That night she was doing something and I went out with cricketers John Emburey, John Snow and Graham Johnson. But I got back in time for a drink with Laura and we have hardly been apart since. Although I have never managed to get away with an eight quid lunch again.

We were a bit concerned that it was just a holiday romance so nothing 'happened' in Florida although we did get close one night. It was just as well we resisted for there was only one way out of my room and that was straight on to the pool. The morning after that night the breakfast room was closed for a conference and the entire party was moved to the pool. Had she stayed she would have had to walk out to face them all the next morning.

When we got home we met to go to a film (not that we saw much of it) and then a Chinese meal. Eighteen months later I took her to Paris on Valentine's Day and proposed over a candlelit dinner on the Seine. It all sounds very romantic until I tell you that, although she accepted, she cried for the rest of the night.

We haven't actually got round to tying the knot yet. It doesn't worry us, only everyone else.

Incidentally, on our first night together in Laura's Fulham flat I had a nasty shock. When I woke up I had paralysed legs. As I looked down a black cat was lying on one ankle and a white one on the other.

They were Fiona (white) and Jasper (black). Fiona was found under the floorboards and adopted Laura in 1987. She was only a year old. Fiona, not Laura. Soon after she had four kittens. Fiona not Laura. Three were given away. By Laura not Fiona. Jasper stayed and they are both still around.

In the spring of 2003 the cats moved to my country oasthouse for their retirement. Of course you have to keep them in to start with so I spent two months as a cat's lavatory attendant. When they go out they don't go hunting. They are Fulham cats after all. I expect they are paying someone to do it for them. We love them, and they love us dearly though Fiona, who has been Laura's soulmate through all her heartaches has nearly died twice. Once, when we nearly had to cancel a trip to Menorca because Fiona was so ill, Laura revealed that she has been paying private vet insurance all their lives. She said that, if we had to cancel, the insurance would not only cover her holiday but mine as well. I was amazed.

'That's better than my travel insurance,' I said. 'What's it called?'

'Supercat.' I'm thinking of getting some for me.

When she (Fiona not Laura) was not taking her four pills a day hidden in her food we went back to the vets. Fiona has to have special LD food for her liver while Jasper, who has a slight kidney ailment, has special tins of KD. The vet said that we ought to give Fiona some new food called AD. We asked what it was for. He said, and I swear this is true, that it was for anorexic cats.

So what is it that Laura sees in me? Who knows? It's a mystery to everyone, including me. What do I see in her? Well, she's lovely, inside and out, very loving and still brings an almost childlike magic to major occasions, especially Christmas and birthdays.

Of course, she is a woman, so she does drive me mad from time to time, not least because of all the good works she gets involved with after which, because of her need for sleep, she can collapse for days on end. However, she is also great company and very funny, not always intentionally. After a drink she does try to tell an occasional joke, sometimes one of mine, but has hardly ever been known to get one right.

Then there are the Petalisms. I leave you with one example. Two years ago we went on another Taverners trip to Aberdeen for the Gavin Hastings Classic. We arrived on the Friday ready for cricket on the Saturday and golf on the Sunday. At our hotel we were given a welcome pack which included, of course, some small bottles of whisky. We were all in the bar near midnight and we were wondering whether to get to bed or have one more for the road. There was great indecision about what to do when Laura helpfully piped up: 'I know,' she said, 'why don't you all go back to your rooms and get out your little miniatures?' There was a silence, then a Laura scream as the inference hit home, and we all fell on the floor. Needless to say we had to have another drink.

First Half

6. KICK-OFF

'Always cast your bread upon the water. You never know when it might float back as a smoked salmon sandwich.'

Lew Grade

I've got this friend, Dick Ayers, who runs a company called Touchline Promotions from his kitchen in Shooters Hill, south-east London. Dick, who started life in an advertising agency but quickly got fed up, is one of life's great eccentrics. When he left advertising he went off to run two bars (although not at the same time) in Calafjell, near Barcelona. When he came back and started his company he began by selling cheap promotional gear. Not the sort of gear I would want in the house. Yet, amazingly, it sells. He has a creative flair and has spotted many market opportunities over the years.

In the late 1970s he hit upon the idea of selling stickers, badges and the like to FA and Football League Cup semi-finalists and finalists. He would go around the various teams' local newsagents, often on his Raleigh fold-up bike as he had been positively breathalysed. He must have done well because once he was stopped by a motorist who warned him that fivers were flying out of his back pocket as he cycled along. At other times, when he was on foot or using public transport, he would be accompanied by his collie dog, Addick – so named because of Dick's lifelong addiction to Charlton Athletic, sometimes called the Addicks.

DOG ON THE PITCH
Back before the Valley was converted into the superb stadium it now is, you could wander in free of charge to watch the reserves. One mid-week afternoon Dick did just that, and Addick the collie went with him. The dog was never on a lead in his life, and wandered up and down the empty terraces while Dick watched the game. Charlton Reserves were playing Watford Reserves, for whom Luther Blissett was making his debut. In the second half, while play was in progress, Addick strolled on to the pitch and cocked his leg against the goalpost. Dick said, with some pride, 'Great dog. He did it at the Watford end.'

Dick's various badges would have terrible puns written on them. Some are a bit dated now, such as those for the 1975 West Ham v. Fulham FA Cup final: FLOAT LIKE A BUBBLE, STING LIKE A HAMMER; HAMMERS BUBBLE AND SQUEAK FULHAM; BILLY (Bonds) BITES YER COTTAGE LOAFERS; HAPPINESS DAY IS MERVYN (Charlton's assistant manager Mervyn Day was the Hammers goalkeeper). But my favourite related to the Fulham goalkeeper Peter Mellor. It was around the time of the court furore surrounding D.H. Lawrence's novel *Lady Chatterley's Lover*: MELLOR IS A GAME KEEPER. For Manchester United against Southampton in 1976 there were MAN UTD – (Mick) CHANNON FODDER and LOU MACARI – BIONIC HAGGIS. And for Liverpool against Borussia Mönchengladbach in the 1977 European Cup final in Rome: POPE PAISLEY RULES ROME, REDS BITE YER KRAUT KNEECAPS (not of course politically correct now) and TOMMY SMITH BITES YER ANYWHERE. But the best, or worst, of all was the badge for the 1978 World Cup final between Holland and hosts Argentina, which coincided with the musical *Evita*: DON'T CRUYFF FOR ME, ARGENTINA. In those days you could produce such things without needing permission to breathe in terms of royalties.

Lawrie McMenemy, then manager of Southampton well before his ill-fated move to Sunderland, actually called Dick to see what percentage his club was getting from all the cup final merchandise he was selling. Dick told him there was nothing in it for them, but that it was good news for the club in terms of promotion and publicity. Lawrie invited him down for a meeting and actually offered Dick the job of commercial manager. Dick declined.

THROW-IN

'There are two things that should never have left Southampton: the *Titanic* and Lawrie McMenemy' – Sunderland chairman Bob Murray.

Once Dick got his car back he started to sell such merchandise to football clubs. I had given him a copy of the tape I had made at the Bank of England FC dinner, and during one visit to Ipswich Town he had a meeting with their commercial man, Mel Henderson. Dick discovered that Mel, now a local journalist in Suffolk, knew me as he regularly tapped me up for a free car ferry ticket on the Felixstowe–Zeebrugge route every time Ipswich had a dinner. Being a good PR man, he always invited me along as a guest, which virtually no one else who was the recipient of my generosity did. To be fair, I, as a football fan, always went to the Ipswich dinners. Most of the other things I supported with free car ferry tickets – fêtes, fairs, the Women's Institute – I wouldn't have been seen dead at. Dick told Mel that I was a good after-dinner speaker, and although Dick takes the credit for opening this door quite wide, it was not entirely down to him. Dick told me that Mel would be asking me to speak, but in fact Mel was not going to use me just on Dick's advice, for reasons I fully understand.

I once did a rugby dinner in the Rose Room at Twickenham, for example, with the famous toastmaster Ivor Spencer. Things went well, and when I sat down Ivor went to the mike and said, 'Once again, your appreciation, please, gentlemen, for Bob "the Cat" Bevan.' I stood up again, modestly received my applause, gestured my thanks to Ivor, and resumed my seat.

'Well, gentlemen,' Ivor continued, 'wasn't that wonderful? Well, now we have some entertainment for you . . .' This was instantly picked up by the audience. A roar hit the room, and Ivor couldn't continue. I got up and pretended to walk out. It was some time before order was restored. I could see how it had happened: the menu had read 'Guest speaker – Bob "the Cat" Bevan; Entertainment – XYZ Show Band'.

What is the point of all this? I hear you ask. Well, the show band weren't in the Premiership of bands. Some guy had seen them at his golf club, they had gone down well and been booked. It is a mistake so often made. You just cannot take someone from an event like that and expect them to operate alongside top-class full-time entertainers. It's like putting a team from the Ryman League straight into the Premiership.

Mel Henderson knew this only too well, and when I hadn't heard anything I called him. He clearly felt a bit nervous, but as one of his benefactors I put him on the spot a bit. He must have accepted the situation because my name was shown on the menu. The meeting between Mel and Dick was clearly a stroke of luck for me, but, with this phone call, I made my own luck. The other speakers that night were *Daily Express* football writer Steve Curry (now with the *Daily Mail*), Essex cricketer Ray East, and Jim Rosenthal, then a Radio 2 sports journalist but now ITV's Grand Prix presenter. In the chair was John Motson, and, as it was a Monday night, manager Bobby Robson and all the team were there too. It was a particularly memorable evening because Ipswich were the FA Cup holders at the time, having beaten Arsenal 1–0 at Wembley in May 1978, and it was the first time I had actually touched the famous old trophy – always a magical moment for any true football fan.

In those days I still used notes, and my eyesight must have been better than it is now because they are all written on the back of business cards. I have kept them all, carefully filed – until, of course, the day I stopped using them. How I wish I'd still kept a record of what I'd used on every occasion since. Perhaps I'll start again? Unlike my debut at the Old Wilsonians, where I can hardly see the laughs, the Ipswich material looks quite good from the prompt notes I can decipher. In fact, 25 years on I'm still using some of the jokes. For example, in one sequence I say, 'I never thought I'd be at a dinner with the FA Cup. Nor be introduced by the best football commentator on TV.' Applause from the audience. Motty is sucked in and thinks I'm being generous. 'And until tonight I'd always thought MC stood for Master of Ceremonies. But now I realise it stands for something completely different. And the first word is Monumental.' Motty took all this in good part, as does everyone else. However someone once did get the hump when I said he was referred to in the *Guardian* as a cult. I had to explain to him that if you *really* meant it you wouldn't say it.

I have to pause here and state, for the record, that I *do* think Motty is the best in the business. He really loves the game. Is besotted with it. A really true professional. On the field, however, he is not quite so sharp. A few years later I initiated an annual game between the Commentators and the Old Wilsonians which was a high-quality match and sometimes got a little nasty. Alan Parry and Jim Rosenthal can certainly play, and Martin Tyler played for Corinthian Casuals as a kind of white Dion Dublin. Motty, however, was more our 6th XI standard, although he did score against me once. He tapped in when I missed a corner – not a new experience for me. He did say later that he couldn't miss a foot from the line; I had to tell him, 'I don't think you were as far out as that.' Worse than letting the bloody thing in was, for me, the fact that he never lets me forget it.

At the dinner, I soon moved on to my own football prowess. Our level of football is under the auspices of the Amateur Football Alliance, which is affiliated to the FA. Some 50 years earlier Ipswich themselves had been at this level in the Southern Amateur League. In fact, they played this sort of football from 1907 right up until 1935. Although football fans talk about the rise of Wimbledon being the most spectacular, I think Ipswich's rise must count as even more amazing. Just 27 years after leaving this minor amateur league – and bear in mind they lost eight years when competitions were suspended because of the Second World War – they won the old First Division, just a year after promotion, in the process pushing the previous season's champions and FA Cup winners Tottenham Hotspur into third place. Bear in mind, too, that Spurs had just become the first team in the twentieth century to win the League and FA Cup double and had added Jimmy Greaves to their squad. I saw Ipswich win 3–1 at Tottenham during their 1961/62 championship season, and despite playing in some really old-fashioned kit, they were an excellent side. They outplayed Spurs on the night. Their manager was Alf Ramsey. Whatever happened to him?

I actually spent one season, 1966/67, away from the OWs with West Wickham in the SAL. Then it was a much higher standard, both in terms of play and facilities, with all the big business houses, as shown in the 1934/35 league table, still in membership along with other major insurance companies. That season I played left-half in West Wickham's 5th XI (they had six sides), and we came second in the First Division to Midland Bank. Even though the football was better, I still missed my mates and went back to the OWs the following year. I immediately became skipper of the 4th XI and quickly moved myself back to *right*-half.

While discussing this with an elderly colleague at work, I discovered that he had played for Merton, who are still in the SAL today. This chap, Brigadier Jimmy Green, told me all about playing in the 1920s when Ipswich were in the league. He said that the crowds were huge. Many thousands. Most people did not have cars, DIY had not been invented and the family life was not so demanding. So Saturday football was the big male outing of the week. Jimmy told me that the gate was so large that they opted, despite the distance and inconvenience, to play both their home and away games at Ipswich simply for their share of the receipts. They also had to take a suit for the dinner after the game and were still able to get home by public transport afterwards. Those were the days!

I'm not sure how interested my Ipswich audience was with some of this, but they soon perked up when I did an original gag about the cup final. Ipswich had played really well and had dominated Arsenal for much of the game. 'Arsenal centre-forward Malcolm Macdonald said to the referee after about twenty minutes, "Can we have a new ball, ref?" The ref said, "What's wrong with the one we've got?" Supermac replied, "Ipswich are playing with that one."' I also told a joke I'd heard on the radio a few weeks earlier which went down well for years afterwards. During the war, Churchill was on his way to the BBC in a cab where he was due to make a speech. When he arrived he said to the cabbie, 'Wait for me, my man.' The cabbie retorted, 'I'd rather not, guv. Old Churchill's on the radio in ten minutes and I never like to miss one of his speeches.' Churchill was so moved that he handed over, through the window, a £10 tip, which was, of course, an enormous amount of money in those days. The cabbie looked at it, then said, 'Oh, all right, guv. Sod Churchill, I'll wait.'

After this, I went into the hopelessness of my game. Much of this material had initially been written by my friend Brian Robinson.

PLAY STOPPED – ANORAK ON THE PITCH

Here are the Southern Amateur League's First Division tables during Ipswich Town's first and last seasons. The season they left, you will note, they only finished fourth.

1907/08	P	W	D	L	F	A	Pts
New Crusaders	16	13	2	1	80	15	28
Richmond Association	16	11	0	5	39	25	22
Ealing Association	16	7	5	4	47	37	19
Civil Service	16	7	4	5	28	20	18
Casuals	16	6	5	5	36	29	17
Eastbourne	16	6	4	6	35	46	16
Ipswich Town	16	5	4	7	36	40	14
Townley Park	16	2	3	11	25	46	7
Croydon	16	1	1	14	12	83	3

1934/35	P	W	D	L	F	A	Pts
Hastings & St Leonards	22	15	4	3	68	26	34
Civil Service	22	12	7	3	40	29	31
Cambridge Town	22	13	2	7	48	30	28

Ipswich Town	22	11	4	7	50	40	26
Catford Wanderers	22	9	5	8	52	52	23
Lloyds Bank	22	10	3	9	47	49	23
Barclays Bank	22	8	4	10	46	49	20
Merton	22	6	5	11	26	39	17
Midland Bank	22	6	4	12	34	50	16
Westminster Bank	22	6	4	12	30	48	16
Eastbourne	22	6	3	13	41	47	15
Bank of England	22	4	7	11	43	66	15

Having been to so many other clubs' dinners, I initiated the revival of Old Wilsonians FCs in the 1970s, and they were held at our club in Hayes. I had also worked out who were the best speakers and all played in the Southern Olympian League. Neither the SAL or the Old Boys League had any speakers of quality. I have immodestly referred to us as the Famous Five. The others were Geoff Brown of Old Grammarians (brother of the former Fulham, Watford and Barnet striker Bobby Brown), Brian Robinson of Old Parmiterians, Del Steward of Old Monovians and Les Williamson of Old Owens. Brian was a ginger-haired Old Parmiterian left-back; he is still their president and leading light, though today he is neither hairy nor ginger. As I have already said, even after meeting many full-time professional writers, I have never come across anyone who tops Robbo for comic invention.

A year or two before the Ipswich dinner I had invited him to come and speak at our dinner. He had obviously got some background on me, or maybe he had watched me play, or maybe both. I was already known in the club as the Cat (with considerable irony), but on this night he brought the whole image to life. He was the one who decided I was called the Cat because I gave my defence kittens. He added a second reason which I'd best not reveal here.

What he said next was to be the basis of my act at Ipswich and the foundation from which everything would flow. (Little did I think then that a quarter of a century later Robbo and I would be walking through the House of Commons to write material together for the Leader of the Opposition.)

'Last week,' said Robbo, 'he arrived at the ground early and he felt the need to loosen up. So he got changed. Then he went outside and broke into a walk. He was there in his Peter Shilton jersey. His Peter Shilton shorts. His Peter Shilton gloves. His Peter Shilton glasses. A bit of Peter Shilton elastic holding them on at the back.' It was all new stuff, and it brought the house down. Later on he suggested that I might be retiring through illness and fatigue – 'The whole of the team are sick and tired of him' – and that my gloves were up for sale in the weekly newsletter: 'One pair of goalkeeping gloves. Hardly used.'

As I sat there listening to this material for the first time, I thought to myself, 'As he's giving me all this stick, I think I'm entitled to nick this.' A day or two later my PR antenna clicked in as I realised that 'the Cat' would be my brand name and that henceforth I would always be advertised as Bob 'the Cat' Bevan. But for my grandfather's name change it could have been Bob 'the Cat' Tenenbaum, which doesn't have quite the same ring to it.

I went on first at Ipswich, and the applause was rapturous. My fellow speakers, all of whom have remained friends, never followed me again. Bobby Robson, the players, Jimmy Hill, Terry Neill, all came up to me afterwards to say well done. I made a mental note to call Dabber Davis the next morning and let him know what had happened. Surely now this was the start of my professional career as an entertainer?

Well, nearly. I would have to wait another year for the final breakthrough.

NO LOVE LOST BEHIND THE GOAL

'It's better to tell an average story brilliantly than a brilliant story averagely.'

Anon.

It was on my 50th birthday, a Sunday, that Fred Price came to my house for the last time. Laura and I had been in Australia for six weeks and I was torn about whether to have a party or not. In the end I decided against it and went to play football for Lloyds Bank Golden Oldies. What else do you do on the morning of your 50th? Our friends Viv and Derek Taylor (he was a director of Oldham Athletic and chairman of the Yorkshire Lord's Taverners) had arrived on the Saturday for a birthday meal, and to my surprise Derek came with me. I did notice that during the game he spent most of the time watching the next pitch and failed to see all of the seven I let in. Merton clearly were unaware it was my birthday.

I live in an old oast house in Kent, which is half a mile from the road down a track. When we got back home, at the top of the track there were some balloons. By then I had forgotten it was my birthday and remarked that it must be a party for one of my neighbours' six kids. As we drove down there were more balloons, and they were red and blue – Crystal Palace colours. 'At least they're the right colour,' I observed to a still deadpan Derek. As we came through the wood to where the view opens out and you see my house, all became clear. There were dozens of cars parked around it, each bearing red and blue balloons.

I had been done. Several ladies, all friends of Laura's, poured out of the front door to photograph a startled Cat. Using my years of experience in PR, I uttered the immortal words, 'Any of *my* friends here?' I'm not sure she's got over that yet. All my friends *were* there, including Robert Newey, with whom I go to watch Palace. We share the same birthday – he's asked me to point out he's much younger – and I asked him to help me cut my cake which was in the shape of a

Crystal Palace shirt. Ironically it had been made at the Charlton bakery, but you can't have everything.

Let me pause here to give you the background on Fred. He was a very funny guy who brought smiles to everyone's faces the minute he entered a room. He was also an excellent sportsman. I was in my teens when I first saw him playing for Bromley in the Isthmian League. In fact, he was in their championship winning side in 1960/61. They played at home to St Albans on Saturday, 6 May 1961; it was a 6.30 kick-off on FA Cup final evening. They won 4–2, and Eric Nottage scored a hat-trick. How do I know? I was there and I've got the programme. (Sad man that I am, I have kept every programme of every game I have ever been to.) Pricey also played for Charlton as an amateur, and for Bexleyheath and Welling in the semi-professional Southern League, again as an amateur. He was unlucky not to get a few amateur international and Olympic caps, but there were several good keepers around at the time. Later on I came to know him, along with Eric Nottage, Les Nelson and others in that team, when I started playing veterans football. They played for Old Bromleians. I greatly enjoyed telling them that I used to watch them 'from my daddy's shoulders'.

Humour can be a great ice-breaker, and Fred was a master of the art. After I cut my cake and the cries of 'Speech, speech!' went up, I was a bit overcome and couldn't speak. At least not until Pricey called out, 'He's bloody useless when he's not being paid.'

There were so many stories about him, and others that he told. It didn't matter how many times you heard them, you still laughed. Not only did he play with the veterans, he carried on in the lower sides on Saturdays as well. One Saturday, when he was playing at Norman Park, Bromley, he went to collect a ball from the bushes behind the goal. There he heard someone trying to attract his attention. 'Pssst!' came the noise. 'Pssst!' In the undergrowth, he spied a woman.

'I've got to speak to George,' she said.

'You can't,' said Pricey. 'It's an Old Boys cup tie and we're in extra time.'

'Tell him I'm here,' she begged.

Fred went back on to the pitch and told George – name changed, for obvious reasons – who said he'd leave it until full-time. When the first period of extra time finished, George shot into the bushes. He had been having an affair with this woman and she had come to tell him that his wife had found out.

George returned to the pitch, finished the game and said he would have to pop home. He handed Fred the beer whip, saying, 'I'll be up the club soon.' What he said to his wife we shall never know, but the marriage survived and George was at the club an hour later to take back the beer whip.

Continuing the bushes theme, we were playing cricket at Bromley Common once and we were getting a hiding. Fred went into the undergrowth with a crowd of other fielders to look for the ball. After a while, someone spotted that Pricey wasn't moving.

'I've found it,' he said. 'We'll just hang around a bit longer to slow 'em up before lunch.'

'You prat,' said one of the others. 'It's a limited-overs game.'

We were standing in the bar at the Old Bromleians after another veterans game and Fred and Les Nelson were reminiscing about a London Challenge Cup tie under poor floodlights against Brentford reserves in the late 1950s. 'I remember playing under these terrible lights and they got a free-kick,' Fred said. 'I lined the wall up perfectly yet somehow it went in like a rocket. I don't know how it got through, and I got an almighty bollocking from [Bromley secretary] Charlie King.'

Les said he remembered the incident, and the bollocking.

'How it got in I still don't know,' Fred repeated, shaking his head.

'I can tell you,' said Les. 'I ducked.'

'You what?'

'I ducked. Well, it was a heavy ball in those days, and he didn't half tonk it.'

Fred then issued his own bollocking, 25 years late.

Another of Fred's traits was his inability to get a joke right. He laughed at most gags, but I often wondered if he always understood them. I told him one once which I had read in the most unlikely of sources, the *Financial Times*. A PR man was on a visit to Czechoslovakia, and on his arrival in Prague was met by a high-ranking official who took him into the mountains on a hunting trip. During this outing they were attacked by a bear which killed and ate the high-ranking official. The PR man escaped and made it back to Prague. The local police decided that they could not have bears eating high-ranking officials and demanded that he go back with them into the mountains to seek out and kill the man-eater. They soon came across a male and a female bear. They asked the PR man which one had attacked and eaten the high-ranking official, and the male bear was identified. So they shot it and cut it open, but there was no sign of the remains of the high-ranking official. They then shot the female bear and opened her up. Sure enough, there were the remains of the high-ranking official. The moral of the tale is 'never trust a PR man when he says the cheque is in the mail'.

I met up with Fred a few nights after I had told him this story.

'Bloody useless, your jokes, Bevin [he always deliberately mispronounced my name]. I told it at work today and nobody laughed.'

'It's the way you tell 'em, Pricey.'

'No it's not. You're bloody useless, Bevin.'

A few days later I was driving three or four people somewhere and Fred was in the back. I heard him start to tell the joke. Eventually he got to the punchline. I heard him say, 'And the moral is, never trust a PR man when he says the cheque is in the post.'

He died far too young from prostate cancer, but he was still able to stop us from getting too sad. I called from the car when he was in hospital and nearing the end. It was a sad conversation, and we experienced a rare awkward silence. He sensed I was upset.

'Never mind, Bevin,' he said, 'I've left you me stamp collection.'

'I don't collect 'em.'

'I know,' he said.

7. EARLY GOAL

'Get your first tackle in early – even if it's late.'

Ray Gravell, Welsh rugby international

Apart from the occasional telephone call from Mel Henderson, I was not aware of the impact my appearance at Ipswich had made, nor would I be for another year. The agent Dabber Davis continued to ignore me, so I went back to my car ferries job and appeared at the various amateur football dinners still without pay. At least now I had the added confidence of knowing that I could go out to an audience that had never heard me and do well. I also knew that I had a unique brand of material that would be especially popular at football dinners.

As far back as 1974 I had started to think I might be able to do it, even before Major Bob Gray's assessment of me at the Lloyds Bank FC dinner three years later. In 1977, when I was working at Townsend Thoresen, the marketing director had received a letter from Harry Swales, agent for, among others, show jumper Harvey Smith. Harry, an extrovert Yorkshireman with a huge moustache and side whiskers, started to look after the England football team during Bobby Robson's reign. He also became the agent for Bryan Robson and Ryan Giggs, again among others. In 1974, Harry was seeking sponsorship for Harvey's horses. If this was not the first such idea in that particular sport, it was very nearly so. If we decided to go ahead, Harvey would be jumping on Townsend Thoresen Dobbin, Townsend Thoresen Ned, and so on.

Generally speaking, sponsorship was not something our company got into. It's very difficult to quantify, and decisions are often based more on the marketing director's ego than on any commercial reason. So I was quite surprised when I was asked to follow this up. I called Harry Swales, who, though I didn't know it then, is a leading light in the Variety Club. 'Why don't you come up and meet Harvey and discuss it with him?' said Harry. As I started to consider whether I wanted to go all the way to Yorkshire, he hit me with a sucker punch. 'On Sunday night we're holding a Variety Club tribute dinner to Don Revie [the manager of Leeds United during their great days with Billy

Bremner, Jack Charlton, etc]. Harvey's coming, so why don't you come and join us?' I needed no second invitation.

On Sunday I caught the train from King's Cross and settled down to read the detailed sponsorship proposal and all the Sunday papers. If it hadn't been for the length of the journey I might not have got to the *Sunday People*. There, on the front page, was a picture of Harvey Smith in a wrestling ring. As I read the story it appeared that Harvey had taken up this sport as well. Professionally.

When I got to the dinner I saw, live for the first time, a whole host of people I had only previously watched on television. Ten years or more down the line I would come to know them all, some of them well. Hosting the event were Michael Parkinson and David Coleman, speaking were Joe Mercer and Stanley Mortensen – the hat-trick hero from what is not totally fairly described as the Matthews final, when Blackpool beat Bolton 4–3 after being 3–1 down. Stan was an excellent after-dinner speaker, not only that night but on the many subsequent occasions when I would work with him.

I remember sitting there with Harvey Smith thinking how much I would like to address this audience. But it would be romantic to say that at that moment I determined to break into this scene. It was more a case of wondering if I ever would.

It became an even more special evening when Eamonn Andrews appeared and did *This is Your Life* on Don right there and then. As a result all sorts of other big names appeared, including the manager of Leeds' biggest rivals, Liverpool's Bill Shankly. After this was all done they actually got on with the dinner, and the speeches went on well into the early hours. I sat next to Harvey throughout and asked him about his wrestling; he confirmed that it was true. I said that we would be worried about him getting injured and not being able to ride his horses.

When I got back to London I wrote to Harry Swales and said we would be happy to sponsor the horses for the figure quoted. However, I said I wanted to insert a rider – not a horse rider – stating that payments would be made on a sliding scale based on the quality of the events. There would be no payment due if Harvey were unable to appear. They didn't take up this offer, but Harry and I have remained friends to this day, and I subsequently appeared at many functions with Harvey, who was no mean performer himself after dinner.

* * *

During the 1966 World Cup, Martin Peters was hailed by Sir Alf Ramsey as being 'ten years ahead of his time'. That label dogged him throughout his playing career and I guess he could have lived without it. Similarly, during the 1970s Crystal Palace were due to be the Team of the Eighties under Terry Venables. We Palace supporters have had to live with that for a quarter of a century. Needless to say, it was the kiss of death. Chairman Ray Bloye suddenly decamped, and El Tel followed (to Queens Park Rangers) along with some of our best players.

But if the 1980s never came for Palace, they certainly came up trumps for me. As I entered the new decade I still had not secured a paid engagement, despite my efforts and a growing feeling that I was good enough. Then, out of the blue – and I still have no idea how this guy heard about me or found my address – I had a telephone call from one Michael Jackson. The Isthmian League's Harlow Town were the FA Cup giant-killers of 1979/80. They had drawn at Leicester and then beaten them in the replay. They were putting on a charity dinner organised by Mike, who was a friend of the Harlow chairman, Danny Norris. Mike was also a policeman who had risen to the rank of inspector the last time I heard of him, and who subsequently appeared as a friend/minder of Frank Bruno.

My debut was scheduled for Monday, 31 March 1980. We agreed a fee of £150 but I was not to tell the other speakers as I was the only one getting paid. I was subsequently to learn that Mike Jackson was a bit of a 'belt and braces' man. He always booked too many speakers, just in case one of them died a death, and his evenings always dragged on too long. They started late, had an overlong auction and more than one comfort break. It used to be the custom at dinners that nobody left the table at times other than during the official break. Those days are long gone, and I always try to convince organisers not to have one as people get up and down all the time, even during my act, maybe *especially* during my act.

INJURY TO MORE EXPERIENCED PLAYER

My good pal Barry Cryer tells a story about experience. Some years ago the great cellist Rostropovich stormed out of a poorly-run studio one afternoon to be confronted by the manager who demanded to know what was wrong. Rostropovich told him in no uncertain terms. At this, the manager drew himself up and said that he had had 30 years' experience running a studio. 'I doubt it,' said Rostropovich. 'I think you've had one year's experience thirty times.'

Some years later, Mike Jackson booked me for another charity event along with Christopher Martin-Jenkins, Alan Simpson and Harvey Smith. This particular evening turned into one of the worst. Chris had spoken and left, and Alan was thinking of heading off but stayed to hear me. I got up at 11.45 p.m. and was determined not to do more than 25 minutes as Harvey Smith, who was a very big name then, was still to come. About five minutes into my routine former boxer Terry Downes, with much drink on board, started to reel around the room shouting. Normally this would call for a few of my carefully rehearsed ad libs – 'that's the trouble when cousins marry', or 'trouble with you, mate, is you're drinking on an empty head'. However, do bear in mind that this was the former middleweight champion of the world. I tried instead to ignore him and carry on, even though he was a bit 'in my face'.

THROW-IN
All his family are boxers – but his mother's a cocker spaniel.

At this point one of the punters went over and started to remonstrate with Terry, saying something along the lines of 'excuse me, old chap, but I'm trying to listen to this amusing fellow and would be grateful if you could resume your seat and show a modicum of quiet'. I've cleaned that up considerably. All hell broke loose. People had to be held back and dragged away, and I sat down and watched it all with some amazement. When order was restored I did another ten minutes to an audience far more interested in checking out the protagonists than in listening to me. So I handed over to Harvey. He also did just enough to get the money before we headed off home. It's no fun getting home at three a.m. when you have to get up for the proper job the next morning.

THROW-IN
I know nothing about boxing. I used to think Sugar Diabetes was a Welsh heavyweight.

That spring the company secretary at European Ferries had reminded me that if I failed to take my holiday by the end of the financial year I would lose it. I was in between relationships and felt like a break, so I decided to take my car to France and the Italian Riviera for a couple of weeks. I'm quite happy with my own company, but by the second week I was getting a bit fed up and decided to come back early.

I arrived home on Thursday, 27 March 1980, four days before my speaking debut in Harlow. As I put my key in the door, I could hear the telephone ringing. These were the days before mobiles and answering machines – at least in my house. What would have happened had I not come back early, or even ten minutes later that afternoon, I'll never know.

Unlike when watching a corner or cross come over, I got to it in time. It was Mike Langley, chief football writer for the *Sunday People* and that year's chairman of the Football Writers' Association. After my triumph at Ipswich in 1979 I had attended the 1980 dinner as a guest, thanks again to the free car ferry tickets. Unlike previous years, I was now regarded as part of the 'in crowd', so after dinner all the speakers and the various celebrities invited me to the late-night drinking party. During this session the chairman of Ipswich, John Cobbold, who was very merry as usual, called me a word beginning with 'c', and I was rather taken aback. Jimmy Hill and John Motson hurried over and told me not to worry. 'It means he likes you,' Jimmy said.

Mike Langley, who was at the dinner, and whom I still had not met, had gone to bed early in the hotel down the road. Like me, he had been unable to get a room in the Copdock Hotel where the dinner was being held. Partly due to a hangover, but mainly because the hotel – and I hereby name and shame the Post House – forgot my early-morning call. I rang my office to cancel the appointment I was no longer going to make and went outside for a cab to the station. That's when I saw Mike. He, too, was going to Fleet Street and he offered me a lift in his car. We got on well during the trip, but he had never seen me speak and he gave me no indication that he would ever be making the call I was now taking.

He wanted to know if I was free on Thursday, 8 May.

I was, and it was to change my life.

8. GOLDEN CHANCES TO SCORE

'Before I speak, I have something important to say . . .'

Groucho Marx

I told my colleagues in the office about my booking for the Footballer of the Year dinner, but I can't say they were overly impressed. I was not too put out by this. I was too busy. It was not only my first day back at work with two weeks' events to catch up on and a few grumpy directors, who always begrudged other people *their* holidays, to cope with. It was also the day of my first-ever paid engagement. I was nervous to a degree, but nowhere near as much as I'd been back in 1967, nor as nervous as I was to be in the future. I had, I think, what Barry Cryer brilliantly describes as 'creative apprehension'.

That night I would earn three times what I had earned during the day but I recalled that I was not to mention the £150 to any of the other speakers.

These days I would want to know who those other speakers were, and the running order. In March 1980, I didn't think to ask. I turned up at this modern hotel in Harlow to find a packed house and several well-known footballers. One of them, Tottenham's midfield player John Pratt, was to be the first speaker. Following him would be the legendary athletics commentator and coach Ron Pickering. I would go third, and last would be a comic, Mike Felix. He had been the drummer with the McGill Five, who'd had just the one hit – 'Mockingbird Hill'. Mike is also a good pianist, and can be seen today in bit parts in TV dramas.

What is the difference between a comic and an after-dinner speaker? I hear you ask. It is true that we get paid substantially more but a northern comic once came up to me and asked the same question. I said I didn't know. He looked at me coldly. 'About two grand,' he said. He had a point, but he's only 80 per cent right. These days I'm quite happy to walk out on to a cabaret floor or a stage, but it was not always so. It isn't the way I came up in the profession. Equally, a lot of comics find it hard to work behind a table. Even Jim Davidson, when he did the PFA Awards in 1983, came up to me before the dinner and asked me (yes, me!) for advice. 'Is there anywhere I can move about?' he asked. In those days the dinner was at the Hilton on Park Lane, before it was forced into the bigger Grosvenor House along the road.

'You'll do well to get a seat, let alone move about,' I replied. 'It's packed out.'

'I don't like it if I can't move about,' he said.

Of course, when he stood up he did brilliantly. Now he says he feels much happier doing after-dinner work.

Barry Cryer also drew my attention to another difference. When you're doing a cabaret, you quite often change with the band and are offered a light ale and a few sandwiches while the guests finish their meal. If you're doing the after-dinner speech you will leave your hotel room – sometimes a suite – not only to sit on the top table but also to join the chairman for pre-dinner drinks in his penthouse.

When I arrived in Harlow I knew none of this. I sat with Mike Felix and Ron Pickering, looking forward to getting up and willing John Pratt and Ron to get on with it. As usual, I had to sit through a long auction and several wee breaks. Finally, I was on.

There is pressure enough speaking at a dinner as it is. When you're taking someone else's money it can blow the lid off your cooker, at least in the early days. I decided to use the opportunity to road-test some of the material I was planning to use at the Footballer of the Year dinner, and it went down really well. Looking at the length of my notes now, I'm sure I made an error in outstaying my welcome, at least as far as Mike Felix was concerned.

THROW-IN

I said to the referee during one game, 'What do you think of us, then?'

'Not a lot,' he replied. 'You're all holding it too long. Except you.'

At this point I shall drag you away from Harlow to Oldham Athletic FC and thence to Rochdale, where I had learnt from my mistake at Harlow.

Oldham was a memorable night for two reasons. Firstly, I realised that I had a funny voice – up north, at least. As I was telling one of my Old Wilsonians 7th XI stories, I noticed I was getting a laugh every time I said 'well' in my south-London-cum-cockney accent. It's hard to write it down, but if you're not from London you cannot say it as we do. The only example I can give you is when we say 'wot' instead of 'what'. I started to play on this and threw in plenty of extra 'wells', all of which got a laugh. Rather like a much-loved catchphrase. As a result I went down extremely well and really hit the audience's funny bone.

In the audience was Tommy Cannon of Cannon and Ball fame, along with his agent Stuart Littlewood, who was also agent for the famous Welsh entertainer Max Boyce, among others. Tommy came up to me afterwards and told me how well I'd done. I replied that I really appreciated his kind remarks, and added, 'especially coming from you'. He seemed amazingly flattered by this. We became instant mates and went off to have a late drink. He told me that Max Boyce had told him about me, and I said that I would like to meet him, as I had always been a fan. Stuart Littlewood said Max had indicated that we could not work together as we were too similar, both doing sport. I thought to myself that I wouldn't mind being as good as Max Boyce.

A few months later I received a call from Tommy, who had recently become chairman of Rochdale. He said he was sponsoring a big dinner in Rochdale town hall and that he would love me to be the speaker. He said he would like me to stay with him, but as he already had a house full he would put me up in a hotel near his house and collect me on the evening.

I headed north on the day determined to do a good long turn with my full act, which by now included some props. At the empty bar in the small and, to be honest, slightly seedy hotel in which I had been booked I ordered a drink and sat chatting to the barman. He seemed to know who I was and what I was doing there. After a while he told me that he had played football. It turned out he was the former Southampton and Sheffield Wednesday player Jim McCailliog. Almost an hour passed with no sign of Tommy. Jim said he couldn't understand it as he only lived down the road. Neither could I understand how he could have forgotten to pick me up but eventually we called for a cab.

I walked into Rochdale town hall. Everyone was seated, enjoying their first course. As I looked across the packed hall I saw that the top table was up on a stage. Tommy was seated in the middle. To his right was, to my amazement, Max Boyce. It was clear from the look on

Max's face that he had no idea I was appearing too. Tommy made no apology for not collecting me, and I can only assume he hadn't told Max who else was on with him. I walked through the whole room carrying the bag of props, which I would normally have sneaked in before the audience turned up.

After dinner I went first, but I did no more than 30 minutes, leaving the field clear for Max as the star, despite the fact that nothing had been said between us beforehand.

Afterwards we all went to a nightclub, with me carrying the props I hadn't used. The audience must have thought it rather odd. In the club, Max took me to one side. 'That was very good of you not to do too long,' he said. 'Very professional.' We've been good friends ever since, thanks to the lesson I learnt on my first professional booking in Harlow Town.

CORNER KICK

Not all referees are lacking in a sense of humour. One actually said this to me after a Veterans game at Lloyds Bank: 'I nearly booked you for time-wasting today.'

I was taken aback. 'What?' I said. 'When was that?'

'When you came out for that corner.'

When Mike Felix had finished his spot at Harlow, the big moment arrived. I was paid. Mike Jackson handed me £150, in cash, and it was in – you've guessed it – a brown envelope. I'm happy to tell you it because I declared this and all my other payments. I like to sleep at nights. As soon as I could, I headed for the toilet. Not for a comfort break. We'd had enough of those. I just wanted to look at my first payment. Nobody else was in the toilet, but still I locked myself into a cubicle and opened the envelope. I stared at its contents. After all these years somebody had finally paid me to perform. I think I punched the air and shouted, 'Yes!'

Then I heard someone come into the toilet. After a moment or two, I heard a voice.

'That you in there, Cat?'

My God, I thought. Is this door made of glass? Suddenly I remembered I was not to admit that I was being paid. After a pause, I nervously confirmed that it was me.

'Counting your money?'

I couldn't believe it. This door must be see-through.

'No, no,' I stammered. 'Charity job tonight.'

'Leave it out,' the voice said. 'You blokes don't work like that for nothing.'

I assured him again that it was not a paid job, but I really don't think he was convinced.

In my panic, I had missed what was a flattering remark. He clearly thought I was a professional. But I'm ashamed to say I stayed in the cubicle until several minutes after he'd gone. To this day I have no idea who it was. But if he's reading this now he will, at last, know the truth. I told Ron, John and Mike the story some years ago and they all laughed. I think we were all being paid. It was simply the organiser trying to stop us comparing fees.

I was to come across Ron Pickering a few more times before he sadly died prematurely. At around this time there was a TV series that still gets mentioned, even though it has long since finished. It was called *Superstars* and it involved many sporting heroes competing against one another in half a dozen different sporting pursuits. It got quite a lot of coverage, especially when Kevin Keegan injured himself falling off his bike during a race. Former QPR player (or should I say genius?) Stan Bowles became famous for scoring the lowest points total ever and clearing a field when he kept accidentally touching the hair trigger on his pistol. Stan was largely too busy drinking the free booze and calling his bookies. Townsend Thoresen sponsored it, but I never got to any of the events as the marketing director, Bryan Thompson, usually had all the best trips himself. Quite often these *Superstars* shows were filmed overseas in exotic locations. Bryan was a terrible groupie, and I think he was jealous when I continued to work there during the day while speaking at dinners during the evening and meeting and becoming friendly with famous people.

One night we brought one of our ships up the Thames and anchored it opposite the Tower of London to hold a few promotional events. I had organised a big party for travel agents, topped off with fireworks. Unbeknown to me, Bryan had invited Ron Pickering and his wife Jean, and he trotted Ron over to introduce him to me, clearly hoping that I would be hugely impressed. Apparently, Bryan had said, 'I must introduce you to our PR director,' and Ron had dutifully walked across, not realising it was me. Before Bryan could utter a word, Ron said, 'Hello, Cat. What you doing here?' Poor Bryan was shattered.

I should also apologise to those of you who might have had a few problems on buses going over Tower Bridge at the time. Whenever we brought a ship up the Thames the captain would call me and check what time we needed them to arrive. Of course it was always subject to the tide, but whenever I could I would ask them to come up during the morning rush-hour as we would get plenty of mentions in the traffic report on Radio 4's *Today* programme. Sorry about that.

This is a rather natural link to a tour Ron and I did with Olympic athlete Daley Thompson and famous *Today* presenter and scourge of the politicians John Humphrys. For a couple of weeks we travelled the country on behalf of Marley Extrusions (plastic drainpipes to you). Looking back, we were an unlikely quartet from totally different backgrounds, although Ron and Daley obviously had athletics in common. But it was a good format. The guests would arrive for a presentation by John, who would then introduce Ron. He would then do his excellent motivational chat about training athletes and talk a little about Daley. After a few minutes he would then say something along the lines of, 'Well, I don't know why I'm doing all this stuff when we can hear from the man himself. Please welcome Daley Thompson.' This was a total surprise to the guests, who had expected to hear only Ron, John and me. After Ron and Daley had done their routine, which was again interesting and funny, lunch or dinner would be served. Then John would stand up and say, 'Well, we've had one great athlete, now here's another . . .' And I would walk on. My opening line was 'When Daley and I were out training this morning . . .' It always got a laugh.

In fact, one day fiction turned to fact. The four of us always spent our spare time together doing different things in the afternoon. One day, for what seemed like an eternity, Ron took us around an area where he used to live. Frankly, it was quite boring, and he got plenty of stick about it for the rest of the tour. On another day, in Manchester, Daley took us to the Adidas factory. Daley was received there like a god, and we were told to help ourselves to whatever we wanted from the shelves. How I wished I had known about this in advance so that I could have given it some thought. As it was, I picked up some stuff I did not need. But I did take a pair of their top-of-the-range football boots. Previously I had had to change mine every two years, but these lasted until I retired. In fact I've still got them and I'm planning to wear them in a charity match soon.

I also picked up a tracksuit, and I was to use this the next day.

PLAY STOPPED – FOREIGNERS ON PITCH

Much as I love the Olympics, I now get confused by all these new countries, as I proved in a pub quiz only the other night. I knew that Sri Lanka used to be Ceylon, and I knew that Zimbabwe used to be Rhodesia. But I had no idea that Iceland used to be Bejam.

Daley's training schedule for the Olympics was amazing. He would start at 9.30 a.m. with a 45-minute warm-up, train, do a 45-minute warm-down, then have some lunch. He would do that again in the afternoon, and again in the evening. So he spent a total of four and a half hours warming up or down in addition to his training. Every day. And he only took a couple of days off a year.

When the tour got to London, Daley's contribution to our spare time was to get his trainer in. All of us followed, as far as we could, his warm-up and warm-down routines. Afterwards I crawled back to my room and collapsed on to my bed without taking off my brand-new Adidas tracksuit. Half an hour later I had recovered, and I felt as good as I have ever felt in my life. Daley said it was because the exercises had pumped blood through every one of my muscles. I can understand why they call fitness a drug. It was a real high.

9. FELL OVER THE BALL

'He could make the ball talk. It invariably said goodbye.'
> John Ford, writing about my outfield play in the
> Old Wilsonians FC weekly newsletter

Before we move to the big night of the 1980 Footballer of the Year dinner, let me give you a better idea of the ability of this footballer, about to address the gods of our national game. I lay before you two reports from the Old Wilsonians newsletter. The first is not typical, and you can almost hear the surprise as the writer, Pete Davis, scribbles away.

Saturday, 12 January 1970

Old Wilsonians 5th XI – 2 Old Finchleians 5th XI – 1

My partial recovery from a nagging ankle injury saw me able to answer Steve Wisson's call to play for the 5ths against top-of-the-table Finchleians. The previous week's 9–1 drubbing did not bode well, but when the team finally lined up for the kick-off it became clear that the result would be a lot closer this time.

The scoring opened after an unsavoury incident when Ian Bailey was hacked down for the second time just inside the area (the first having gone unnoticed). This gave skipper DAVE CUNNINGHAM the chance to slot the ball home. I only wish he had. His weak shot was saved but not held by the keeper, giving Dave a second bite of the cherry, which he took.

Finchleians took umbrage at our scoring and started to play with more urgency. I am loath to say it, but it was during this period, lasting about 20 minutes, that Bob Bevan decided to keep us in the game with a string of fine saves worthy of any club keeper. He held everything they threw at him, including a fierce near-post cross that he clutched out of the air, much to the amazement of the whole team.

The second half saw us under renewed pressure from Finchleians who were becoming frustrated by our offside trap. Our second goal is a bit of a mystery to me, except that it came from a swift break-out and OW charge resulting in GLEN HANDS scoring.

After that Finchleians became more frustrated and more aggressive, but we held out. It was not until five minutes from time that Finchleians pulled one back. It was a most unfortunate goal as Bob Bevan was unable to hold a bobbling back-pass and was left with no alternative but to bring down their centre-forward as he rounded him with the ball loose in front of goal. The last five minutes were to be our finest hour, with all defending well.

The whistle went, leaving us 2–1 victors over the league leaders. The game was a pleasure to play in with no arguing or bickering – not from us anyway. Good games from all who played, with the defence of Tony Brighton, Cy Giles and Dave Cunningham playing very well indeed.

I cannot close without mentioning my 'Man of the Match', Bob Bevan, who will rarely play such a good game at such a crucial time and so deserve a clean sheet and yet lose it so tragically.

You will gather that such a report was sufficiently rare for me to keep it in my scrapbook.

———————

MATCH HALTED BY BAD WEATHER

Brian Stapleton, writing in the Old Wilsonians newsletter about a frozen pitch: 'I wouldn't say the pitch was slippery, but we had a job to turn round at half-time.'

———————

Much more common was one report that recently appeared in the 'All Our Yesterdays' section of the newsletter, where the editor runs a page from a 25-year-old edition. It was written by one of the best report writers during my playing career, Brian Stapleton. In it, he refers to an operation I had. This was a rather late-in-life circumcision, which I tried to keep quiet about until someone found out and spilt the beans. It prompted me to send this short piece to the newsletter:

The Cat Has Been Doctored, or a message from Jumpin' Jack Flash
OK, OK, so I know that but for this I'd be in the 1st X1. And I know that you all know why I've not been around. And I can tell

you I am only just beginning to see the funny side of it. At times like this you know who your friends are, and thanks for the many get-well cards and phone calls.

The whole thing has not been without its lighter moments. Like when the doctor in the hospital said, 'Let the air get in when no one's around,' and dubbed me the flasher of Orpington.

'I'll get you a gown instead of those pyjamas,' said a nurse.

'A dirty old mac will do,' I said. Come to think of it, *he* [one of our players was called Mac] didn't send me a card!

There were some wonderful get-well messages. 'More than one way to skin a cat,' said Chris Cowell. 'You're a cut above the rest,' wrote his brother (or it might have been 'cat above the rest'. No, perhaps not.) Two other friends noted, 'The first cut is the deepest,' and 'It's no skin off my nose.' Top of the pile, though, was John Matthews with 'Makes the coming easy – and the going back' [a variation on a British Rail slogan at the time – 'makes the going easy and the coming back']. Mind you, a close second was the gift from Dicky Ayers [Old Bromleians and OW squash star]. It was a huge orange on which he had inked in large letters ISRAEL.

The Cat

Meanwhile, back to the more common report on one of my performances by Brian Stapleton.

Saturday, 4 March 1978

BEVAN NOT IN SEVENTH HEAVEN

Mayfield Athletic 3rd XI – 7 Old Wilsonians 5th XI – 2

After the match, when a disconsolate Bob Bevan, in the corner of the dressing room, was muttering to himself that he could not remember when he last let in seven goals (his memory seems to have failed him since his operation), we gave him the opportunity of writing the match report. He said he had not got the time, so when I pointed out that I would have to describe his perform-ance, he got worried and made me write down 'the true account' (sic) of Mayfield's 'seven great goals'.

This game was a vital one in the promotion battle, with ourselves and Mayfield occupying third and fourth places. Unfortunately, for the second week running, we had to start the game without a full side, this time, in fact, playing the entire game with only ten men. This meant we had to adopt revised positions, with Glen Hands and Paul Johnson in midfield, Brian Stapleton at left-back and Bob Bevan in goal!

Mayfield were presented with an easy first goal when an innocuous cross had the Cat in two minds, unsure whether to catch it or push it over the bar. In the end he just pawed it over his head and into the net.

Bob: 'Well, yes, that one was my fault. Caught me in two minds, didn't it?'

Not deterred by giving away goals we could ill afford, Paul Johnson was awarded a free-kick after challenging for a ball in midfield. The kick was floated into their penalty area, Paul headed on and MAX CARTER stretched out a boot to put the ball into the goal. Mayfield, in a repetition of the move that brought their first goal, floated over a similar cross, which drifted into the net at the far post.

Bob: 'Well, you've got to cover the near post, haven't you?' (What was your full-back doing? – Ed. Oh, sorry, Brian – Ed.)

Mayfield's third goal resulted from a through-ball which Bob came out for, realised the forward was going to get there first, stopped, and then watched the ball roll across the goal to be knocked into an empty net.

Bob: 'Great goal.'

With twenty minutes left, we reshuffled the team and forced a corner. The kick was taken, Dave Hodson 'knocked' the keeper and DAVE CUNNINGHAM knocked the ball into the net. However, Mayfield came back at us with, as Bob describes it, 'A great shot. The save was better, the ball fell loose, and it was a surprise to everyone (but not me) that the ball was not in the back of the net.' However, one of their forwards was able to regain his composure and stuck it in the empty net.

In the last five minutes, by pushing everyone into attack, we left ourselves open to counter-attacks. Glen Hands missed a tackle and their right-winger smacked the ball into the net as if the goalie wasn't there.

Bob: 'Glen should have got his tackle in.'
A sixth goal.
Bob: 'Offside.'
A seventh goal.
Bob: 'Seven goals. Christ, I cannot remember when I last let in seven.'

THROW-IN

'Our goalkeeper didn't have a save to make in ninety minutes, yet he still ended up conceding four goals' – Joe Royle, Ipswich Town manager, on BBC Online, proving I'm not alone.

As I have said, Brian wrote some really good stuff. Here is an extract from a report he penned about a game between Camden Municipal Officers and our 6th XI which we won 3–2, probably because I was not playing:

The delayed start to this game was due, so their skipper informed me, to the fact that the referee had only been contacted the previous morning. We were somewhat surprised to learn that he required a day and a half to get to the game!

Then we saw him. He trotted out of the dressing room as fast as anyone else could walk slowly and wandered straight on to the pitch where the 5th XI game was in progress. When he reached the centre circle he had a look round, saw the game had started, spotted their referee and realised something was amiss.

John Brittain kindly collected him and led him over to our pitch so that the game could commence.

Further examples of Brian's scribbling come in these two extracts from a game in which I again did not take part, between our 6th XI and Economicals, which was a 4–1 win for us.

CORNER KICK

There was an incident at the Old Bromleians ground once when the Old Wilsonians 1st XI went on to the wrong pitch and actually kicked off against Old Bromleians 6th XI. They played for a good ten minutes before the mistake was spotted. It is embarrassing to relate that the score was still 0–0.

Having been away for a couple of nights, drinking, playing golf and . . . drinking, I returned home at about 1.30 p.m. on Saturday. I had my lunch and contemplated the day out I had promised my wife. At 2.15 I received a telephone call from [captain] John Hemmingway asking if I would play football. I asked Celia if she would mind if we skipped our previously arranged trip.

'Not at all,' she said. 'I mean, what is a first wedding anniversary if not just another day. Can you drop me off at my mother's?'

'Of course,' I replied.

So I packed my kit, she packed her suitcase, and another season had begun . . .

After a report of the game, he concluded:

At half-time Martin Taylor, who had been competent in goal, informed me that he would not be available for some weeks as he played chess for Kent. I tried to convince him that our football was like human chess and that he was the king at the back and if he were beaten we would lose. Our full-backs were like bishops, not letting anyone pass. The midfield were like knights, all over the place but with no clear direction. The forwards were like castles, running up and down in straight lines. And, of course, we've got our queen in John Hemmingway.

Brilliant stuff. But Martin, also known as 'Claw', still went and played chess. He now lives in Houston, Texas.

_____

THROW-IN

During our schooldays long hair was the fashion, and Martin Taylor had the longest, curliest and fullest head of blond hair I've ever seen. A joke I told at one of our dinners at the time went as follows.

Martin Taylor was having his hair cut the other day and the barber had been clipping away for about twenty minutes when he said to Martin, 'Did you used to go to Wilson's Grammar School?'

'I did,' Martin replied. 'How do you know?'

'I've just found your bloody 'at!'

_____

Finally, I have come across another old newsletter in which there appeared a report in verse. I have always found it easy to write poems, as you will discover. In the following the names are unimportant, except that it might be useful to know that Alex Pepper is a fellow keeper.

VERSE AND WORSE: Old Wilsonians 4th XI – 2 Old Bealonians – 2

I was due in the 5ths last weekend, down at Fulham, a change
· from up north,
When I got a call from old Houghton, who said, 'You're back
once again in the 4ths.'

So I sallied forth in my Cat car, while the tea lady sat there and
sniffed,
For just to make sure of my grub, I'd decided to give her a lift.

At our ground they all greeted me warmly, not as usual, like an
old leper;
I could only assume by their greeting they all thought they had
Alex Pepper.

There was no score in the first half, after one 'great' save I got
cold,
And watched them all run in the distance, except Rayworth, who
is far too old.

After half-time they scored twice, and I saw a lot more of the ball,
While Tyson was constantly chipped, for they spotted he isn't
that tall.

Then RICH CHAPMAN beat the offside trap, and twice made their
'Cat' look a mug;
The second was made by Paul Johnson, whose mention should
earn me a jug.

I look forward next week to a new game, with another skinful of
liquor,
And a groan from long-suffering team-mates, as I nauseatingly
say, 'Hello, skipper.'

Cat Laureate

'I'LL BE BACK ON THE 2.35'

'It was a woman that drove me to drink, and, I'm ashamed to say, I never wrote to thank her.'

W.C. Fields

As teenagers, we all have to try a smoke and a drink. These days maybe it's earlier and even more experimental. But let's not go there. My first, and pretty much my last, cigarette was a Strand. I was impressed by the advertisement showing a guy in a trench coat. In today's parlance, it looked 'cool'. Fortunately, I didn't like the taste, and apart from a few cigars and even a pathetic attempt at a pipe I have kept away from tobacco. Nor have I tried anything else. Nor do I have any plans to do so.

At the other end of the scale, I have always been drawn towards pub and club culture. I have had several friends who have suffered from alcoholism, which is most definitely an illness. Fortunately, whatever the make-up of the metabolism that causes the craving they have, it is not present in me.

My first drink, at the astonishingly late age of sixteen, was a brown ale for 1s. 6d. at the leavers' supper in the Old Wilsonians club. But sociability rules in Old Boys sport. It isn't just the rugger-buggers who have jugs of beer flying around. Old Boys football is much the same, and I look back with some horror on the days before the breathalyser when I would drive across London full of ale after an away game. I'm not proud of it, but in those days we all did it. Fortunately, I have always been and remain a social drinker. I don't drink much at home, and almost never alone. But there have been a few occasions when I have been far more social than I should have been, and one of these took place fairly recently.

As president of the West Kent Lord's Taverners, I was summoned to an informal lunch meeting in Tunbridge Wells at the offices of a local jeweller, Harry Collins. He is not only jeweller to my Petal, he is also jeweller to Her Majesty the Queen. A glass of wine and sandwiches were to be provided. As I am also president of the village cricket club at Bells Yew Green, I get parking rights in the local pub, the Brecknock Arms, which is next to the station. So, as a former drink-driver, I took the mid-morning train to Tunbridge Wells, telling the landlord I would be back on the 2.35. A phrase that was destined to pass into legend.

En route to the meeting I called into Marks and Sparks to pick up two pairs of trousers; then, carrying my executive green carrier bag, I headed for the jeweller's. Packed into a room with wall-to-wall security cameras, for two hours we discussed everything but the one item on the agenda, finding it hard to concentrate for too long as we had excellent views of the various young women calling in at the shop downstairs. Our concentration was further weakened by a zooming-in device we all managed to operate quite successfully whenever Harry went out of the room.

Jeweller Harry is a generous man, but the supply of sandwiches was somewhat limited. The same could not be said for the wine, but even that had run out by mid-afternoon. Unfortunately, there was a wine bar next door, so we repaired there. Each of us purchased a bottle of wine, maybe more.

By 5.30, still with only liquid taken on board, we were getting bored so we hailed a couple of taxis to take us to the Black Horse in Pembury. I had heard a great deal about this pub, its excellent seafood restaurant and its jolly landlord, but had never got round to visiting it. In the weeks that followed, the landlord, Gary Coldwell, son of former England and Worcestershire fast bowler Len, was to perform what I said on entering and other people have told me that it was a fairly accurate impersonation. Sadly, or perhaps fortunately, my remarks cannot be adequately described with the written word.

During the next four hours, much of which is a blur to me, several interesting events took place. Freddie Cook, a member of the committee, who is many inches shorter than me, apparently decided to try on the trousers from my M&S bag, which, miraculously, was still with me. Finding them a far from ideal fit, he crashed head-first on to a concrete step outside but rose again unhurt, as often happens when someone is drunk. He was destined to fare less well during the rest of the evening. By ten p.m. we were being pushed into cabs with instructions given to the drivers as to where we lived. By then, you see, we were not sure.

I got home in one piece, still with my carrier bag, and was found naked and unconscious on the bed by my Petal when she arrived home. Freddie Cook was not so lucky. Having waved goodbye to his cab in Crowborough, he found that he had left his coat and his keys at the jeweller's. His wife was out, so he tried the front windows, but they were all secure. He then went down the side of the house and climbed rather shakily over the fence. Although he got over, he fell straight into the compost heap and cut himself quite badly – not a good idea in a compost heap. Pulling himself together, he tried the downstairs windows. No joy. He then got a ladder and wobbled up to the first floor where he found a window he could open. He hauled himself through and crashed on to the carpet where he thought he might stay for a bit.

During the previous week there had been an attempted burglary at one of his neighbours' houses. Consequently they were all in Neighbourhood Watch mode. Freddie's uneasy ascent of the ladder had been observed by a lady next door, and she had called the police. For the second time in a week the road was filled with sirens and blue lamps. It didn't wake Freddie, but the hammering on the door eventually did. Spraying blood and compost everywhere, he staggered downstairs to answer the door. It was double-locked, and without keys he couldn't open it. Discussions then took place through the letterbox. The police were far from convinced with Freddie's explanation until a second police car arrived in which, fortunately, was the husband of his cleaner. He vouched for Freddie's identity and his social lifestyle, and the road returned to its slumbers.

Freddie, exhausted by the experience, went back upstairs and laid his bloodied, composty body on the bed. Soon after, his wife returned. There was no car, and the door was double-locked – clearly Freddie had not yet arrived home. But when she got in there were rather a lot of lights on and a cold draught coming from the open window upstairs. There was also a terrible smell and a strange noise coming from somewhere in the direction of the bedroom, and – Oh my God! – a ladder leaning against the back of the house.

So she called the police.

I heard all this the next morning from Freddie. I had tried to get up twice, but at eleven a.m. I was still in bed. 'The wife's not talking to me,' he moaned, 'the neighbours aren't talking to me, the cleaner and her husband are definitely not talking to me . . .'

I had my own problems. In the early evening my Petal said, 'Are we going for our usual Friday night meal at the pub?' I thought a hair of the dog might be helpful so I lamely offered to get the car out. Only then did I realise where it had last been parked.

As I walked into the pub, the landlord greeted me. 'Miss the 2.35, did we?'

10. GAME HELD UP – WEIRDO ON PITCH

'We are not permitted to choose the frame of our destiny. But what we put into it is ours.'

Former United Nations secretary-general Dag Hammarskjöld

Now that you have a grasp of my playing ability, you are probably asking why on earth I bothered. Why didn't I go and do something I was good at? So before we move on to the Big Night – and we will, I promise – let's have a look at what sort of supporter this most famous of football audiences was about to encounter.

What is it about football that so attracts me? It's a fair question, and I don't know the answer. I simply can't tell you where my love of the game came from. None of my family was interested. I can just about recall having a conversation about Brentford with my Great Uncle Alf, but that's it. My earliest memory of football is of it being something my father used to bet on. He had a weekly perm with Vernons until the day he died. I used to play a game with his unused Littlewoods coupons, on which I first saw the name Crystal Palace. (The other name that was to catch my eye, although I can't remember where, was Dulwich Hamlet. It also happened to be the name of the primary school I was attending at the time.) I used to fill in imaginary scores, then I moved on to a more sophisticated game of my own invention. I would fill endless exercise books running league and cup competitions. I also played Subbuteo, the table football game. In fact, mine was Newfooty, which was the forerunner by about twenty years. A guy in Tunbridge Wells, near where I now live, updated the game and called it Subbuteo. It's not a name that trips off the tongue. Its origin stems from the fact that they wanted to call the new game 'The Hobby' but were unable to get the name registered. A hobby is also a species of bird, the Latin name for which is *Falco subbuteo*, hence the name. Even many anoraks don't know that.

When I was eight we got our first television, or rather my grandmother who lived downstairs did. Like so many others she bought it for the Coronation, and lots of people from our road came over to watch the twelve-inch black and white screen. Sadly, it arrived too late for the 1953 'Matthews' FA Cup final, but I did watch the 1954 match between West Bromwich Albion and Preston North End. Ronnie Allen was centre-forward for WBA and Tom Finney was on the wing for Preston. I sat in a darkened room, on my own, lapping it up as the Midlands side won 3–2. FA Cup final day thereafter became one of the highlights of my year. The following year Newcastle United beat Manchester City, Jackie Milburn scoring early on in a one-sided game. Then, in 1956, I saw the previous year's runners-up beat Birmingham City in a game during which German goalkeeper Bert Trautmann broke his neck but played on. In years to come I would get to know all these stars, and Ronnie Allen, Tom Finney and Jackie Milburn would all be at the upcoming Football of the Year dinner.

In those days a cup final ticket was something only to dream of. I never thought I would get to one. I am actually ashamed to admit that I ended up declining one not so long ago because of the aggravation of getting to and from Wembley. That was not the case in 1966. Old Wilsonians FC were entitled to one ticket, and the secretary, undertaker George Croucher, offered it to me because of all the work I had done for the club. It was for the Everton v. Sheffield Wednesday match. Both teams had performed poorly that season, and it was billed in one newspaper as 'The Cup Final Nobody Wants to See'. Tickets were still like gold dust, though, and as I felt sure I would never get to one again I hopped on my Honda 50 motorcycle and went to watch Everton stage a dramatic comeback. After being 2–0 down they won 3–2, previously unheard of Cornishman Mike Trebilcock scoring twice. I had a terrible view, standing right down at the front overlooking a corner flag, but I enjoyed the occasion.

Destiny then took a hand as I decided to try my luck in some better football at West Wickham in the Southern Amateur League. One evening in May 1967, the secretary, Alan Glen, telephoned me and asked me what I was doing the following Saturday. I said I was due to play cricket. He then told me that their one cup final ticket was always given to a fully paid-up member by ballot, and my name had come out. I think they were a bit gutted as I was a relatively new member, but I went and saw a memorable match: Tottenham, complete with my hero Jimmy Greaves, beat Chelsea 2–1. Greavesie didn't score, but Jimmy Robertson and Frank Saul did, while Bobby Tambling notched up one for Chelsea. The day was especially emotional because Dave Mackay, having come back from two broken legs, went up to collect the cup for Spurs.

YELLOW CARD

Tony Hateley, father of Mark, and a good header of the ball, played for Chelsea in 1967. He subsequently went to Liverpool before being sold. Manager Bill Shankly, so the story goes, held a press conference during which a journalist asked, 'Why are you selling Tony Hateley, Mr Shankly? He's very good in the air.'

Shankly thought for a moment, then said, 'Aye. But so was Douglas Bader.'

Note: Douglas Bader was the famous fighter pilot who lost both legs in the war. If you've got to explain them, are they still funny?

West Wickham were even more gutted the next season when I went back to the Old Wilsonians. However, that paled into insignificance a few years later when the same Alan Glen, fearing that he had cancer – wrongly, as it turned out – was found hanging from the clubhouse rafters by one of the lads who had gone to open up the clubhouse one Saturday lunchtime. A sad end for a good lad who did a lot for the game.

But I get a little ahead of myself. Apart from the cup finals in the mid-1950s, I watched several youth international games, which were shown live on BBC early on Saturday evenings. That was when Jimmy Greaves, a little lad and a prolific goalscorer, first caught my eye. If I could see just one player again, it would not be Denis Law, Bobby Charlton, Bobby Moore or George Best, much as I admired them. It would have to be Jim. That's when I began seriously to think that I would like to go and see a game live. But who would take me? The family weren't interested, and while most fathers would take their lads to football, mine was only really keen on boxing and snooker. Years later, when I had a spare ticket to Crystal Palace, in the directors' box, and asked him if he wanted to come, he declined. 'I'm not really bothered,' he said. 'I don't mind coming to cup finals and things like that, though.'

Things like that? What else is like a cup final?

Eventually I was to get to my first match but through an unusual source.

When I attended Dulwich Hamlet Primary, I used to have to walk about a mile to and from school along Court Lane. It was quite a long trek for a weedy little lad like me. One day, one of the kids, Derek Curtis with the German mother, mentioned someone called George. 'We get a lift from him sometimes,' said young Derek, and so, not knowing any better, I started to walk up Court Lane with him. Sure enough, a few days later this large black Hillman Minx drew up and loads of us piled in.

George Brown was a tall, thin, bespectacled local councillor with a long nose. He was well spoken, and clearly had a good position at the council to have a car like a Hillman Minx. He lived at home with his mother in Burbage Road. Whatever his job entailed, it enabled him, several times a week, to cruise up and down Court Lane picking up little kids. I know. Scary, isn't it? My parents knew all about this bloke giving us lifts and clearly thought nothing of it. In fact, once, when my mother spotted me on my own in George's car, she turfed me out and got in herself as she wanted to talk to him, as a local councillor, about a problem she had with my grandfather's grave.

To be fair to George, I never heard about him ever doing anything untoward, and I quite often spent time alone with him in the car. He certainly never touched me or made me feel in any way uncomfortable. But, looking back, it's hard not to believe he must have had some problems to behave the way he did. One day, my mother showed me the local paper, which was carrying a small picture of George. He had been found dead in a flat in south London, and the strong inference was that he had taken his own life.

It seems strange now that people could be so innocent, but clearly my mother was. That was until the local scoutmaster took his troop on an outing to a river and made them all undress in order to 'get used to being in the nude together'. There was uproar in our street, although I wasn't involved in the trip. I had already been slung out of the scouts. They said they couldn't have a Seconder in the Kingfisher patrol missing scout evenings just to watch the 1958 World Cup.

The scoutmaster certainly looked a bit odd to me. Ugly, with thick spectacles. I saw him in the 1980s in Holborn outside a camping shop loading up an old Bedford Dormobile, just like the one he had when

I was a kid. It was about that time that I read his name in the *Daily Telegraph*. He was in court on an indecent assault charge.

I never liked him, but the opposite was true with George. When I said I wanted to go to watch Dulwich Hamlet, he said he would take me. Sure enough, on Saturday, 29 October 1955, at about 1.30 p.m., the black Hillman Minx pulled up outside my house and I clambered in with a whole load of other kids. How do I know the date? Because I still have the programme of course.

I remember the game as if it were yesterday. We stood behind the goal (something I never do now out of choice) and I saw for the first time the famous pink and blue shirts of Dulwich Hamlet. You can actually buy replicas from a company called Toffs in Newcastle. I'm wearing one now as I write. But I should warn you that that delivery took even longer than it takes me to come out for a cross. Dulwich were at home to Wycombe Wanderers in the Isthmian League, and they lost 4–2. I can still see, in my mind's eye, Dennis Anderson, Dulwich's centre-forward, sustaining a nasty cut and being led from the field with blood pouring from his head. No substitutes, no floodlights, so a 2.30 kick-off. There must have been at least 3,000 people there, as there were for most home games. Sometimes Dulwich even had 800 for the reserves.

Such crowds were remarkable when you realise that Crystal Palace, Millwall and Charlton were all nearby, not to mention other local senior amateur teams. Corinthian Casuals, for example, played just up the road at the Kennington Oval. Yes, the Oval. On the far side, away from the main pavilion and, of course, the cricket square. That year Charlton were in the First Division and a fleet of special buses actually ran from Dulwich to the Valley. Yet Dulwich still had these big crowds in a huge ground that could hold up to 26,000.

PUNCH-UP

Ryman League club Windsor and Eton full-back Mike Murphy was suspended for the 2002/03 FA Trophy fourth-round tie against Aylesbury. His manager, Dennis Greene, said that he had thought of signing former Olympic boxing champion Audley Harrison, but changed his mind when he realised that Audley had no experience of going beyond the fourth round.

I went to the football a few more times with George, but he didn't go to every game so I started going on my own. My parents then began to realise how keen I was, and after Christmas, my father, no doubt under pressure from my mother, said that he would take me to Charlton. Just how much pressure she put on him is clear from the fact that we were only to go to football together on three more occasions. He came to the 1990 FA Cup final with me when Palace got there, but didn't bother with the replay. He came once to Crystal Palace, but I think the lunch was the main attraction, and as a kid I once got him to come to Dulwich Hamlet. He came to watch the game against Kingstonian on 12 November 1955. On the away side's team sheet you can see the name A. Busby. Not remarkable in itself, until you realise it was Sandy Busby, son of Sir Matt. I know because I sat next to him at a dinner years later and he told me that the Ks used to fly him down for each game. 'You were strictly amateur, then?' I said, tongue in cheek. Wisely, he failed to answer, but gave me an enigmatic smile. He remembered the 1955 game, which was hardly surprising: at half-time the score was 4–4, and it ended 6–6. The fact that my father never came again does rather emphasise that nothing would ever get him interested in the great game. He even went shopping with my mother on World Cup final day in 1966. I bet they were the only people around the shops in Catford that day.

FOUL THROW

Here is an insight into dealing with football club directors. One of my best friends is Lennie Lawrence, now Cardiff City manager, who will forever be remembered for managing Charlton through all their tough times and taking them into the old First Division, even though they were ground-sharing at Crystal Palace. He had also managed Middlesbrough, Bradford City, Grimsby Town, Luton Town and is now doing great things at Cardiff City.

Over Christmas 2002, Cardiff lost 2–0 at Luton. After the game manager Joe Kinnear invited Lennie into his office for a drink. They were sitting there with Luton coach Mick Harford when the Luton chairman came in and sat down. He said to Lennie, 'What did you make of it, then?'

There was an awkward silence until Lennie said, 'Why you asking me? I'm manager of Cardiff.'

'Oh, are you?' said the chairman.

Lennie said, 'You should know. You sacked me!' (I've cleaned that up.)

Even so, on Saturday, 18 February 1956, Dad and I caught the special bus from Dulwich and went to watch Charlton lose 2–0 at home to Arsenal in the fourth round of the FA Cup. There were 66,000 there, and they didn't close the gates. How do I know the date? Silly question. Mind you, I have wondered over the years about how I could have persuaded my father to buy a programme. On looking at it again, I have to assume that someone gave it to me, because it has been written on.

Playing that day were two of my goalkeeping heroes, Charlton's Sam Bartram and Arsenal's Welsh international Jack Kelsey. Sam was reckoned by most people to be the best uncapped goalkeeper in the land. These days, on the rare occasions when I go to the Valley, it still seems strange, as you turn the corner into Floyd Road, not to see the sign SAM BARTRAM SPORTS over his shop.

Years later, when Mike Langley of the *Sunday People* was elected Sports Writer of the Year, his colleagues, one of whom was Sam Bartram, held a small lunch in his honour and asked me to go along and say a few words. Afterwards we went to the Press Club where I ended an extremely boozy day playing snooker with Sam. Who would have thought it?

FREE-KICK

In 1982 I spoke at the Press Club Travel Night with Sir Peter Parker, then chairman of British Rail. I was still head of public relations for European Ferries at the time. We owned Townsend Thoresen Car Ferries, while British Rail had Sealink, our main competitors. At that time Sir Peter had had problems with Ray Buckton, leader of the rail unions, and Mark Thatcher had become memorable for getting lost on a desert rally. Travel News reported the following week: 'Bob Bevan had some bad news for Sir Peter. He said that the good news was that Ray Buckton had decided to emigrate. The bad news was that Mark Thatcher was driving him to the airport.'

While I can point to many other instances of meeting later in life those players I had seen as a child, two people who were destined to become very good friends were playing in this Charlton side. To be accurate, one of them was on the programme but pulled out through injury. He was Derek Ufton, who not only played professional football and had one full international cap against the Rest of the World in 1954, he also played cricket for Kent and understudied legendary wicket-keeper Godfrey Evans. At left-back that day was Syd Ellis, and he was to become a great pal. Sadly, Syd died in 2002. He was a very young 67, and from the day he retired he put so much back into the game, running the local Boys Brigade football side among many other things. He also had the distinction of playing in the first-ever England under-23 international, in Italy in 1955. That was to be the end of his representative honours, and he moved on to Brighton to replace their Fulham-bound star England left-back Jim Langley. Syd ended up playing at Guildford City, along with, coincidentally, my friend Mickey Stewart. He marked all the great right-wingers: Stanley Matthews – whom he played against on Stan's 40th birthday – Tom Finney and Peter Harris of Portsmouth. Interestingly, Syd said that of the three Harris gave him the most trouble because he was so quick. These words, which I spoke at his funeral, show what a great character he was:

Whenever Syd and I met we always had a laugh, so I wanted to remember him today with a smile.

The sad news which Syd's brother Frank called to give me a couple of weeks ago caused me, like all of you I'm sure, to think back to my first meeting with Syd, and I was astonished to realise it was 35 years ago.

These days I earn my living as an entertainer, but I did have a proper job once, which is how I met Syd. On 1 January 1966 (in those days we still went to work on New Year's Day), I joined a company called Maclean-Hunter as assistant editor of a travel magazine, and across the corridor were the advertising offices of the company's most successful publication, *British Printer*. Syd was one of their top salesmen. I can still see Syd back then, with the Dickie Davies white stripe that fell into an eyebrow. Someone once said he looked like a badger. Well, if he did, he was a very friendly badger. He had a cheeky face and a twinkle in the eye which meant that you were never far away from a laugh or being on the end of one of his wind-ups.

For although Syd was a very kind, caring man, as we all know, he had a wicked sense of humour. I know he would have found it very amusing today to know that when I leave here I have to have an operation for a hernia. For he did find great amusement in the fact that I was at the opposite end of the fitness and sporting ability scale to him. And the very first occasion when we spent time in each other's company, he 'did me up like a kipper'.

For six months he was just a guy I nodded to in the corridor. But in the summer there was a company cricket match at Hampstead and Syd and I were picked to play. I was also told that this bloke lived near me and would give me a lift home in his company car. During the game, whenever the ball came near Syd he seemed to flick it up and juggle it with his feet. So when we were in the car going home I asked him if he was into football. He said he used to play and then asked me about myself. I told him that, being much younger, I still played, and I regaled him with some of my exploits with the Old Wilsonians 5th XI in considerable detail. When I ran out of things to tell him I asked him who he used to play for. He said, 'Oh, I only played locally.' He dropped me off in Catford, and that was that.

A few weeks later the new Littlewoods Pools annual arrived and there was a picture of Stanley Matthews being chased by a left-back. I looked at the left-back's face and couldn't quite place him, although I was sure I knew him. A few days later I passed Syd in the corridor and it clicked. I'd better not tell you today exactly what I said to him. But it wasn't to be the last time he was to turn me over.

I left the company two and a half years later, but somehow we always kept in touch. It's hard to know why – and you don't stop to analyse a friendship until a day like today, when you're forced to.

We didn't see each other that often, and, as Iris Ellis will confirm, it sometimes took half a dozen phone calls or more before we found a time when we were both at home. But the measure of a good friendship is that however long it is since you last met, you pick up as if you'd only parted the day before.

I'll remember many other things about him. How I was ten when I first saw him. The first professional match I ever saw was at Charlton, and Syd was playing. I've still got the programme. Derek Ufton, who is here today, was also in the programme but he didn't play. Even in 1956 his knees were playing him up.

The only time I have not been pleased to see Syd was when he turned up unexpectedly behind my goal when I was playing at Charlton Park. His Boys Brigade game had finished and I was playing for the Old Wilsonians 4th team away to Old Colfeians. When Syd appeared we were 3–2 down. During the fifteen minutes he watched me I let in the fourth, fifth, sixth, seventh and eighth goals of my afternoon. I don't know if Syd tried not to laugh, but if he did, he failed miserably. And, as a parting shot, he said he didn't think he ought to let his boys watch me as it might not be good for them.

I remember inviting him to Stanley Matthews' 75th birthday dinner, at which I was speaking, and how he took Stan's book along for him to sign. [Stan] wrote 'to my pal Syd' across that famous picture of Stan being chased by Syd. It was only when Syd wrote a piece in the Charlton programme the weekend after Stan died, and he mentioned the evening and 'my good friend Bob Bevan', that I realised how much my invitation had meant to him.

And I remember his delight watching me struggle up and down Shooters Hill golf course while he strolled easily over the hills. No wonder they call one of them 'Heart Attack Hill'. I only went once. I always made him come to my flatter course after that.

And I'll remember him as someone who always brightened up my life whenever we met or spoke. How he took a lot of pleasure from everything he did. And how he always seemed to put back far more than he ever took out. It's a cliché, but true nonetheless, that, like the old song, 'You Don't Know What You've Got 'Til It's Gone'.

When Frank called two weeks ago, I had just been looking at my 'things to do' list on my desk. It had 'April 1 ring Syd for golf'. I haven't been able to bring myself to cross it out yet. It reminds me of him – of how much, like all of you, I shall miss him.

After I'd watched that game, and Syd, at Charlton in 1956, I returned to Dulwich and went there most Saturdays, including reserve games. These were the last golden days of amateur football. In my first year as a Hamlet supporter they reached the semi-final of the Amateur Cup. In the quarter-final replay at Dulwich 13,000 watched them beat West Auckland Town 3–0. Left-winger Tommy Jover came out of retirement and scored twice. Today he is club president, and still attends most home games. Tommy thinks the crowd was so big that day because, in those days of less media coverage, many people thought that the Hamlet were playing the more famous Bishop Auckland.

At Stamford Bridge, despite a full League programme, 26,000 saw Hamlet lose to Corinthian Casuals in the semi-final. I went with a crowd of lads in George's Hillman Minx and we were packed in behind the goal. Now, gates were huge in those days, so 26,000 means it was only half full. So why were we so hemmed in? I think Roman Abramovich owes us a few quid. Plus interest. The Casuals did well that day because they lost their amateur international centre-forward Jack Laybourne early on but still won 3–1. Famous Essex and England cricketer Doug Insole played for them on the wing while West Indian wicket-keeper Jerry Alexander played left-back. They went on to the final, in which they met Bishop Auckland, who were going for their third successive win. After a draw in front of 80,000 at Wembley they headed to Middlesbrough for the replay the following Saturday. The Casuals' star inside-forward, Mickey Stewart was on a cricket tour in the West Indies, and it was decided to fly him home for the game. After a tortuous journey the plane was late and he missed the kick-off. The Casuals lost 4–1.

GOAL-KICK

The under-employed goalkeeper of Bishop Auckland was Harry Sharratt, who died in 2002, and was such a great entertainer that he had a half-page obituary in *The Times*. If Bishop were winning easily, as they often were, he would throw the ball to the opponents. At other times he would watch the game sitting on his crossbar.

Most famously, when they were winning 12–0 against Kingstonian in an Amateur Cup tie, he stood by his post and allowed the opposition to score three consolations.

Best of all, when they were hammering Shildon in a Northern League game on a very wintery day, he built a snowman on his penalty spot. The referee booked him.

Then, before the end of that 1955/56 season, I plucked up the courage to knock on Bert Mew's door. And I'm glad I did, because it led to one of my most vivid football memories and provided me with a treasured possession.

11. FOUND TO BE AN ANORAK

'We can do no great things. Only small things with great love.'

Mother Teresa

All us kids were scared stiff of Bert Mew. He was a burly CID inspector who lived in my road, a former Dulwich junior and the ground steward at the Hamlet. But he was quite kind to me as he knew I loved going to football. In answer to the squeaked question 'Please, Mr Mew, can I come and sell programmes at Dulwich Hamlet?' he replied that I could, next season.

Then he asked me whether I was free that coming Saturday, and I said I was. Bert told me that the British Army were playing the French Army at Dulwich. These were the days of national service, even for professional footballers, so they had to play for the Army ahead of anyone else. A big crowd was expected, even though there was, as usual, a full League programme. Dulwich, for some reason, had decided not to sell tickets in what they called 'the enclosure' in front of the main stand. This was a strange narrow strip that ran along the whole length of the pitch, and you actually stood about three feet below the level of the pitch. Bert asked me if I would like to be a ball boy in this area. Needless to say, I agreed. No tracksuits in those days. Just your ordinary clothes.

I have, of course, got the programme, on which I have, unfortunately, written the score. The last time I ever did such a thing. It was only in later years that I realised the identity and importance of the legends for whom I was retrieving the ball. And it is only in looking out this programme now that I have realised something even more significant.

What a team the British Army had. The programme gives only rank and initials, but most of them you will have heard of, even if you're a lot younger than me. In goal was Lance Corporal A. Hodgkinson. Alan went on to play for England and is still a top goalkeeping coach. Full-backs were Lance Corporal J. Armfield of Blackpool – Jimmy was in England's 1966 World Cup squad and can now be heard every week on BBC Radio 5 – and Signalman G. (Graham) Shaw of Sheffield United and England. At centre-half was Driver B. Foulkes of

Manchester United. Bill had played for England against Scotland two weeks earlier and was in that great United side destroyed by the Munich air crash a couple of years later. Fortunately, he survived. The wing-halves were Trooper S. (Stan) Anderson of Sunderland, who forced another Busby Babe, Signalman E. (Eddie) Coleman, to play 'out of position' at left-half. Sadly, Eddie was not as fortunate as Bill Foulkes in Munich. There were also two Scottish wingers, described in the programme as Gunner A. Hill of Clyde – 'a strong, robust player' said the pen picture – and Private A. Crawford, who had scored twice for Hearts in the Scottish Cup final a week earlier. Up front was Tottenham's Lance Corporal D. (Dave) Dunmore. The inside-right was Lance Corporal A. (Alfie) Biggs, a prolific goalscorer for Bristol Rovers, and at inside-left, also moved from his normal left-half slot, was one of the greatest players who ever drew breath: Private D. Edwards. Duncan, too, had played against Scotland a fortnight before and was to be another victim in Munich.

Surely this team would be unbeatable. They weren't. They lost 3–1. Three of the four goals were penalties, and Duncan Edwards scored one of them for the Brits.

But playing up front for the French – and I have only just realised this – was someone who would become even more famous than Edwards. He also scored two penalties for the French. In the programme he is shown simply as 'Soldat 2 Cl J. Fontaine', but he was, in fact, Just Fontaine, who scored thirteen goals for France in the 1958 World Cup finals in Sweden. This is still a record, even though more games are now played during the finals. In fact, nobody else has got near him. Only Gerd Muller of Germany has made it into double figures, with ten in 1970.

At the end of the game, Bert Mew managed to get many of the signatures of the French players in my autograph book, and Fontaine may just be one of them (though, like most footballers' signatures, they are almost impossible to read). But the one I wanted most, even then, was Duncan Edwards. Apart from being a player who was without any apparent weakness, he was for many years the youngest player to play for England. He held this record until Michael Owen made his debut; Owen in turn lost out to Wayne Rooney. On this special day, I was in behind the scenes for the first and last time. As Edwards came out of the dressing room, Bert asked him to sign my book. Through the open door at the end of the corridor I could see a cab, engine running, standing outside for him. I was hugely impressed, and I remember thinking that he must be very rich and important to have a cab waiting. I can see him now, in a rush, kit bag in one hand, raincoat over his arm. But he stopped, put them down and signed my book. Legibly, too. There is no doubt whose autograph it is, and I still have it.

'Sorry,' he then said, 'got a train to catch.'

How were Bert and I to know we would never see him play live again? Less than two years later he was dead.

In 1957, true to his word, Bert got me into the programme-selling team. From a little hut behind the main stand we would be given a hundred programmes and a shoulder bag for the cash. The programmes, printed in blue on pink paper, comprised just one sheet (slightly smaller than A4 size), folded. They cost three old pence (1.26p). Once our batch was sold, we returned the bag to the hut and stood there while the money was counted out, then given a fresh supply. It was my first job. It paid well, too. A shilling (5p) a game, free programme and free entry about ten minutes after the start. I used to pray that there would be no goals until I got into the ground.

This was really the beginning of the love affair.

For the next six years I followed Hamlet everywhere. There were several coaches running to every away game, and in the 1958/59 season I saw 50 out of their 56 games. Three of the six I missed were in the Channel Islands on tour. And I did see other games that year. I would slip into Millwall and Charlton for an evening game, and I also made my first visits to Palace during that period. I was so keen that over Easter in 1959 I saw five games. On Good Friday morning I went to watch Fulham, placed second in Division Two, meet Sheffield Wednesday, who were top. Jimmy Hill had not scored all season and was not selected until someone failed a fitness test just before the kick-off. Fulham won 6–2 and Jim scored a hat-trick with his head. That afternoon I went to watch Arsenal play West Ham at Highbury. I saw Dulwich on the Saturday afternoon and again on Easter Monday morning, and that afternoon I went to watch Palace.

But Dulwich remained my number one. I can still recite the 1958/59 team to you, if you're not careful. It's a funny thing, the mind. Ask me what I did last week, and I'm struggling.

THROW-IN

When I spoke at the Centenary Dinner of Dulwich Hamlet FC I was, at the time, presenting BBC Radio 5's *Six O Six* show. Amazingly, more than half of the 1958/59 team I remembered so well were there. Centre-half Dennis Joyce even came up and asked me for my autograph on the menu.

'This turns the clock full circle,' I remarked. 'About thirty-five years ago I ran across the car park to get your autograph.'

He suddenly looked anxious. 'Oh dear,' he said.

'What's wrong?' I asked.

'I hope I gave it to you. I used to get a bit miserable and refuse.'

I was pleased to assure him that he had signed.

That 1958/59 season was the club's most successful, post war. They came second in the Isthmian League to Wimbledon. This was also the season when Tooting and Mitcham had an amazing giant-killing run. After beating Bournemouth and Northampton they were drawn at home to First Division high-flyers Nottingham Forest. That May, Forest would lift the FA Cup at Wembley, beating Luton with ten men after their winger Roy Dwight broke his leg. No substitutes then. Incidentally, Roy is Elton John's uncle. I've met them both: Elton in the Savoy, and Roy at Crayford dog track, where he used to work. How many families have a social gap that wide? He called me not long ago about doing a cricket dinner. Roy, that is. Not Elton.

Let me pause here to set the scene a little and give you a taste of the scale of Tooting's achievement. Isthmian League sides were not semi-professionals; they were amateur sides, or, more likely, 'shamateur'. Most clubs paid their players. Even so, often they still did not manage to beat legal semi-professional sides in competitions such as the Southern League, let alone full-time professionals, and certainly not teams from the top division in the land. Well, Elton's uncle, Roy, nearly didn't get to the fourth round, let alone Wembley, because Tooting, on a frozen pitch, gave them one hell of a game and drew 2–2. Forest's goals were both lucky. Left-half Ted Murphy was harshly judged to have handled in the area, and then he put through his own net. Yet Hamlet still finished above Tooting in the league that season, despite Tooting coming to Dulwich one late summer's evening (no lights, kick-off 6.30) and winning 8–2. I was distraught. For days I said to my mother, 'I can't believe it. Eight–two!' Not that she understood what I was going on about. My misery lasted until two weeks later when Dulwich went to Sandy Lane, Tooting, for the return evening game and won 3–1. After that they didn't look back. At least for the rest of that season.

We lived in hope of getting to the FA Amateur Cup final. Dulwich had won it four times before the war and had had two players given full international caps – not amateur, *full*, a most rare occurrence – but after 1956 they missed out until amateurism was scrapped. My main ambition, however, was to see Hamlet in the first round proper of the FA Cup. It had last happened in 1947 – I couldn't remember it; I was two at the time – when they lost to Northampton.

In 1995, the *Daily Express* asked me to write a series following a team through the cup from the early rounds, and I was only too happy to agree. Unfortunately, the sports editor then left so the series was never finished. In fact, it lasted just a couple of games. Needless to say I decided to follow Dulwich, but as they had a bye in the preliminary qualifying round I was despatched to watch Southwick play Littlehampton Town.

I started my piece with the story about selling programmes and how I had come to go to Dulwich in the first place, and how Bert Mew had got me Duncan Edwards' autograph. Then I wrote the following:

Life moved on. I started playing Old Boys football, discovered the delights of Crystal Palace and left behind my non-League roots – although Dulwich was always the first result I looked for.

Now only one thing is missing from the jigsaw. I've always dreamt of the day when I might see them play in the first round proper of the FA Cup. This season they have a chance. I've even checked out the opposition.

I headed west through Brighton on to the A27 to Southwick. I'd have missed it if I'd blinked. As I entered Southwick, I noticed that the fish bar carried the sign FISH AND CHIP SHOP OF THE YEAR 1988. It was closed for lunch, which was not a healthy barometer of the crowd expected for the preliminary qualifying round clash with Littlehampton Town and the right to visit Dulwich Hamlet in the first qualifying round.

In the second half, I walked around the ground. When did you last do that at a football match? The Southwick Kop, all five of them, had moved to the other end. I asked them why they did not go and watch Brighton. They looked shocked. 'It's bad enough watching this lot,' came the reply.

They had a point. Littlehampton were awful, and Southwick were worse. The 1–1 draw was a triumph of mediocrity. The whistle went. The gate money of £181 was registered and the crowd of 47 headed home. I waited three minutes for the traffic to clear and left. Southwick won the replay with an own-goal.

Hamlet, meanwhile, have made a dream start. They share the lead in the Isthmian League with last year's champions, Enfield. Paul Whitmarsh, who signed from Stevenage, has scored seven goals in six games, and Nigerian Joseph Odegbami is starring in midfield. Even Southwick's veteran Northern Ireland striker Gerry Armstrong will surely be unable to save them from a hammering. I'm looking forward to the game with the same eager anticipation I had 40 years ago.

The last FA Cup tie I saw there was in 1962. Hamlet made it to the final qualifying round, losing 2–1 at home to Southern League semi-professionals King's Lynn. Lynn went on to win at Coventry, their manager was sacked, and Jimmy Hill took over to launch the Sky Blues. Jimmy took them from the Fourth Division to the old First, and they stayed in the top flight, despite many narrow escapes, until 2001.

OWN GOAL

'If the Titanic had been painted Sky Blue, it would never have gone down' – Coventry City chairman Brian Richardson in 1999.

Since then, Hamlet have not been near the FA Cup first round. Sainsbury's are in the car park of the old ground, and Duncan Edwards' penalty spot has long faded. But on Saturday I shall go to football again with Mr Mew . . . burning with that long-held ambition.

My 'hammering' forecast was right: Dulwich won 7–1, and then beat Chatham Town 2–1, but went out to Bognor 4–2 in the third qualifying round. Three years later Hamlet did reach the first round proper, beating Newport (Isle of Wight) 3–2 in the fourth qualifying round. Then they lost at home to Southport in that long-awaited tie. I was at both games, sitting with Tommy Jover and Bert Mew, both of whom still go to this day.

12. GROUNDSMAN SWEEPS UP AFTER ANORAK

'If money is the root of all evil, give me a cutting.'

Anon.

My mum was standing in my bedroom at Dulwich looking worried. I had just left school and was getting changed to go out. Her concern was of the 'whatever will become of you?' variety. My one O level in English Language had precluded me from applying for a job in a bank, where you needed a minimum of four. Thank God! 'Don't worry, Mum,' I said. 'One day I'll earn a thousand a year.' Although she didn't live to see many of my successes, she did at least get to see me earn £20,000 a year in a proper job. I often think of her during a busy period. I kept a full diary for the year 1998, and I see that I did four functions at the end of one week. Although one was a charity dinner, I still picked up around £8,000 in 36 hours. Who would have believed it, Mum?

DIRECT FREE-KICK FOR BEING SCYTHED DOWN

Comedian Ronnie Corbett is always teasing me about the number of jobs I get. This stems from a time when he heard that I did a lunch and a dinner in one day. This is not totally exceptional, but he has latched on to it whenever we meet or if he drops me a line about something.

A few years ago we were at a party together talking to legendary golf commentator Peter Alliss. Ronnie was pulling my leg, as usual, and then joined another group. When he'd gone, Peter asked me what it was all about. I told him, 'It's just his little [pardon the pun] joke. Don't tell him,' I continued, 'but I once did three jobs in a day. I did a travel industry lunch, then Tony Berry [former Spurs director and then chairman of his Blue Arrow company] sent his chauffeur to take me to speak at a late lunch at the Café Royal, and then I did a dinner at the same venue.'

Ronnie overheard this, and rejoined us. 'Three jobs in a day!' he spluttered. 'That's not possible . . .' On and on he went until I had to interrupt him.

'Listen,' I said, 'I probably didn't earn as much in those three gigs as you do in one.'

He went quiet. Then he said, with his usual immaculate timing, 'Would you take the word "probably" out of that sentence?'

When I left school most of my friends were going into insurance, but not with any real enthusiasm. I had no idea what I wanted to do, but the family said I had the 'gift of the gab' (little did they know) and would make a good sales representative. Driving around the country in a company car appealed to me, and after several refusals I got a job as a trainee rep with Nicholls & Clarke, a builders merchant in Shoreditch High Street, east London. I earned £5 15s. (£5.75p) a week less tax. Out of that I had my bus fares and my daily lunch of 1s. 6d. (8p) and the £2 I gave to my mother. Every day I got the number 78 bus from Dulwich and sat on the top deck, taking in everyone else's smoke (smoking used to be permitted on the top deck). Whenever we crossed Tower Bridge we'd see large ocean-going cargo ships loading at the quays. One day I would arrange for it to open and cause the sort of hold-up I had frequently cursed years earlier. But these were bad for me at the time as, it was the only point in my life when I had to clock on and off.

Nicholls & Clarke was a family firm. I have no idea about the Clarke, but there were two Nicholls. They were both tall and bald. One was very old and bent ('Old Mr Sam') and the other wasn't ('Young Mr Sam'). I was put in the general sales department and spent my day liaising on the telephone with customers and reps, writing up orders and taking them down to transport for delivery. Travel would eventually broaden my mind, but my mindset then was still in school mode, and I lived for clocking-off time.

I befriended a nice young lad with ginger hair called David Robertson. He was Young Mr Sam's nephew so was obviously destined for stardom. Like me, he was into football, and on my seventeenth birthday (26 February 1962) he invited me to Tottenham to watch them play Dukla Prague in the European Cup. Spurs skated over a snow-covered pitch and won 4–0, although for some reason my hero Jimmy Greaves did not play and Dave Mackay played inside-left. This was also my first sight of the legendary Danny Blanchflower. Eighteen years later he would be my co-speaker at my first Footballer of the Year dinner. After that I sometimes went to watch midweek games at Tottenham. During this time I also took half days out of my valued two-week holiday allowance to see England play internationals at Wembley. No floodlights, so afternoon kick-offs. It was there that I watched, for the first time, Bobby Robson – a man who would play a big part in my future – winning some of his twenty caps.

Despite my 'just a job' attitude I must have impressed someone because I was asked if I would like to become the assistant to the transport director. It was an awesome moment to work for someone who was on the main board. I can't remember what his first name was, but I wouldn't have used it anyway. He was 'Mr Greenaway', and a nicer man you couldn't hope to meet. I would sit with him in his office, along with another elderly guy whose job I can't recall.

Mr Greenaway was quite often out and about and the other guy was always wandering round the factory, killing time. So I was forced to take a few executive decisions when problems arose. Mr Greenaway was quite impressed by this, and when Young Mr Sam needed an accounts assistant I was offered the job. I took it because my money shot up to £7 per week, but it turned out to be a pretty miserable existence, only a few steps up from being Dickensian. Six of us worked in the office on the other side of the glass from Young Mr Sam. Bent over the ledgers each day, the manager was a miserable bloke called Pinchbeck. The only thing that kept me sane was a good guy called Tom Matthews. He was number two to Pinchbeck and a supporter of the famous but now sadly defunct club Walthamstow Avenue, which played in the same league as my team Dulwich Hamlet.

We did speak while Pinchbeck was in the room, but not much. Whenever he went out of the room the sun peeked through the clouds. We started to have a chat and a bit of a laugh with another friendly woman and a none-too-bright but nevertheless very pleasant Irish office boy called Pat. It was like being back at school. The minute Pinchbeck reappeared, however, we would all go quiet, although sometimes the secretary, a miserable woman, would sneak on us.

I put up with it for a year, then asked to move on. They put me in the sanitary department with a Jewish bloke called Woolf. He was a pleasant enough guy but was not really interested in me, and the feeling was mutual, although what I don't know now about S bends and U traps isn't worth knowing.

I was starting to look around for something else, and then something happened that made me believe in fate. While browsing through a financial paper I did not usually read, I spotted an advertisement: 'Trainee journalist wanted. Apply J.D. Prince, Editor, *Lloyd's List and Shipping Gazette.*' If there was one thing I could do, it was write. What's more, I *enjoyed* writing, so this advertisement appealed.

INDIRECT FREE-KICK

I was walking the dog through the graveyard, and the vicar came along and said, 'Morning.'

I replied, 'No, I'm walking the dog.'

I suppose I must have written a decent letter because I got an interview with the editor himself. If Mr Greenaway was a nice man, then Jack Prince was Mother Teresa. He was tall and thin with a small moustache, a kind face and sympathetic eyes. Over the many years I would know him I never heard anything other than good things spoken about him. Absolutely everyone liked him.

I'm not sure I did a very good interview, in fact I'm pretty sure I didn't. Despite this, he took me on. Many years later at his retirement party, which I attended not only as a former colleague but also as the director of public relations for a major plc, I asked what it was he'd seen in me all those years before (I still called him Mr Prince; I never could bring myself to call him Jack). In his usual kind manner and with his normal friendly smile, he said something about the promise he'd seen in me, but he said it in such a way that I got the feeling he was as amazed as everyone else about what I had achieved.

Lloyd's List salary was not much better than where I'd come from. In those days they did not pay National Union of Journalist rates. In fact, they ignored them. We were on the standard pay scale of the Corporation of Lloyd's, which owned and published the paper. None of this bothered me, though. It was an exciting move as I became a trainee sub-editor on not just a daily newspaper but the oldest daily newspaper in the world.

Lloyd's List is all about transport, and when I joined many of the pages were taken up with shipping movements. These long lists were compiled daily by a whole horde of people sitting a floor above us – a job that can't have been much better than working in the accounts department at Nicholls & Clarke. I should make it clear here that the

Lloyd's Register of Shipping has nothing to do with *Lloyd's List*. The *Register* is just what it says: every ship in the world is listed therein, and it's published annually (or at least it was, if it isn't on some computer disk or CD by now). At the front of *Lloyd's List* were three or four pages of editorial. This was the glamour bit of the paper. At least we thought it was. As a result, we were the subject of some jealousy.

As the most junior staffer, I had to write the Casualty List every evening. At about five p.m., having selected the juiciest accidents and having been careful not to word it in such a way as to apportion blame – 'was in collision with' as opposed to 'crashed into', for example – I had to take it up to the shipping office for it to be checked by one of the senior men. Most of them were OK, but there was one guy called Bartlett who seemed to take some delight in picking up on any mis-spelling or grammatical error. I think of him every time I write 'occurred'. It has two 'r's, while occur has only the one. Funny how things stick in your mind.

We also had a 'waiter' called Bill Prince. There were loads of these guys at *Lloyd's* doing the menial jobs. Bill later became a taxi driver and did 'the knowledge'. He picked me up years later and gave me a free ride. His job was to make the tea, run errands, collect the tapes from the Press Association machines upstairs and send copy in the old-fashioned air pressure tubes to the printers below our offices. It was all hot metal in those days; all our stories were set in lead, proofed and sent back up for us to check. When Bill wasn't there the most junior member – me for about eighteen months – would add these duties to his own. One of these was taking copy down from correspondents dotted around the country. They would call in and one of us would have to put on the headphones and take their words down using the typewriter. I was, and still am, a two-finger man, but I became quite quick and accurate after the number of bollockings from these correspondents about my lack of speed, and from the news editor, who had to decipher my manuscript and often told me to re-type it. Accuracy was a byword, and every company name had to be checked from reference books, not just the first few times but every time. All hell would be let loose if even so much as a comma was missed out from '& Co., Ltd'. It was excellent training.

By and large it was a happy place, and to varying degrees pretty well everyone got on. During the lull between six p.m., when the last copy went down, and seven p.m., when the copy and page proofs came back up, a heavily contested penny and comb football game took place on a big desk which we highly polished to make the surface smoother. There was a big league, and even the more senior staff joined in. Until there was a huge row one night and it was banned.

THROW-IN
Why is abbreviation such a long word?

Our hours were 1.30 p.m. until eight p.m., and we had to work on Sundays and bank holidays, even Boxing Day, for which we did get some overtime. However, I started to think about using my mornings more fruitfully and tried one or two part-time jobs, such as gardening. None of these lasted too long, until I saw an advertisement for part-time Kleen-e-zee brush salesmen. In the early 1960s it was unusual for women to go out to work so being a door-to-door salesman was still a worthwhile job.

I went for an interview at Herne Hill in a very shabby room over a very shabby minicab office with a very shabby and miserable-looking Mr Simmonds. It was one of my shortest interviews as I was immediately appointed. I asked how many brushes I would have to lug round. 'None,' he said. 'These days we sell from a catalogue and you deliver the goods two weeks later.' Commission was good, too. Part-timers got 40 per cent, and if I wanted to go full-time I could have 45 per cent. We agreed to meet the following Monday at nine p.m. on Frien Road, East Dulwich, where I would start my training. I was looking forward to this. Some proper sales tuition at last.

As you might expect, Monday was cold and wet. Mr Simmonds looked even more miserable. He knocked on a couple of doors and got the bum's rush. He then got the real hump. An old lady came to the third door we tried and clearly wanted nothing from us, but he was determined. He didn't actually put his foot in the door, but he might have had she tried to shut it on him. Eventually he browbeat her into placing an order for a tin of polish. I'm not sure who was most relieved to end the negotiation, him or her. At this point he announced that my training was complete. I stood in the street somewhat stunned. 'Is that it?' I said eventually. He said that it was, handed me my catalogues, and announced that he was off for a nice hot coffee.

As he turned to go, he said something that was to haunt me through the rest of my days. 'Remember,' he said, 'always to go on to the next door. That could be your sale.' That remark has been both a burden and a Godsend. It was probably what made me persevere with my speaking, despite setbacks such as those with Dabber Davis.

Over the next two weeks I was to do rather well in my new part-time job. Bex Bissell carpet shampoo machines were a new fad. Dulwich was also changing, and there were plenty of West Indian immigrants settling around south London, most notably, of course, in Brixton, which was nearby. During our last eight years in Dulwich we had West Indian neighbours. My parents weren't too pleased, and there was obviously plenty of prejudice. Fortunately that has always passed me by, probably thanks to sport, which breaks down most barriers. In fact, as a young teenager I got on so well with them that they asked me to go and play Lambeth League park cricket with them. The captain, Mr James – we never called him anything else – and I were the only white players in the side. How I never lost my good eye on those pitches I shall never know. Makes me go cold to think about it.

The Kleen-e-zee Brush Company had launched their own carpet cleaner, but it did not have quite the sophistication of the Bex Bissell, which had a tank on top and looked rather like a vacuum cleaner. Our version was a foam roll on a pole and a separate bottle of shampoo. I decided to push this product and it started to sell well, not least to all the big West Indian ladies who were much impressed by my chat, whatever it was. At 30 bob a time (£1.50) they were a fraction of the Bex Bissell, and I would pocket twelve shillings from each sale. Two weeks later my father had to get the car out to help me deliver my first batch of orders as it would have taken me several trips on foot. All the orders were accepted and paid for, except one. You've guessed it – the old lady said that she hadn't really wanted the tin of polish forced on her by Mr Simmonds. I hadn't the heart to tell her she had signed the form. I thanked her, said that I completely understood, and gave it to my mum.

'LOOK AT ME WHEN YOU'RE READING THIS, SON'

'A good laugh is sunshine in a house.'

Anon.

Dick Ayers – he of the five-pound notes flying out of his back pocket as he cycled around the East End – has given me advice all his life, nearly all of which I've ignored. But once he said to me I would be funnier if I kept a straight face. Why I listened to him on this one occasion I can't tell you, but I did. I studied some videos of my heroes, Tommy Cooper, Frankie Howerd, Jasper Carrott and Eric Morecambe. People say I sound like Tommy Cooper, but I especially liked Eric. Maybe it was the glasses. Michael Caine, in an acting masterclass, said you should watch others and steal from them. Not their material, their mannerisms, to see if they suit you. He said they would probably look totally different and nobody would guess where they came from.

I'm saying no more – too many secrets.

I first met Eric through Jimmy Savile (a story to come). After that I was hoping to get to know him as he was quite an active Lord's Taverner. Everyone said he was as funny off screen and stage as he was on. Eventually I did see him again, but it wasn't through the Tavs. He was to be one of the guests at the 1984 *Sunday People* Merit Awards and Eve of Cup Final banquet. I would do 20 minutes, then host the evening and introduce various award presenters and my hero. I chatted with him during the evening, and he seemed such a pleasant guy. Kevin Keegan was also on the stage with us when I let Eric have the microphone to announce the award. Eric began to speak, then looked round at Kevin, did a double take and said, 'Just a minute.' He pulled Kevin to the centre of the stage. In his most creepy, charming voice, he said, 'I didn't know you were here,' and then, going right over the top and pretending to be impressed, he added in a pleading voice, 'Would you please sign this piece of paper for my son?' Kevin duly autographed it and handed it back to Eric. Eric looked at it, looked back at Kevin, looked back at the piece of paper, screwed it up and threw it away. It brought the house down. It was a mark of not just a great comic but also a great clown.

I was due to speak with Eric and Christopher Martin-Jenkins of *Test Match Special* fame at a Tavs Eve of Test dinner in Birmingham a month later, but sadly Eric died in the interim. A few months after he passed away I had lunch with his son Gary, who recalled his dad coming home and rattling off some of my football gags. I felt proud at this, yet cheated in some way that I would never see him again.

When we turn the TV on at Christmas, I think we all still feel cheated. It's never been the same since he went.

13. PITCH CLEARED – GAME ABOUT TO RESTART

'Growth begins when we begin to accept our own weakness.'

Anon.

I was earning far more from selling carpet cleaners to West Indian ladies than I was from my proper job, but I was completely knackered by the time I got to the City at lunchtime. This despite still being fit and thin. It would also be fair to say that while I loved the *Lloyd's List* job, I was, despite the excellent training, a bloody awful sub and proofreader. As people came and went I was tried on other senior jobs. I did the tanker charter column for about six months under the direction of a very nice man called 'Midd', as in Middleton. I can honestly say that, despite everything, I still haven't got the first idea what I was writing about.

This was probably the least rewarding period of my time with *Lloyd's List*, and I would come into work on my Honda 50cc motorcycle with less joy than hitherto. This little machine had changed my life. I had upgraded from a Mobylette moped, one complete with pedals, which was a bit uncomfortable. I had briefly flirted with an Aerial Leader, a huge machine I'd mistakenly bought from a colleague at Lloyd's. Not only would it not start, I was still so weedy that I couldn't get it up on its stand. I had to endure the embarrassment of having to get my mum to help me. In the end she lent me £50 to buy the Honda, and it never let me down. Nor did I ever fall off it – sober anyway. It also made me money. As any of my friends will tell you, I love a league table. If I'm getting a bit noisy, put me in a corner with one and I'll be absorbed for ages. My Honda 50 league table showed me how much I was saving every time I went out. It was a great little machine. Strangely, when I sold it to my friend Mike Kendrick it never went again.

It was about this time that one of the most sought-after jobs became vacant. There were two 'outside staff' who sat in the front office along with the editor's secretary; these were the only nine-to-five jobs, loosely speaking, on the paper. They were the reporters. They went out to press conferences and on various visits to ships and launchings. Mostly these were in the United Kingdom, but some were abroad. Denis – only one 'n', if you knew what was good for you – Burgess was the long-standing chief reporter, and his assistant was a chap called David Prior. Prior had come down from university to work for a year before going into the Church, where, I understand, he remains to this day. He was a jolly chap and played a very good standard of hockey for Spencer, who were one of the top sides then. As his year was coming to an end, a replacement was needed. Everyone wanted the job, and the rest were seriously put out when it was given to me. They saw it as being earned by default rather than on merit, and they were probably right.

As it happened, I turned out to be a good reporter. I always wore a suit, I got on well with people, and I refused to be overawed by the national newspapers' shipping reporters (they still had them in those days). My first days were not auspicious, however. I failed miserably on my first mission, which was a source of great delight to all my colleagues who had missed out on the job. I was sent down the Thames to look at a small coaster. At this distance I can't remember what was so newsworthy about this little vessel, and I couldn't remember much about it when I got back to the office either. I'd unwisely joined the very sociable captain, who'd produced various unusual bottles from a not very impressively stocked drinks cabinet. I was unused to strong drink. They took one look at me when I somehow got back to the office and sent me home. Next morning, Jack Prince, in his kindly way, suggested that I bear in mind that this was far from the last occasion when I would be offered a free drink. Not only was this sound lifelong advice, it also meant that I was not going to be quickly kicked back to the subs desk.

Further trips followed. One that sticks in my mind is a bitterly cold January visit to Hull to look at a new trawler operated by Boyd Trawlers, headed by a larger-than-life Yorkshireman called Tom Boyd. Put up in the station hotel, I got drunk on Scotch for the first and last time with the other press guys. Next morning, with the mother of all hangovers, I was roused at six a.m. and taken round the fish docks, which were a good deal busier than they sadly are today. We then headed off in a taxi, and I opened the window to avoid throwing up, only to be met with a heavy smell of fish. I survived until about 8.30, when they took us to the Fisherman's Club for breakfast. When a nice piece of smoked haddock arrived with two large fried eggs on top, I had to make my excuses.

THROW-IN

During one visit to Nantes for the launching of a Normandy Ferries vessel, the speeches were interminable, as they tend to be in France. Even worse, they were in French. *Lloyd's List* had a rival transport newspaper in those days called the *Journal of Commerce*. Their reporter was an elderly Scotsman called Bill Coulter. Deciding that there weren't enough laughs in any of this, and noting the absence on the toast list of any reply on behalf of the British guests, Bill decided to act. He could speak a little French, and fortified by this and plenty of our hosts' local wine, he got to the mike and delivered a joke in French. It wasn't a bad one. In fact, it was quite a good one. But it might have gone down better had the punchline not been an Englishman saying to God, 'Who do you think you are? General de Gaulle?'

As I progressed well in the job, I was given my first overseas assignment: I had to cover the maiden voyage of a new North Sea car ferry operated by the England–Sweden Line. This would be only the second time I had been abroad. At the age of seventeen my old school friend Len Bateman and I had gone to Rimini for two weeks, but that was it.

I set off for Heathrow and met up with the rest of the press party, among whom was the late John Petty of the *Daily Telegraph*, with whom I got on rather well. I thought I would hang around him while I learnt the ropes, but when I came back from getting a newspaper there was no sign of him. I waited for announcements, not realising that there was a departure lounge as well as the one I was in. By the time I had sorted out the system, the plane for Gothenburg had gone. Disasters – and at that moment 'disaster' was not too strong a word – can often lead to something positive. Despite my total lack of experience, I found out that I could still get to Gothenburg before sailing time via a connecting flight from Copenhagen. Fortunately, I had this information to hand before I made my highly embarrassing call to the office. Most people, including the editor, thank God, found it all highly amusing, and I was applauded on to the ship by my fellow journos about twenty minutes before the MV *England* sailed. Ironically,

I've been to Copenhagen six times now, but only to change planes. I have still never left the airport.

It may be a cliché that travel broadens the mind, but it was certainly true in my case. Experiencing how other people lived prompted me to examine and make judgements on my own country. I was also mixing with some intelligent and experienced people, and this was rubbing off. Rather like footballers who compare their wages when they go on international duty, I started to realise that, while my national press colleagues were not earning a fortune, they were doing a good deal better than I was. My feet began to itch.

CORNER
Why do people who believe in reincarnation leave their money to other people?

Outside work I was producing the Old Wilsonians' Association magazine. For years, a guy who rejoiced in the name of E.G. Camden Pratt had run the whole association, including the magazine. He also ran Pratt's News Agency, but was about to retire from work and outside interests. His OW jobs were split into three, and I, as the only journalist, was asked to do the magazine. It was a professional production, if slightly old-fashioned, but I set about redesigning the cover to give it a lighter feel. A copy was given to each of the 500 schoolboys. Advertising revenue was my responsibility but at this stage I had not the slightest idea about advertising supplements, so it was somewhat remarkable that I invented one. I decided to run a careers supplement in the middle of the magazine, and I wrote to several leading banks and institutions. It took off. There were sixteen pages in one issue with all the major banks and insurance companies advertising. Royal Assurance took a double-page spread.

I was starting to become aware of my strengths, and decided that a career magazine delivered free to south London schools could be a winner. I persuaded the printers of the OW magazine to provide me with a dummy issue in return for a guaranteed print contract when it took off, as it surely would. Then I arranged for the *Observer* careers editor Joy Larkham to lend her name to the editorial, and in my spare time I started selling. Several OW advertisers took options on the first edition, and the Post Office booked a whole series. Many of the schools said they would be pleased to take copies. I dreamt of owning a red estate car with the name 'Career Focus' down the side as I delivered the copies three times annually.

I had also started to look around for a job that paid me more than *Lloyd's List*. Having always loved animals and the countryside, I was mildly interested in a request to go and see a Mr Arthur Greenhalgh, director-general of the Shorthorn Society of Great Britain and Ireland. He was impressed by what I had done for the OW magazine, and by my career in general. He was looking for a press relations man who could also edit the monthly publication the *Dairy Shorthorn Journal*. I said that I was interested in the money but that I had started to travel abroad and I did not wish to give that up. He told me that with the *Dairy Shorthorn Journal* there would be frequent trips to Canada and elsewhere.

So in July 1966, just after England had won the World Cup, I joined the Shorthorn Society, and, at the age of 21, was able to go home and tell my mum that I was now earning £1,000 a year.

14. HANG ON, THERE'S A COW ON THE PITCH

'Even if you're on the right track, you'll get run over if you just sit there.'
Will Rogers

I don't know if there is a name for it, but some people have a tendency towards one-upmanship that compels them to top whatever you say to them. Unfortunately, Arthur Greenhalgh had it. If you told him you had received 30 Christmas cards, he would have got 50. If your father had won the MC, his would have got the VC – and bar, if they awarded it. Consequently, I didn't get on a trip to Canada; the furthest I got was Peterborough, for a farm walk. I was also unaware that the Dairy Shorthorn was a dying breed. Although it was a good multi-purpose animal, suitable for beef and dairy, it had now been overtaken by the black and white Friesians, which are now known as Holsteins, and most other breeds too. Before the war the Dairy Shorthorn had held sway, and whoever produced the TV series *All Creatures Great and Small*, based on the books of the vet James Herriott, certainly did their research. In these programmes – you have to go to satellite to see them now – all the cattle are the distinctive rust and white Dairy Shorthorns which would have dominated the herds then.

Still, I did churn out six issues of the *Dairy Shorthorn Journal*. Churn out – geddit? If you want to know about milk yields and butterfat content, I'm your man. And I did one of my supplements, which no previous editor had thought of. Up in Cheshire lived one of the best of our herds which was owned by the Duke of Westminster. I went up to see them and wrote a huge slab of copy about them backed by advertisements from all their suppliers. Arthur said it was the first time for years that an edition of the magazine had made money. He was probably right, although of course you couldn't totally trust him.

FREE-KICK

A farmer went out one morning and found his cows all frozen solid. He called the vet, and the vet turned up with a little old lady. She bent down and whispered in each of the cows' ears and they all revived.

The farmer said to the vet, 'That's amazing. Who is that woman?'
The vet replied, 'That's Thora Hird.'
(I sat next to Dame Thora when I spoke at a Grand Order of Water
Rats Annual Ball in 1998. What an interesting and talented lady she was.
When she died, *Private Eye* did a very nice but respectful cartoon
showing her going up to heaven on a chair lift.)

After just six months it was time to move on again. I was offered
more money to stay on at the journal, but I was keen to get back into
travel. I saw an advertisement for a magazine called *Travel Agency*
published by a Canadian company, Maclean-Hunter, based in the
heart of London's West End in Old Burlington Street. *Travel Agency*
was quite a successful monthly magazine as it was competing with just
one weekly, *Travel Trade Gazette*. There was another monthly, *Travel
World*, but it was a poorly produced and supported publication. There
were two jobs going – editorial assistant and deputy editor. I applied
somewhat ambiguously and would have been happy with either. I
can't remember when the interview was, but I do remember the time
– 4.30 p.m. This was fortuitous in view of the editor's fondness for a
glass or two. Neither do I remember much about the interview, but a
week later I landed the deputy editor's job.

On 1 January 1967 – no public holiday then – I stepped into the
travel business proper.

Editor Gordon Wharton had a dramatic effect on my future. He
taught me about layout and how to write creatively, and he got me
into coloured shirts. Some twenty years later he would come and work
for me, but don't let's race too far ahead yet. Gordon also taught me
how to drink, and I'm lucky that my metabolism is such that it did
not lead to the illness of alcoholism. I certainly gave it every chance.

On my first day, Gordon told me there was a French Railways party
that evening and that it would be useful if I went with him so he could
introduce me. I'd never drunk champagne before, and it certainly
flowed. When we left, Gordon wanted to go to the pub so, eager to
impress the new boss, I went along. Pints of bitter on top of
champagne are not to be recommended. By this time my parents, with
whom I was still living, had moved to Bellingham. When I'd groped
my way to Blackfriars, I found the station spinning around. I crawled
in to work the next morning with one of my worst ever hangovers.

Not long after I joined, Gordon went off on a trip to Australia and I was left to run the magazine. I was thrown in at the deep end but still managed to have a bit of a row with the publisher, Dennis Holman, our ultimate boss, who wanted me to run some editorial on the Holland–America Line in return for them increasing their advertising. I stood on my editorial dignity but eventually had to give way.

The fourth member of the team was the new editorial assistant, Peter Elliott. Tall, good-looking, but could be unreliable. Although I'm sure drink slowed me down a bit, I can't recall that it ever interfered with my work. Still, we did have a bloody good time.

I have to admit to throwing my toys out of my pram at a travel agents conference in Bournemouth once. These were massive hospitality affairs, every company trying to outdo the other with dinners, parties and special events. Obviously journalists were invited to just about everything. We took it in turns to cover the business sessions, and I was due the morning off. I ambled into breakfast to find Dennis and Peter slipping down their bacon and eggs, still in their dinner jackets from the night before and still very pissed. Peter was due to be covering the session but I had to go and do it, and I was not best pleased. I would have sought out Gordon to provide Peter with a severe bollocking to go with mine, but he wasn't even back himself yet. Gordon was not the most organised person in his personal life. He was on his second marriage, which was also doomed to failure, and I would even often have to sub him until the end of the month.

CROWD GIVING US THE BIRD

A magician is working on a cruise. The captain's parrot is ruining his act. Every time he does a trick the parrot announces how it's done: 'It's not the same hat', 'There's another bunch of flowers under the table', and so on. One day the ship hits an iceberg and sinks. The parrot finds himself sitting on a piece of driftwood with the magician. They don't speak for hours. Eventually the parrot says, 'All right, I give up. What have you done with the ship?'

I had two-and-a-half happy years at Maclean-Hunter, and when we went from a paid-for magazine to a controlled circulation (free to specified people in the industry) it really took off. We were magazine of the year in the company. Sadly, in between the announcement and the presentation lunch, Dennis was fired. To this day I'm not sure why, but we were up in arms and were all threatening to walk out. Despite his own problems Dennis went out of his way to talk us out of doing this. Something I shall always admire him for. A new guy came in from another publication. Nigel Foster was a nice enough bloke, but not the extrovert character we'd been used to, and he had a bit of a hill to climb. Rather unfairly, since the money should of course have gone to Dennis, Nigel was to be the recipient of a quite healthy cheque as a result of our award. On receiving the cheque, Nigel shared it with the rest of us. He wasn't trying to buy our loyalty, he just thought it was the fairest thing to do. It was a nice gesture, and we respected him for it. It wasn't the money, it was the fact that he didn't have to do it.

After Dennis went, the magazine wasn't the same. I thought I would try my hand at the advertising side and asked for a transfer, which I got. This meant I had to resign from the Chapel (house committee) of the National Union of Journalists. One day in the corridor I met the Father of the Chapel who was also editor of another of our publications, *Packaging News*. He said he was sorry that I was moving to the advertising side and added that he thought I was 'prostituting my art'. I replied that there was 'not much bleedin' art in *Packaging News*'. He never spoke to me again.

Not long after I moved across, Dennis Holman, who had gone to Reed Publishing, was in the throes of launching a rival weekly to *Travel Trade Gazette*. It would be called *Travel News*, and is now known as *Travel Weekly*.

TRAINER ON THE PITCH

When I moved into advertising, Maclean-Hunter asked me to take an assessment test. Strangely, they didn't bother to ask their journalists to take it. This is what they said about me (bear in mind that I had been a successful journalist for six years and was already starting to do after-dinner speaking): 'Of superior intelligence, with good arithmetical and clerical skills, good sales sense, some idea of how to activate people and good visualising ability. Ambitious, you would probably work hard to be successful but you should push yourself harder and not expect things to come easily to you. Your judgement about practical affairs needs further seasoning, and your vocabulary and verbal skills are weak and should be improved to help you become a successful salesman with future advancement.'

Dennis set about recruiting Gordon and the new editorial assistant who rejoiced in the name of Jonathan Conquest. They also asked me to join them. I was thinking about it when, after just nine months selling space (during only one of which did I exceed my target) I was headhunted to go into public relations.

15. PLAY TO RESTART ANY MINUTE

'Non-executive directors are like bidets – no one knows what they're for, but they add class.'

Michael Grade

Hertford Public Relations Limited was based at 193 Fleet Street. It was, as I would subsequently tell my many visitors, above a pawnbroker's and next door to a bookmaker's. It was up four flights of stairs, too, with no lift. The major account was Townsend Car Ferries. They had just bought Thoresen Car Ferries and were planning to launch the new brand name Townsend Thoresen Car Ferries to fight the nationalised British Rail company Sealink. I vaguely knew Phil Holt, who interviewed me for the job. He had recently been named in a trade journal survey of PR people, which had said that Tony Bennett of P&O was the best (he would subsequently come to work for me, not with happy results) and Phil Holt 'always phoned back'. With my background of writing about car ferries for both Lloyd's and *Travel Agency* over the past seven years, a time during which drive-on, drive-off really began to establish itself, I was considered a good candidate for account executive. So in August 1969 I moved into public relations.

There were about a dozen employees in the company and four directors: the chairman, the Marquess of Hertford, Denys Hamilton, who handled the Atlas Copco business, Phil Holt and Bryan Thompson. Bryan had worked on national newspapers and had started the company with the Marquess, Hugh Hertford. Hugh knew nothing about PR and had a major stately home called Ragley Hall near Stratford-upon-Avon. He had a very aristocratic speech impediment and referred to it as 'Wagley', as we also did when he wasn't within earshot. Bryan had been taken on by Townsend to move to Dover as marketing director, although without a seat on the main board, which was something he would never get. The other directors (except Holt) and the rest of the senior staff did not welcome the fact that he was on the Hertford board, but Bryan was not a straightforward man, as I was to discover. Having said that, I did learn a great deal from him about promotion and press relations. In a way, initially at least, I regarded him with some respect, almost as a father figure. Holt, however, I was not to have much respect for as I felt he was a selfish man. Whenever we went to Dover, the much-sought-after mileage costs always went to him. Lunch always had to be when and where he wanted it. Unfortunately, it was often a pint and a greasy meal at the Cock Tavern. It was at this point, not surprisingly, that I started to put on some weight.

My first assignment was to write the press release announcing the new Townsend Thoresen name. My second was to go to Southampton one Saturday morning to mastermind a presentation to the 100,000th car to travel to Cherbourg since the service started. This may not seem like much of a story now, but in 1969 it was quite innovative and most of the local 'stringers' (reporters) of the national papers turned up along with both local TV stations. They asked me if I was going to select someone, but I said I would play a 'straight bat', and whichever car was the actual number would be halted at the top of the ramp. A nice surprise for them, I thought.

THROW-IN

Someone once asked me, 'What's the lightest you've ever been?'

I replied, 'Six pounds five ounces.'

This event was important on two fronts. Firstly for me as a new PR man, secondly for relations between Townsend and Thoresen. There was not much love lost on either side. Townsend regarded Thoresen as spendthrifts who did not run their operation on sound economic lines; Thoresen regarded Townsend as cold, hard accountants with no real feel for their employees. They were probably both right. Hertford PR had been forced on Thoresen and their PR company lost the contract. They always regarded me as a 'Townsend man' no matter how many times I pointed out that I had arrived at the birth of the joint name and that I was neither a Townsend nor a Thoresen man but a Townsend Thoresen man. It was an argument I never won.

Thus, Thoresen people could scarcely conceal their delight when the following appeared in the *Daily Sketch* after my first visit, under the heading PR STUNT THAT WENT WRONG:

The captain of the cross-Channel ferry and shipping line officials were all smiles as they stood on the quayside. Newsmen and TV crews waited eagerly for the 100,000th car to go aboard the holiday ferry. The car's driver had won a free pass from Southampton to Cherbourg, and the captain stepped smartly forward to break the good news and hand over the documents.

But that was when the ceremony – held yesterday by Townsend Thoresen at Southampton – began to go badly adrift. For the lucky driver was Air Marshal Sir Gilbert Nicholetts, who was setting off for a continental holiday. He stopped for a few seconds at the imposing sight of Captain Fynn Magnusson, then he snapped, 'I do not want the publicity. I am a shareholder in the company. I will not pose for pictures.' And with that the 67-year-old air marshal took the pass and drove smartly on board the ferry, *Viking II*.

Last night, flustered public relations men hired for the occasion by Townsend Thoresen were puzzling in a Cherbourg hotel over what went wrong. One of them said, 'It was all very, very embarrassing. We weren't to know he was a shareholder, or that he would shy away from publicity.'

What the *Daily Sketch* failed to mention was that alongside the 67-year-old air marshal was a rather attractive young lady. Of course, I make no suggestion that there was anything untoward going on. She might have been his daughter, his niece, or his secretary on a genuine business trip. However, if I am not correct in this assumption, then you don't need a great deal of imagination to envisage the horrific scenario of someone 'playing away from home' on a naughty weekend to be suddenly confronted by TV cameras and the national press.

It could have been horrific for me too, but fortunately Holt had come with me – maybe to get the mileage – so he couldn't distance himself from the event as much as he might have liked to. As it turned out, Townsend Thoresen would dominate the next fourteen years of my life.

After a year, Holt, who spoke excellent French, albeit with a 100 per cent British accent, announced he was leaving to run the London operation of the French Government Tourist Office. I was hoping to get his job and was disappointed when they said they were going to get someone else in. But they were keen to keep me, and offered me a big rise and a directorship of Hertford PR. All this was pushed through by Bryan Thompson as a non-executive director of Hertford, and it caused more resentment of him there.

The 'someone else' was Geoff Morgan, a nice enough bloke who was brought in from Chrysler and instantly made a director. He was made about as welcome as a fart in a spacesuit. His first day was not a good one on all fronts. In addition to his chilly welcome, I found out later that on that very day he'd been told by his actress wife Sandra Payne that she was leaving him. To be fair, he tried hard, but he was not a man's man. He could be a bit smarmy which made him appear insincere – something he certainly was not. The fact that he didn't drink in a heavy drinking culture was, however unfairly, another black mark.

One thing I learnt from Holt was the value of attention to detail and the need to double- and treble-check when organising a major event such as a ship launching. These events were legendary for their organisation, and I was lucky enough to inherit Hertford's experience for the sixteen I was destined to run. Geoff had brought in a new secretary who used to work for him in his previous job. This was another lead balloon within the consultancy, and it was pretty obvious that he had started an affair with her. They rather poked fun at my wish to back-check all arrangements at every turn, which was to prove a disaster at one event. If a table plan for 400 starts to go wrong, you can hit real problems. Having said that, I liked Geoff, and we largely got on well. He was a decent bloke and a good deal easier to work with than Holt. We shared the mileage for a start, and it became a running joke that he drove too fast in his MGB and I drove too slowly in my Singer Vogue.

Geoff also went to work on presentation. We did the offices up for a start. Having sat opposite the chain-smoking Phil Holt for twelve months it was a relief to be with a non-smoker. When the decorators came to wipe down the paintwork we couldn't believe the muck they took off the ceiling above where Phil had sat for several years. We started to make more as well by adding mark-ups to services we supplied and earning commission on hotels at the many events we staged.

We gradually became a little unhappy about the section of the company run by Denys Hamilton, which was not earning the money it should have been. Neither were we too happy with the quality of staff – inexperienced but attractive young women – he was employing. After a bit of a row over these issues, Denys resigned and took his entourage with him. This left Geoff, the marquess and me running the company.

Geoff was also very supportive to me on a personal level. In 1971 I started going out with Denise Harvey, one of Denys Hamilton's girls. We got engaged and were due to be married in June 1972. We weren't really suited though and, about six weeks before the wedding, after all the invitations had gone out, she had the courage to pull the plug. Nevertheless I was in quite a state when Geoff picked me up the following morning to take me to a meeting with Bryan Thompson in Dover. He helped me through it over the next few days and, after a heavy night out with the lads culminating in an all-night brag school at the Q Club (a snooker hall in Beckenham), I felt ready to get on with the rest of my life.

My mother had liked Denise and was almost as upset as I was (maybe also because she'd already bought her frock and hat). On the day when I should have been getting married my parents were on holiday; they sent me a nice letter to arrive on the morning itself. That same day we had flash floods in Catford. It was unheard of, but it meant I couldn't get out of the house. It was probably the loneliest day of my life.

FREE-KICK

'My love life is terrible. The last time I was inside a woman was when I visited the Statue of Liberty' – Woody Allen

-----

Not long after that I moved out of my parents' house into a one-bedroom flat in Bromley for £9,000, and my life started anew. I even invited my parents to sample my newly acquired cooking skills one Sunday. I brought the chicken to the table and laid it before them.

'Actually,' I observed, 'it doesn't look quite right.'

'No,' said my mother. 'It's upside down.'

Despite our friendship, my irritation with the fact that Geoff had come in over me failed to totally disappear. Bryan Thompson was also starting to suggest, rightly or wrongly, that he was not performing too well in certain areas. In the end this all got to Geoff, and he announced he would leave after the launching of our latest car ferry, *Free Enterprise VII*, in October 1972. At about the same time Hugh Hertford's agent at 'Wagley' was taken ill and was forced to retire. As Hugh couldn't get him out of his tied house, he decided to go back and run it himself, and it was agreed that when Geoff left I would be in charge of the Townsend Thoresen account. I would become managing director with 50 per cent of the company, and Hugh would have the other half as a sleeping partner.

It is worth pausing here to have a look at my new business partner. Hugh was born in another age. He might have been called by some a popinjay. Maybe he was, but you were never quite sure whether his actions were unwitting or whether he was winding you up. Certainly he dressed very expensively, and his marriage to a French countess had produced four children. I met one, Harry, when he was seven, Harry. Sorry, 'Hawwy'. I have to say it was difficult to take in the fact that this snotty-nosed kid was the Earl of Yarmouth. I also think Hugh had another life. Postcards used to arrive at the office for him from overseas. They were sent by what appeared to be serving merchant seamen, some of whom were barely literate. 'Another of those postcards for you, Hugh,' I'd say. He would give me a foppish smile, thank me a little too profusely, and shut the door.

In my early days at Hertford PR we were all invited up to 'Wagley' for a firm's outing over a Saturday lunchtime. Hugh's home is still a wonderful place, and it's open to the public. The gardens are magnificent, as you would expect of something designed by Capability Brown. The ballroom is the second largest room in the land, so he told me, and was used for the Grand Ball scenes in the BBC 2 production of *War and Peace*.

I had set off in my dark green Ford Cortina. (It actually turned out to be two Ford Cortinas welded together. We only found this out when a policeman knocked at my mother's door, putting the fear of God into her. Amazingly, I managed to sell it soon afterwards to an Irishman who was leaving the next day to go back to Ireland. As I never heard from him again, I assume he and the car made it to the ferry.) En route to 'Wagley' I broke down, but I managed to fix the problem and arrived late, covered in grease. Having spent a lifetime pricking the bubble of pomposity, Hugh's butler was an easy target for me, and we developed an instant dislike for each other. A normal bloke would have said, 'You're a bit late, mate. Had a bit of bother?' Hugh's man said, in a most disdainful way, 'Everyone else is here, sir.' I put on my roughest London accent, held up my grease-blackened hands and said, 'I've 'ad a bit of bother with the old motor, mate. Anywhere I can clean up?' He led me to a toilet grudgingly and rather pointedly served me last for the rest of the day.

Hugh, who always pleaded poverty despite his great pile and 1,000-acre farm, was a larger-than-life character. His pride and joy was a Sunbeam Tiger, which he drove in what I can only call an optimistic manner. He believed that immediately over every hump-back bridge was a three-lane dual carriageway. I was even glad to get back into Geoff's MGB. Hugh was, so he claimed, directly descended from Henry VIII's third wife Jane Seymour. When Geoff was still there we three partners had lunch together one day in the Cock Tavern.

'Are you actually in line for the throne, Hugh?' I asked him.

'Oh yes,' he said. 'If all the woyal family were killed in a plane crash, I'd be king!'

I'm still not sure if I believed him.

He always seemed to laugh only after we'd started. At the same lunch, which was just before Christmas, he used another of his famous phrases – 'buzz off', or in his case, 'buzz orf' – and went right over the top. 'I must buzz orf early this afternoon. We're thwowing a party for the staff at Wagley.'

'How many people do you actually employ up there, Hugh?' asked Geoff.

Hugh paused. 'D'ye know, I haven't got the foggiest idea. Until one thwows a party for one's staff one never knows how many one employs.'

He exceeded that only once, and I think, or at least I hope, he was joking. One Monday morning he arrived at the office and said, 'D'ye know, I bought the childwen down to the House of Lords at the weekend. They wan awound and absolutely shweiked with delight.' He paused for thought, then added, 'I suppose it's the only place in London that wemotely wesembles their home.'

In October 1972 the unthinkable was threatened when Roland Wickenden, chairman of European Ferries, the group that owned Townsend Thoresen, went off sick with influenza. Roland was a very nice and hugely talented man. Especially for an accountant. He didn't like public speaking, but when forced to perform he did very well. His performances at the AGM were brilliant. There wasn't anything he couldn't answer about any aspect of the company. He was hugely respected by the press, and because he didn't say a lot, everything he did say was seized upon and used. It made press relations very easy. We were largely in control of what was written about us. This, too, was a man who was never ill. His absence would be a blow. But when the Friday of the launching of the *Free Enterprise VII* came, he was fit enough to travel and seemed his usual cheery, friendly self.

Geoff was looking forward to his last launching, and then to getting away from all the problems. I was looking forward to working a little more closely with Roland, for, by the following Monday, I would be in sole charge of the company's public relations, and I was still only 27.

WHEN BOB MET JIMMY

'When are you going to stop earning money and start making it?'
Sir Jimmy Savile, to me

A friend of mine asked me if I'd seen the BBC programme *When Louis Met Jimmy*. I hadn't. The friend said that he thought Sir Jimmy Savile had come out of it not too well, that the programme had revealed a strange side to him. When I saw it at a later date I could see what he meant, but by the end Louis Theroux had actually decided that he quite liked Jimmy, albeit somewhat despite himself. Jimmy is certainly difficult, if not impossible, to analyse, which is exactly how he likes it. He is an ace persuader – and I mean that in the nicest way – it's hard not to enjoy being persuaded by him.

In the 1970s Jim was at the height of his powers. Among his programmes was a two-hour show broadcast on Radio 2 every Sunday afternoon. It was recorded at the BBC on Friday mornings, leaving him free for his weekend. From time to time he would record it around the country, which was a throwback to an earlier programme he'd done called *Savile's Travels*. It was a kind of pop version of Radio 4's long-running but now defunct programme *Down Your Way*.

In 1973, as Townsend Thoresen's PR man, I was trying to kick some life into a Belgian holiday village we owned at De Haan, a coastal village that lies between Ostend and Zeebrugge. It was a good-value holiday camp but low on luxury and facilities. Noting from the *Radio Times* that Jimmy's producer was a man called Ted Beston, I sent off a letter to him suggesting that De Haan would be a good venue for one of Jim's trips. Back came the original letter with a huge P.T.O. scrawled on it – how I wish I'd kept it. On the reverse, Jim himself had written in his sweeping and flamboyant hand a note saying I should come up to the BBC the following Friday at two p.m. to see him after he had recorded his show.

Shaking off the annoyance of missing my normal heavy lunchtime session in Fleet Street's El Vino's wine bar, I went. It was to be the start of an interesting and formative period of my life.

When I entered the basement studio it was full of people. Most were handicapped, some were in wheelchairs, and others were just hangers-on. Jim greeted me warmly. 'Now then, now then, how do you do, Mr Bob?' I told him about the holiday village and what I had in mind; he replied that I was knocking at an open door as he hated flying and that, as he never stopped working, this would be like a little holiday for him. At the time he had a good relationship with P&O, and he told me how he had just come back from Gibraltar after yet another free cruise.

Later, when the studio cleared, I told him that I knew the Gibraltar Minister of Tourism, a Mr Abrahim Serfaty. Jim boasted how he'd kept him waiting on the quay while he seduced a girl in his cabin. He left nothing to the imagination.

'Now then, now then,' he said eventually, 'back to your 'oliday camp . . .'

'Village,' I corrected him. A mistake. After that he always called it a camp, and our ships 'boats'.

''Ow we going to travel?' he asked.

I told him I had a very nice Hillman Hunter company car and that I would drive him over, leave him there for however long he wanted to stay, and then collect him. He didn't think so. His image required big cigars and a Rolls-Royce. The BBC did not pay him to do his programme, they gave him a Rolls-Royce every year. But he hated driving himself, and on the few occasions he did he never went above twenty miles per hour. He drove me once, and it was absolutely true. Therefore we would need a chauffeur, a Rolls-Royce, a friend or two he might want to take with him, and me. We would go as a team and we would all stay together from start to finish.

'Now then, now then. As I work for the BBC I am not allowed to charge you any money for the fantastic honour and privilege and all the publicity I am about to bestow on you. Therefore, when I get off your boat I will have as much money in my pocket as when I got on.'

I was starting to wonder if I was going to get this past the marketing director. I asked if we could use his Rolls-Royce, but he looked at me as if I was stupid and shook his head in disbelief.

'Deary, deary me. Use my Rolls-Royce? And put all those miles on the clock?'

A few weeks later, we set off. I had hired a large Rolls-Royce with a chauffeur called Harry. Jim told him the rules at the outset. He would always wear his suit, his tie and his hat. Also on board was an attractive girl called Carol and another guy called Bob. Carol was a well-spoken, bluestocking charity worker. When we got back I took her out, and she was good fun. The other Bob, whom I never really took to, was one of Jim's entourage who seemed to be a feature of his life. On board, Jim wanted the best of everything, except drink – he has never touched alcohol and drinks copious quantities of Coke. During the crossing I tried to spend as little as possible while Jim hammered my expenses for all they were worth. This became something of a long-running joke between us.

At De Haan, we got off to a slightly difficult start when Jim headed to his chalet for a nap. They had just been repainted, but God knows what with. He rushed out again, his eyes streaming and, apparently, stinging.

'Fooking hell! Fooking hell!'

'What's up, Jim?'

'There's some fooking stuff in those 'uts. They've done me fooking eyes in!'

Soon we were settled in new quarters. I was next door to Jim, separated from him only by the chalet's wafer-thin walls. At this time, there was much speculation about Jim's sexual preferences. He had been briefly engaged to Polly Brown from a pop group called Pickety Witch, but he told me that that had just been a publicity stunt. Some thought he might be gay, others had darker stories. Personally – and there were many subsequent trips and meetings – I came across no evidence of his having anything other than a healthy interest in adult ladies of various legal ages. If anything else were true I feel sure it would have surfaced by now. That first night in De Haan I heard more than I wanted to of his activities as the blue stockings flew off.

To my mind, he didn't have a great deal of respect for women. He used them for his own ends and would be fairly indiscreet. When I first met him he claimed he was having an affair with a titled lady (whom I won't name), but when it came to a serious relationship worries surfaced about someone else spending his money unwisely. During one interview with a woman journalist who asked him if he regretted never being married, he answered, 'Well, I must admit that

I do come home sometimes and think how nice it would be to have the old slippers by the fire, a pretty lady waiting and a nice meal.'

The interviewer leant forward, eyes softening. 'Do you really?' she said.

'Yes,' he replied. 'And that lasts for about ten minutes.'

During the trip we went running together and had some lengthy conversations about life in general. Jim, a Catholic, would make Mass several times a week and always spoke about God as 'his mate'.

'I have a chat with him several times a day,' he would say.

'But at the end of it all, suppose there's nothing?' I asked him eventually.

'Then I haven't lost anything, and I'll have lived a decent life.'

It became pretty clear during the trip that he loved the limelight and would only disappear into his chalet for an occasional rest. When I had to take his passport to reception I slyly took the opportunity to check his age (then a closely guarded secret). I was amazed to find he was already well into his forties (now, of course, he's in his seventies).

Our strange little team spent four days eating and drinking around Belgium on my expense account. Everyone had to be at every meal, including Harry the driver. In one expensive restaurant Jim insisted that Harry have his first oyster. Harry's face was a picture as he stared at it for some time before plucking up the courage to swallow it. It was a memory Jim and I laughed about for years afterwards.

One day we went to a place called Brendonk, the site of a German concentration camp which the Belgians had kept as it was. It was quite a chilling experience. I'd heard that at Auschwitz there is no bird song even though it is in the heart of the countryside. This place had a similar atmosphere. We went into the old courtroom, still festooned with Nazi flags. 'Fooking hell,' Jim observed, 'I bet a few hearts sunk in 'ere.' He'd summed it up well, and he did quite a moving piece into his recorder for the show the following week.

On our return to England we kept in touch and occasionally went for a Chinese meal together in the Edgware Road. I always paid, but it wasn't too severe as Jim liked to have a meal of starters – which I had to admit was a great idea.

A year later, I suggested that we go off to the Normandy beaches for another programme, so we set off again. This time the driver was a big guy called Colin who was good value. Harry had never really got our jokes, but Colin was the opposite. He laughed at everything. The team was smaller this time too, with just producer Ted Beston coming along for the ride. Jim enjoyed it, and as usual was recognised by all the Brits. However, one night we drove into the Normandy countryside and walked around a fairground. Although the French stared at this eccentric, bleached-haired bloke in a tracksuit, nobody actually knew who he was.

'Fooking hell,' Jim remarked without any pleasure in his voice. 'Imagine me doing this at home.'

In Belgium, where British television could be picked up, he was quite well known to the natives, but in rural France Jim was out of the limelight, and he didn't seem to like it.

Ted Beston was a great bloke who lived near me in Bromley and greatly enjoyed the by now highly developed interaction between Jim and me over my expenses. One day, when Jim was asleep and Ted and I were having a beer, he said to me, 'Do you know why Jim likes you so much?' I was flattered, and said that I didn't. 'It's because you treat him like a normal person and take the piss out of him. Most people are too overawed to do that.'

This was all the encouragement I needed, and the following day, in the interests of my expenses, I introduced Jim to Les Routiers. For all his claimed knowledge of France I was surprised to hear that Jim had not heard of this classification of great-value restaurants, which was originally aimed at truck drivers. I informed him that if you passed one with lots of trucks and cars outside, that was a good sign, and we should go in. Jim agreed to stop at one. The dish of the day was belly of pork, a fatty dish at the best of times, but not normally as fatty as this one. It was served with white beans, which turned out to be one of Jim's pet hates. He moaned all the way through the meal with plenty of 'fooking hells' between each mouthful. I made great play of how much I was enjoying it and how *typique* it all was. After the meal he was fairly quiet. He had been had, and he knew it, but he would rather die than give me any satisfaction. If I ever mentioned it he would say, 'Very nice, those white beans,' and change the subject.

I had at last got one up on him, and my delight lasted for several weeks before fading from my memory. Not from Jim's. Having allowed a suitable time to elapse, he got Ted Beston to call me.

'Jim wants you to come up for lunch,' he said.

'What?' I was astonished. 'Is he paying?'

'He certainly is. It's all on him, and I'm coming too. Can you make this Friday?'

'I'll clear the diary,' I said.

I turned up at two p.m., after the recording, and once the usual crowd had been cleared out of the studio, Ted came in. He was wreathed in smiles and could barely conceal his mirth as I baited Jim about him actually paying.

'You don't carry cash,' I pointed out. 'How will you pay?'

Jim indulged me. 'I have been especially to my bank this very morning and have drawn out the nelsons [he loved rhyming slang – and just in case you don't know, it's Nelson Eddys for 'readies'] for the entire meal,' he said, patting his tracksuit pocket. 'Now come along or they won't keep the table.'

At this, Ted nearly collapsed, and I was about to find out why. We walked around the corner to an establishment where there was a free table right in the window. It was the only one in this scruffy sandwich bar. Jim, cackling quite horribly, made great play of showing me to my seat and asked me if I wanted chicken or beef in my pie.

'No chance of a coffee, I suppose?'

'You want drinks as well?' Jim countered. 'Certainly. Nothing is too much trouble when I'm entertaining.'

And so the three of us sat at this table in the window of this shabby little shop, in full view of an ever-increasing crowd, no doubt wondering why this peroxide superstar was having such a frugal lunch with two boring-looking blokes in suits. I'd been turned over, and I complained about the quality of my pie. Ted could hardly eat for laughing, and Jim continued to cackle away. 'Eat up now. They'd be glad of this in Biafra.'

During another of our trips Jim told me that he was about to go on television with a version of *Savile's Travels* on the early Saturday evening slot. He said that the BBC had to be careful not to appear to favour us too much over Sealink. Nonetheless, the charmer must have gone to work because I soon received a call for us to provide facilities for an item on a French market in Calais. This time Jim was in his own Rolls-Royce, and we were off again for a couple of days. This particular show was not a great success, although, at the time, Jim claimed it was, of course. He then told me that they were going to replace it with something that was destined to go into the English language as a catchphrase, a programme about making kids dreams come true – *Jim'll Fix It*.

'You're bound to get a kid who wants to steer a ship,' I said, 'so you know whose ship it'll be, don't you?'

Jim'll Fix It hit the ground running and was a huge success. After a few weeks a call came from a lady at the BBC. Jim had been at work again. 'I'm not sure if you will allow us to do this,' she began, 'I know it may be too much to ask . . .' I let her continue, and went along with the charade of which she was clearly unaware. I suggested it would be far from easy to arrange, but after a lot of 'persuasion' I agreed to let a kid steer one of our ships. Yet more massive publicity.

As we were getting quite closely linked with Jim, our advertising agency decided it would be a good idea if he featured on our TV commercials. Jim always handled negotiations for such things personally, so we fixed up a lunch in a private room at the hotel across from the BBC for the agency and myself. We agreed a fee of £10,000 just for the day's filming; any appearance on brochures or point-of-sale material would be extra. As usual, I offered Jim a cigar at the end of the meal. The waiter arrived with a huge box of Romeo y Juliet which he left on the table. Jim picked one out, rolled it around his fingers and, after a lengthy inspection, lit up.

'Well, gentlemen,' he said, getting up from his chair, 'it's been an honour and a privilege to do business with you but now I must bid you good day as I am in serious need of some kip.'

With that, he picked up the box of cigars and went. We were all too stunned to stop him, or even to say anything. My expenses had to be very creative that week.

Once, showing uncharacteristic modesty, Jim admitted that he had no talent. 'I can't dance, sing, act or tell jokes,' he said. But he did say that in all his shows he was a 'one-take man', and it was true. Filming the ad was a breeze. He was very professional.

Jim was by now well aware of my entertainment abilities and encouraged me to go out on my own. 'Why make all this money for other people when you could make it for yourself?' I was constantly impressed by his business acumen, and he certainly shaped my commercial view of life from the time I met him. During one period when top earners could pay up to 98 per cent in tax, he made sure he got paid in kind whenever he could. Charm was a part of his persuasive arsenal. Like the time when he wrote in my copy of his autobiography (for which I had to pay, of course), '2 Bob (as it happens, that's all I make out of him at any one time!!), Man of Destiny, Tycoon, and De Haan!! From his employee!! Jimmy Savile'.

But he was thoughtful, too. He knew I was a big fan of Morecambe and Wise and he called one day to tell me they were on *Jim'll Fix It*, inviting me up to the recording to meet them. He took me into their dressing room, and they were both very friendly towards me. Eric was sitting down and didn't look well, but Ernie was very bouncy. In those days we had a shareholders' perk of cheap ferry trips, which was very popular and highly publicised. Everyone seemed to be a shareholder, though, and at parties I had stopped telling people who I worked for.

'Ah,' said Ernie when we were introduced, 'I'm a shareholder.'

'You would be,' Eric put in. 'Anything to save a few quid.'

I later checked it out on the share register, and he was indeed a shareholder. Under his real name Ernie Wiseman.

Ernie then told me how well the crew always looked after him, as it was difficult being so recognisable. He also told me a moving story about a little boy who was in awe of him and who had followed him around the ship but was too shy to say a word. Eventually Ernie said to him, 'I'm going to have a sleep now so I'll see you later, and make sure nobody comes into my cabin.' A couple of hours later Ernie woke up and went outside to find the little lad still standing there. 'I felt so awful I had to take him off and buy him a Coke,' he said.

This particular show was memorable for something else, too: for the first time I unwittingly got under Jim's skin. One of my team-mates in the Old Wilsonians was a PE master at the school, Dave Wellman. Apparently his real name was Derek, but for some reason he was known as Dave. Jim had written in his book about his time as a professional racing cyclist and mentioned a guy called Derek Wellman. I knew Dave had also done some bike riding and asked him if it was him. Amazingly, it was. He told me that he remembered Jim in those far-off pre-fame days. 'He was always going on about being a DJ, and he had the nickname "Oscar", which for some reason he didn't like.' Armed with this information, when I marched into Jim's dressing room at the BBC I said, 'Good evening, Oscar.' Jim didn't flinch, and completely ignored me. He then left the room. Feeling somewhat chastened, when he came back I was forced into a humiliating, 'Didn't you hear what I said?'

'I heard you.'

'Well?'

'Well what? You've just met someone who's been biking with me.'

With that, he walked out of the dressing room a second time. Neither of us ever mentioned it again.

Towards the end of my career at Townsend Thoresen we built a series of huge state-of-the-art car ferries. The first was called *Spirit of Free Enterprise*, the second *Herald of Free Enterprise*, which was destined to sink at Zeebrugge in 1986 and bring an end to the Townsend Thoresen name. Showing a sense of timing never present on the football pitch, I had left three years earlier. By 1982 I had become friendly with the *Jim'll Fix It* production team, especially the top man on the show, Roger Ordish. I asked him if he fancied having a little girl launch the ship for the programme, and he agreed. Jim would not go on the trip; in fact, he was deliberately missing from most of the *Fix It* films as the children were meant to be the stars and his presence would only detract from this.

These launchings were massive pieces of event management. Apart from the ceremony itself, we would also entertain 500 of our top customers accompanied by senior management and their wives. They all had to be shipped to Hamburg – the only place where we could accommodate everyone in one hotel – then moved to Bremerhaven for the launching. Four days of frantic hospitality had to be laid on, and there was no budget. Still, I had to make sure that the best of everything was always available. Special planes and trains were to be decked out in our logos and company colours, and I actually started planning a year to the day prior to the launching by visiting Munich to look at a train.

At a launch, the sponsor, as the launching lady is called, is fêted with film star-type treatment. At the fifteen previous events I had run, a director's wife had always been in the role, and she would be showered with gifts, not least a hugely expensive piece of jewellery from the shipyard. On top of all this, I now had to look after the *Fix It* film crew and make sure that the little girl was given the full treatment.

Apart from Les Dawson dying the death in the cabaret, everything went like clockwork, and a few months later we headed for the studio where Jim was waiting to record the show with the little girl and the ship's captain in full uniform. We also met up with other performers on the show, among whom was a rather weird young pop group whom we really liked as blokes. They were called Madness. As the programme had one of the biggest audiences at the time it was fantastic publicity, to which we could add a big feature in a book of the show and several repeats, including a spot in a 'best of' compilation.

Jim suggested that a suitable reward for the show's success would be a trip to De Haan. How could we refuse? So, for the last time, we set off in a Roller, this time with Roger Ordish and a production girl. We retraced our steps and revived old memories, Jim insisting, as usual, that the car be parked in the most prominent position wherever we stopped, especially if there was a big NO PARKING sign. We also went back to Brendonk, which was no easier than the last time.

Since then I have seen Jim only once, when he turned up at a Variety Club dinner in Leeds and heard me speak for the first and only time. He was very complimentary, but I was left in no doubt that I was second on the bill. We have also spoken on the telephone, although not for several years. He has moved from his bedsit near the BBC and I have now totally lost touch. I used to be able to reach him via Broadmoor, where he was on the board for a time. He has a somewhat macabre interest in the medical side of life and some Christmases could be found wheeling bodies to the morgue in Leeds Infirmary. But he has done a massive amount of good. Quite often, having made sure that he has been well paid for a particular job, he has insisted on an additional donation to many hospitals up and down the land, especially the spinal injuries hospital at Stoke Mandeville. This was probably due to his pit accident when he was younger, after which he was told he would never walk again. He ended up running marathons. At the time I knew him he was spending so much time at Stoke Mandeville that he had a room there.

When the daughter of a journalist friend of mine was seriously injured in a riding accident and was flown to the hospital by helicopter, I spent several days trying to reach him to ask him to go and see her. By the time I spoke to him he had already seen her four times; he had even met the helicopter when it landed. He'd had no idea, until I told him, that she had any connection with me, or that her dad was a journalist.

A few years back I sent a message to him via a heart surgeon who had performed a bypass on him, but I never heard back. I was sorry. It would be good to have a chat with him again, or to hear one of his messages if he called when I was out. He always fooled whichever secretary took the call. One day I came back from lunch to be told by a temp, 'Your probation officer called.' I knew exactly who it was, but I'm ashamed to say I never told her. She probably still wonders how I got such a good job with my record.

In fact, the last time I heard from him was in 1996 when he wrote to me, on Broadmoor notepaper, after I had appeared on an episode of Terry Wogan's *Auntie's Sporting Bloomers*. 'Robert!' it began. 'Good to know you are a mega-star, as you always have been, but now with national recognition. Will you please get a proper job so we can go to Venice on the Orient Express and back with a Rolls-Royce hired in Venice for four days. Just like the Townsend gig. Great days. Jimmy.'

When I saw Jimmy interviewed by Louis Theroux, the memories came flooding back when he said in a follow-up programme, 'I had his measure in the first ten seconds.' But I'm not so sure. In an interview spot in a minibus Louis actually got him to admit that he did have emotions but was good at masking them. When he finished the show, Louis remarked, 'To my surprise, I was sorry to say goodbye. I had a new-found respect for Jimmy, and although I didn't feel that close to him, I felt that that made me no different from anyone else in his life.' Spot on Louis.

16. DEATH IN THE CROWD

'Nothing is permanent but change.'

Heraclitus, Greek philosopher, 500 BC

I can remember Monday 23 October 1972 as if it were yesterday. I had showered and dressed and come out of the White Cliffs Hotel in Dover. I wasn't sure if I wanted breakfast. I just stared across at the Townsend office at Camden Crescent, half-expecting to find that it had fallen down during the night.

During the weekend we had had our ship launching in Holland. Another successful affair. As usual, our surprise cabaret at the Saturday night banquet and ball had gone down very well. This time we'd booked magician David Nixon and Anita Harris, who had a successful TV series together at the time. David was quite a nervous man, and I probably didn't help when I woke him up in the afternoon, quite accidentally, to give him some names to use in his act. He staggered to his hotel-room door shirtless, to my mind looking quite old and heavy. I think of that moment now whenever I catch my no longer thin body in a hotel-room mirror.

On the Sunday morning, we climbed on board our special train for the journey to Zeebrugge from where we could catch our scheduled ferry service back to Dover and home. I was staying on in Dover for a meeting. It was a jolly train ride. Although we had been let down by the booked modern train, the rather elderly rolling stock they provided, every carriage different, gave us a good atmosphere. As I walked through the carriages there was a card school going on in one, a guest leading a singsong with his guitar in another, and heavy drinking and laughter in another.

I settled down with some press guys for a few sharpeners when a freight customer came to find me. 'Mrs Wickenden has asked me if there is somewhere Mr Wickenden can lie down. He's not feeling very well.' The only place our chairman could lie down was in the catering carriage in a separate compartment. I got the staff to move the French sticks into another area and went to get him. He was sitting asleep opposite his wife, Josie.

'He's asleep now, Bob,' she said, 'so I think it's best to leave him. He wouldn't want to walk all that way past the guests anyway.' She thanked me, and I went back to my seat.

As we approached Zeebrugge, I walked back up the train. Roland was awake and I asked him how he was feeling. He smiled back at me and used a throwaway line I have never used since: 'I expect I'll live, Bob.'

He then got up and went into the toilet. It was where we found him when the train pulled into Zeebrugge. One of our directors, David Bradford, broke the door down. Roland had had a massive heart attack. He was 46.

17. A MINUTE'S SILENCE

'In life, all good things come hard, but wisdom is the hardest to come by.'
Lucille Ball

It goes without saying that the ship was delayed. We left someone behind to deal with the formalities, and then we got everyone on board, including Josie, who had become a young widow only minutes earlier.

The news soon leaked out, and it was as if a cloud hung over the ship. I stood around with the rest. I had never been that close to death before and I felt numb. Then Jim Macdonald, a large and sometimes grumpy Scotsman who was the shipping correspondent for the *Financial Times*, came up to me and laid a kindly hand on my arm.

'Bob, I know you're all upset, but you do realise this is a story.'

'I'm sorry, Jim,' I said. 'I'm not thinking clearly. Give me ten minutes.'

I cleared a lounge on the upper deck, then called for the press to come and join me and Bryan Thompson. Just an hour after I had spoken to Roland, I heard myself talking about him in the past tense. When I finished, I had the even harder task of organising the one telephone on the ship to be used by the press – no mobile phones then. Everyone wanted to go first, so I called for a bit of respect to try to keep the peace. Next day the papers were full of the story, and the shares plunged. 'A ship without a rudder' said the *Financial Times*.

Working next door to Roland's office when I joined were two men: Ken Siddle, an accountant who acted as his assistant, and Geoff Parker, who bought all the duty-free goods for the ships. Neither were directors, but both would one day become chairman. For now, Ken Siddle took up the reins as managing director since most of the main board were non-executive. There was no way that he would become chairman yet as he had not got either the experience or the personality. He was a shy man, very unsure of himself in the limelight, which he hated. At this time Rolls-Royce had gone into liquidation, and this was being handled by accountants Thornton Baker. The man who was getting much of the publicity was Roland's younger brother

Keith. Concerned about the press stories, and seeing that Keith had handled the media impressively, it was decided to appoint him as chairman and make Ken managing director. It could have been a marriage made in heaven – Keith would be the front man while Ken would sit at his desk and check the small print – but it was a move that would bring the company down years later.

I waited to see whether Keith Wickenden would bring his own man in in my place, but when we met it became clear that his brother had thought highly of me and that my future was safe. Keith was instantly likeable, and spookily like his brother. The same laugh, the same mannerisms. But there the similarity stopped. I told Keith how brilliant his brother had been by not saying too much. I told him that the art of PR was to subtly ensure that we controlled what went into the press, whatever tricks they might play on us to get us to reveal more than we should. Additionally, with Stock Exchange rules getting tighter all the time we had to be more and more careful, as a public company, about exactly what we said. Keith was impressed and said he understood now why his brother had thought so highly of me and why we had had such a good press.

From then on he did exactly the opposite of what I'd suggested. If you opened the fridge door, Keith would do ten minutes. He was forever talking to the press without telling me, and he often took decisions without telling the main board. It drove Ken mad, and although he tried to hide the problems, they were there for those of us close to the powerbase to see all too clearly. It didn't help that the head office was moved to Tonbridge while Keith kept his base in London.

Nor did it help that some of the company, with the exception of Keith who disapproved but did nothing to stop it, was awash on a sea of booze. I was sucked into this to a degree. A morning marketing meeting, before the move to Tonbridge, was always followed by lunch in a local Italian restaurant with Ken and as many as could be roped in. We always had plenty on board by the time we staggered back to our offices, if we made it at all. At this point I could have gone down that slippery slope. I did find myself looking to have lunch with someone if there was nothing in the diary that day. A particular friend was Pat Mennem. He was motoring correspondent on the *Daily Mirror* but his appearance was that of a senior army officer. He really should have been on *The Times*. We frequently whiled away two or three hours in Fleet Street's major watering hole, El Vino's. They were very happy if somewhat fuzzy times.

Eventually, a few years later, an incident took place that forced me to re-examine alcohol's place in my working life. By that time I was working directly for the group and I was in the London headquarters before most of the top brass moved to Tonbridge. I thought I would look in on Bryan Thompson as a courtesy. I tapped on his door and walked straight in, as I usually did. He quickly slammed shut the top drawer of his desk and cried out, 'Oh shit!' He'd upset a glass of whisky in his desk. I decided there and then that I would not end up doing that. I went back to our Fleet Street offices and announced that henceforth there would be no drink in the office at any time. If staff had to entertain journalists there were plenty of pubs in which to do so, and if they needed it they could have a membership of the Press Club to drink outside the licensing laws (pubs still closed at three p.m. then by law).

The first indication that Keith was a man who shot from the hip arrived early in 1973. I was watching TV at home one evening when he called me. Although we were on call 24 hours a day for any emergency situation, this was the first time he had telephoned me at home.

'Hello, Bob. How are you?' he said cheerily.

'I'm fine, thanks, Keith.'

'I've just bought an airline.'

He waited for me to be impressed. Instead I was stunned, and said something pathetic like 'I suppose I'd better get a press release out.' I went in to see him the next morning. It became pretty clear that he had done it without any reference to the board. We drafted a release, and he wanted to include such phrases as 'integrated transport system'. I cautioned against this. 'You've got to live with that if it goes pear-shaped,' I pointed out. 'Journalists store up such phrases and use them against us if it doesn't work out.' I was overruled. Well, he was the chairman.

Invicta International Airlines was a poky little company based at Manston in Kent. It was in some financial trouble and was run by a retired squadron leader and another fairly hard-nosed chap. It comprised a handful of elderly aircraft that did occasional charter flights, but it was largely a freight operation. Flying cattle (not Dairy Shorthorns) to the Sudan was one of their main businesses at the time. It was pretty clear on the first morning that Keith had bought a 'pup', but nobody dared say anything. He was still wearing the emperor's new clothes. Not that I said so at the time, but we at Hertford PR should not really have been involved as we only had the car ferries account. There were other small industrial companies in the European Ferries Group, and now we had an airline.

After that press release I did not have much to do with the airline. Not until Tuesday, 10 April 1973, that is. Ken called me at about 12.30, just as I was thinking of El Vino's. 'One of these bloody aircraft is missing,' he said. 'It doesn't look good, and if the worst fears are realised I want you to handle it. These bloody Invicta people can't handle it. If the worst has happened I want Townsend Thoresen's name kept out of it as much as possible.'

They could have picked a better day. I was one account executive down and waiting for a replacement, and the other one was in Belgium on a press trip. Half an hour later, those worries paled into insignificance. And El Vino's would not be visited for some days to come. Flight number 435, a Vickers 952 Vanguard, had crashed near Basle-Mulhouse airport in bad weather. A combination of faulty navigational equipment and poor signals from land-based beacons had seen the aircraft overshoot the runway and come down in a forest. The aircraft had disintegrated except for the tail section; still, there were, amazingly, 37 survivors among the 145 on board. Not that we knew that at that time. On board were women from the West Country, most of them from the village of Axbridge. They had taken off from Bristol for a day trip.

I got hold of my man on the press trip and told him to get himself off to Basle. Then the calls started. We had no crisis management plan for the ferries in those days, let alone for this little airline, so we just used our common sense. At first I took all the public calls, as well as those from the press, but after a few hours I had to call Ken and tell him that I needed some help. Could someone else be deployed to deal with the public? Today, one person couldn't possibly handle all the media, but then it was just about possible. Some of the relatives waiting for news in Somerset were still ringing me and it was hard to turn them away. One particularly nice man, whose name I wish I could remember, asked if I minded if he kept in touch as he felt he was getting more accurate information from me. What could I say? 'Of course,' I said.

It had never occurred to me before that after an air crash people are not necessarily in one piece. That was brought home to me the next day when a father and son, who had been flown out to Basle, disagreed over the identity of their wife/mother. And she had survived.

Invicta, quite uselessly, had three separate passenger lists and we had no idea which was the correct one. By now the national press were camped in my office, and I have to say that they all behaved very well and remained sensitive to the problems throughout. By ten p.m. on the second evening after the crash I spoke frankly to them. 'Look,' I said, 'I'll level with you. I've three bloody passenger lists and we don't know which is the correct one. I know you've got hold of some, but if you publish one and it's the wrong one it will cause untold misery on top of what these people are already going through. We are still unable to tell people whether their relatives have survived or not and you might give false hopes or, indeed, the opposite. Could I therefore ask you to agree not to publish any passenger lists tonight?' Again, I wish I could remember his name, but I do recall it was a guy from the *Daily Mail* who stood up and said, 'Right, lads, are we all agreed that we don't use our passenger lists?' I could have kissed him. They all agreed, but added that I had to promise to get them the proper one the next day. I made the promise, not knowing how I was going to achieve it. One thing at a time, I thought.

I'd told the press about the nice man I was helping to keep going, and I think that helped. As the journalists drifted back to their offices, he called again. I told him that I still had no more news about his wife. 'The kids want me to stay here,' he said, 'but I want to go out there. I don't know what to do.' I said it was hard for me to advise him. Maybe he needed to talk to some friends, but at the end of the day it had to be his decision.

If you have journalism in your bones, there is definitely a buzz associated with being front-page news over several days. You feel unworthy for having such a feeling, of course, because you wish the accident, or whatever, had not happened. However, the adrenalin such a buzz creates keeps you going, and by the next morning I had all the names of the dead and the survivors. After seeing pictures of the crash site, it seemed incredible that anyone had walked away from it. I had to call the nice man and tell him in a faltering voice the worst possible news. He took it quite well, and said he had been prepared for the worst. Then he started to thank me for all I had done. I was so overwhelmed – I feel emotional just writing about it now – that I just broke down. I had been in the office for about 48 hours, and now all the adrenalin seemed to leave me. One of the European Ferries staff members had just arrived from Dover, and he took one look at me and told me to go home. I did, and slept for fifteen hours.

Reluctantly, that weekend I sent a staff member from another account on another press trip for Townsend Thoresen. When he got back I received a complaint from Bryan Thompson: one of the women had allegedly been touched up by my executive. I was furious, and vowed to kick him out, but Bryan persuaded me against it as the woman didn't want to take it any further, which made me wonder why it had been mentioned at all. I talked to my man and he was gobsmacked and totally denied it. He left us soon afterwards to go into politics. He became a Tory MP.

As a result of the air crash, European Ferries decided they needed full-time PR for all their companies. They bought Hertford PR from Hugh and me. I feel Bryan Thompson took advantage of my commercial inexperience (at least as far as the value of a profit-making company was concerned) and browbeat Hugh into accepting far less than we should have got. That was probably the launching pad for what was to become an uneasy relationship thereafter.

Despite that, we did at least get to keep the money we had left in the bank. I had managed to turn the company into profit for the first time since I had been there. We moved to better offices just off Fleet Street which housed only our department. This meant I could keep my independence. I had an increased salary, a company car and a pension. I was told I could even sign my own expenses. When I queried this, Ken Siddle said, rather coldly, 'If we can't trust you, we can always get rid of you.' Over the next few years my staff grew to seventeen, and we had five European and one United States consultancy reporting in to us.

Apart from the ferries, we now had the rest of the group to look after too. This included Larne Harbour and major property investments at home and in the USA. We bought another shipping company, and the size of the ferry fleet rose year by year. We had agricultural interests too, including a cattle lairage in Scotland. I was the only one who knew what it was (still no Dairy Shorthorns, though). In the late 1970s we also bought the La Manga golf complex in Spain and the port of Felixstowe. For the latter we mounted a major campaign to stop it being nationalised. We spent a lot of time in Parliament during this time, and came out successful.

When you get behind the scenes in Parliament, you realise that it's like a great big club. People slag one another off during a debate, then go and have a drink together. Keith had come across this before when we had successfully fought the introduction of the Channel Tunnel in 1974. We even published our own Green Paper which got a lot of publicity. Keith's head was turned after the Felixstowe campaign and he decided to become an MP. We all advised against it. I asked him if he was planning to stay as chairman of European Ferries. He said he was. 'In that case,' I said, 'you won't enjoy it. You will have no power. You will just be a backbencher. You won't even be able to become the most junior of parliamentary private secretaries unless you give up the chairmanship.' As usual, Keith would not be told, and in 1979 he stood for the Tories in the Dorking constituency in Surrey, and became an MP.

'This will end in tears,' I thought as I returned to my office. But a matter of months later I soon put it out of my mind. After all, I had an important dinner to speak at.

18. A GREAT GOAL

'It's never too late to become what you might have been.'

George Eliot

I know I was nervous about the Football Writers' Association's Footballer of the Year dinner in 1980, but not as much as I might have been had I done a bit more homework on the evening. Looking back, I nearly blew it when I asked FWA chairman Mike Langley, during his invitation phone call, if there was a fee. Back then, nobody had ever been paid. Today a payment is made, but although I've done it on three occasions since – a record; only two other entertainers have done it twice – I have never felt able to keep a fee because of what the evening did for me. Once I donated it to the relatives of Mick Leach, the former QPR and Chelsea inside-forward who died in his early forties. He was a great guy, and he managed Dulwich Hamlet for a time. He also scored four against me in a charity match I played at Stamford Bridge. Since you ask, I let in eleven. On another occasion it went to my village cricket club's ground fund.

GOAL-KICK

The other two who have done the FWA dinner twice are the brilliant impersonator Kevin Connelly and comedian Mick Miller. Mick was asked back a second time because the guest of honour that night was Sir Stanley Matthews. Mick had been a professional goalkeeper at Port Vale but was sacked by Stan when he became manager. When I first worked with him, Mick had a brilliant line about his football career. He said, 'I used to play professional football at Port Vale with Ray Kennedy. At the end of the season he went to Arsenal and I went to Pontins.' Not only a great gag, but true!

At this time there were no rival awards, no Professional Footballers' Association Player of the Year. This was the only one. Even now it is still the best football dinner of the year. While the PFA event is virtually ignored by all but the lower division players, this night is the one everyone in football tries to get to.

I went to work as usual on the day and had a couple of meetings, but definitely did not go to El Vino's. I had given little thought to who might be there, what size the audience would be, or anything else. All I knew was that Danny Blanchflower was the other speaker and that Terry McDermott was the Footballer of the Year. Let me run by you those footballers who'd won the award up to and including 1979:

1948 – Stanley Matthews (Blackpool)
1949 – Johnny Carey (Manchester United)
1950 – Joe Mercer (Arsenal)
1951 – Harry Johnston (Blackpool)
1952 – Billy Wright (Wolverhampton Wanderers)
1953 – Nat Lofthouse (Bolton)
1954 – Tom Finney (Preston North End)
1955 – Don Revie (Manchester City)
1956 – Bert Trautmann (Manchester City)
1957 – Tom Finney (Preston North End)
1958 – Danny Blanchflower (Tottenham Hotspur)
1959 – Syd Owen (Luton Town)
1960 – Bill Slater (Wolverhampton Wanderers)
1961 – Danny Blanchflower (Tottenham Hotspur)
1962 – Jimmy Adamson (Burnley)
1963 – Stanley Matthews (Stoke City)
1964 – Bobby Moore (West Ham United)
1965 – Bobby Collins (Leeds United)
1966 – Bobby Charlton (Manchester United)
1967 – Jack Charlton (Leeds United)
1968 – George Best (Manchester United)
1969 – Dave Mackay (Derby County)
1970 – Billy Bremner (Leeds United)
1971 – Frank McLintock (Arsenal)
1972 – Gordon Banks (Stoke City)
1973 – Pat Jennings (Tottenham Hotspur)
1974 – Ian Callaghan (Liverpool)
1975 – Alan Mullery (Fulham)
1976 – Kevin Keegan (Liverpool)
1977 – Emlyn Hughes (Liverpool)
1978 – Kenny Burns (Nottingham Forest)
1979 – Kenny Dalglish (Liverpool)

I arrived at the Café Royal and went upstairs to the VIP reception. As I walked into the room my good eye almost popped out. All but half a dozen of the players listed above were standing there. It is tradition that not only are all previous winners invited every year, but they sit on the top table together. These days it takes a two-tiered top table.

By now I *was* nervous. Mike Langley introduced me to a few people, but my head was spinning. When football people get together they always get on well and have lots to talk about. Since that night, aside from when I've spoken, I have been to all but two of these occasions and am now instantly recognised and am regarded as part of the football world. And most of them call me 'Cat'. But that night, at least for the first few hours, I was an unknown face in the crowd.

When we went into the packed room for dinner I was there in the middle of the top table. Apart from the previous winners, international managers, cup final managers and chairmen were also seated there. I sat between the chairman of West Ham, Leslie Cearns (whose team was due to play Arsenal in the FA Cup final in a few days' time), and the Scottish manager Jock Stein. It was fairly heavy going talking to Cearns, and Jock had much more to say to Billy Bingham, then the Northern Ireland manager, who was on his other side. I managed to eat some of my meal, but it was a fairly lonely one.

When we'd finished eating, Danny Blanchflower stood up. I had heard Danny once before at Ipswich, and he was a lovely speaker. He would start with some gentle material about the Northern Ireland team: 'We had a tactical meeting and decided to try to equalise before the other side scored.' It was good, humorous stuff, until he started to get more serious later on. 'And, you know, life is rather like a game of football . . .' But he didn't get that far on this particular night. The microphone packed up.

THROW-IN

Danny Blanchflower was also famous for refusing, live, to appear on *This Is Your Life*. It was said that, as he had been married three times, the reason he declined was because he wasn't sure which of his wives would turn up. His brother, the late Jackie, a great after-dinner speaker, once said, 'My brother Danny is addicted to wedding cake. Hates women, but loves wedding cake.'

I was panic-struck. I had recently been due to speak at the Southern Olympian League dinner and had written something special which could be used only at that particular dinner. With 600 people waiting for the last speaker, the sound had gone down there, never to return. As the room was so large, the speeches were cancelled. It had left me with a feeling of loss I found hard to understand – I would never know whether that material was good or not. About a year later I read a quote by Dr Samuel Johnson: 'Never leave a man with the burden of an undelivered speech.' I knew exactly what he meant.

This all ran through my mind as I sat there. Was I going to be denied on the biggest night of my life?

Then the sound came back on, Danny wound up, and we awaited the presentation of the Footballer of the Year trophy. For the first and only time to date, however, the Footballer of the Year hadn't turned up. There was no message, no explanation. There was a strong rumour that Terry McDermott had gone racing and not made it back. Liverpool manager Bob Paisley stepped in to collect the statuette on Terry's behalf. 'That's the first blind-side run he's done all season,' Paisley observed.

Then it was me.

They took some time to get the microphone and stand along to me. It got caught somewhere under the table, and it seemed like an age before it was in its proper place. The tension was unbearable, and I almost forgot to turn on the small recorder I had bought especially for the occasion. For the first time for many years I have just listened to this tape, and have decided that I'm lucky – even when I am terribly nervous I almost never sound as if I am.

At last, a rather formal toastmaster stepped up with the gavel. Now or never. Sink or swim. Shit or bust.

'Mr Chairman, gentlemen, pray silence for our guest speaker, Mr Bob "the Cat" Bevan [he pronounced it wrongly as Bev-anne] of the Old Wilsonians Football Club.'

I swear to you that you could hear, on the tape, people saying, 'Who?'

Some sixth sense, which experts have since told me is right, told me to hit them with a big laugh early. Rather like my goalkeeping, however, I came off my line a little slowly. I had been excited to see cameras there recording the events and was disappointed that they stopped the minute I rose. I decided to refer to it.

'You can tell what I'm going to be like. The cameras are already pointing the other way.'

Nobody got it.

'Mr Chairman, honoured guests, gentlemen, fellow football stars,' I continued.

A little chuckle.

'I'll tell you when I say something funny, all right?'

Nothing.

'Mr Langley has asked me here tonight because he feels that your knowledge is somewhat blinkered by one or two fairly minor competitions, such as the game on Saturday. I believe it's the London Senior Cup final, isn't it? Something like that.'

Another little chuckle.

Well, the first three hoped-for laughs hadn't come. If my next line didn't go, I might be facing an uphill battle. Would they bite?

'And so he's asked me here to broaden your knowledge of the game this evening, and to this end I would like to bring you all greetings from Old Wilsonians Wonderful Football Club.'

Nothing.

'Well, thank you very much.'

Big laugh.

'I'll take your good wishes back with me.'

Bigger laugh, even the start of a ripple of applause. I moved in for the kill. In those days I used to swear (not any more – I'm a family entertainer now), so I've cleaned this up as best I can.

'I was warned that speaking here tonight would be rather like making love to a hedgehog.'

Even bigger laugh.

'One prick against five hundred.'

A roar, applause, and even a couple of shouts of 'More!' I was away, but I can't say that I ever really relaxed and enjoyed it, as I sometimes can now. Rather like players who get into the Cup final, or at least those who win it, say that it goes by in a flash and they want to go and do it again. I have since learnt, and was glad I didn't know beforehand, that this is a tough audience: hard-bitten journalists who are not easily impressed, famous football people who have seen it all and done it all, and a few celebrities. When someone completely unknown turns up to speak at a dinner like this, when all previous speakers in this slot have been well known, the audience start to fear the worst. That cry of 'Who?' as I was introduced signifies a cry of despair that the organisers must have got it wrong. But after the first big laughs they relax, sit back and start to anticipate. They look forward to the next line. There is also something special about hearing someone new for the first time, about being there on the night he was first spotted. In years to come many people would take the credit for spotting me, which is all rather flattering.

After the hedgehog gag I stated, not for the first time, how nervous I was. By the time I'd said it for the third or fourth time nobody believed it, and even that was getting a laugh.

'But quite honestly,' I continued, 'I'm so nervous tonight, and it's so difficult for me to follow the previous speakers [unintentional laugh], I'm only glad I'm not anywhere important [big laugh].'

By this stage, even a weak line would get a laugh, such as, 'Quite honestly, it's the only time I've ever been asked to speak in a bloody café before.' I then criticised the food and said that I had been on the Continent and had nearly forgotten about the evening. 'Then I looked in the *Telegraph* for it under "Important Events", but it wasn't there. Eventually I spotted it under "Forthcoming Balls" [good laugh]. Anyway, I'm in public relations [pause, then a big laugh].' I continued with a blue joke about a car ferry captain which brought the house down. During this I did another gag about the captain's posh voice. 'All the blokes who work for us speak like Barry Davies,' I said, which again got a good laugh. For the following line I put on the rough voice of an able seaman, and former West Ham centre-half Ken Brown shouted from the audience, 'No, that was Barry Davies!' which again got a big laugh. I acknowledged him by name. Afterwards Ken seemed flattered that I had recognised him, and he still mentions it now when we meet.

I'd got them. Pretty much whatever I said was going to get a laugh. Years later, Jimmy Tarbuck said to me that I did too much good stuff. Have a good start, a good middle and a good end, then you can go back again with new material, he said. I have never really had the confidence to do that, although I'm not so bothered now if the odd gag doesn't hit the spot. On this night, however, there was no question that everything I had left was good stuff. My next line, according to Lawrie McMenemy, was the best line of the night, and I thought of it as I was standing there.

'But honestly, I'm so nervous tonight. I mean, when you look around – I mean, just look at this lot.' I swept my arm to either side, indicating the previous Footballers of the Year. 'It looks like someone's upset a box of cigarette cards.' This got applause. 'I'll tell you what, tonight I've even had the pleasure of a piss with Jimmy Hill [who was there, and whom I'd not met at that point – big laugh]. I knew you'd be impressed [another big laugh]. We were outside, in traps one and two, and as I turned to go he said to me, "Excuse me, old chap." I said, "What d'you want, chief?" He said, "At the BBC they teach us to wash our hands." I said, "At the Old Wilsonians they teach us not to piss over ours" [huge laugh].' I then did a Churchill story, which also went well, and moved into Mike Langley calling me during *Match of the Day* – all untrue, of course. Then came some football jokes. At this time the troubles in Northern Ireland were at their height and sporting events were being cancelled. I read out a quote from Harry Cavan, who was Northern Ireland's FIFA representative. He had made a Colemanballs with 'The Scots are still refusing to meet us in Belfast, so we may have to compromise on this and meet them halfway.'

After this, I went into my football routine. What? No. You'll have to buy a ticket for my next dinner. What I can tell you is that it laid them out, not least when I started comparing myself with Pat Jennings, who was also there. I know this sounds sad, but on the tape I have timed some of the laughs. On a few occasions I couldn't continue for a full minute. If that doesn't sound long, just put the book down and sit there for 60 seconds.

THROW-IN

Whenever I see Leslie Thomas, author of *Virgin Soldiers* and much more, I always do a gag about him. 'He writes the sort of books that, once you've put them down, you just can't pick them up again.' Now I do it about me.

I finished off with a few more jokes about the hospitality; my audience was now laughing at anything. Even the toastmaster, who did have a rather funny voice, got a big laugh when he announced that they had moved all the coats to the fourth floor. I laughed too, but, looking back now, I don't know why.

I'm so glad I've got the tape and can relive the evening. All through it you can hear Jock Stein and Billy Bingham laughing. At the end,

Jock is full of praise for me. 'Och, you were great, excellent.' Whenever we were at dinners together in years to come he always came over to say hello to me.

Suddenly, everyone wanted to know me. Before long, there standing in front of me was Nat Lofthouse, one of my early heroes. At this time he was commercial manager at Bolton Wanderers. He booked me there and then for a dinner. Jimmy Hill also came up and asked what I was doing the next day at lunchtime. Apparently, when he was chairman of the Professional Footballers' Association he'd used the London offices of the agent Bagnall Harvey. As a result of this Bagnall had used Jimmy to line up 50 international players to go on some cigarette cards. This was the first time players were ever paid for the use of their image. They got £4 each. On the back of this Jimmy had formed the Internationals Club, and they always met for lunch the day before the cup final. He invited me along, and we have been good friends ever since. John Bond, the former West Ham full-back who was then manager of Norwich, said to me, 'You've reminded us all of where we came from. No matter how good we are, or like to think we are, we've all played where you play at some time in our careers.'

A few months later, Mike Langley gave me the best write-up I've seen about my act. The first time I read it even I started smiling. Much of it has been recorded above, but the introduction was as follows:

The most wanted goalkeeper this Christmas is not Shilton or Clemence but a 35-year-old amateur who is blind in one eye. He flounders into action wearing not only unbreakable glasses but also a gum shield.

I sat between Bob Paisley and Ron Greenwood at the Footballer of the Year dinner when Bevan first exploded on to the professional world. The toastmaster boomed, 'Pray silence for Mr Bob Bevan of Old Wilsonians FC.' A tape of the occasion distinctly reveals top-table dignitaries asking one another, 'Who?' But a hilarious half-hour later Greenwood and Paisley rose with 600 other guests to deliver the dinner's first-ever standing ovation for a wind-up speaker. Greenwood said, 'I can see why he's so funny for an audience of pros. It's because he talks about a level of football they've never experienced or imagined.'

I did get one thing wrong on the night: I should have gone off clubbing with some of my new friends. Somehow, my celebration ended up with three people in my hotel room raiding my mini bar: Peter Swinburn from Trust House Forte, whom I've met many times since, Mel Henderson from Ipswich Town, and Ken Montgomery from the *Daily Mirror*, who, by coincidence, is now secretary of the Football Writers' Association. At that time it was run by Dennis and Pat Signy. I was told that, although Pat was there in the reception, she would not be staying as it was a strictly stag dinner and I was horrified to hear afterwards that she was upstairs listening. Even now, I'm never comfortable swearing in front of women. Pat and Dennis didn't mind at all, though, and we also became firm friends from that night on. 'Next year,' said Dennis, 'you're coming as a guest and you'll be on the top table next to Gordon Banks.' Despite the lateness of the evening and the booze consumed, he didn't forget. On the other side of me in 1981 was some non-goalkeeper called Bobby Charlton.

After the guys drank my minibar dry, I lay in bed re-running the evening through my mind. I suddenly remembered the tape. I must have played it two or three times. I think it was only then that I realised just how well my speech had gone down.

The following day I was at the Internationals Club lunch meeting yet more famous players and doing twenty minutes. In the evening I honoured a long-standing engagement at the annual dinner of the East Barnet Old Grammarians of the Southern Amateur League. There was even a connection with the previous night as my friend John Hockey, at that time the agent for most of the major broadcasters such as John Motson, was at both events. He was a silky wing-half for EBOGs. At least that's what he asked me to write. There the similarities between the events ended and I whiled away the early hours with the EBOGs' secretary, Terry Boyce, who still lived with his mother.

Mike Langley had given me a cup final ticket, so the next day I went to my third Wembley final. As I walked around and into the ground to a much better seat than on my previous two visits, several people came up to me to say how much they had enjoyed the FWA dinner. My life had changed for ever. (Trevor Brooking scored the only goal in a drab final with a header past Pat Jennings. He has asked me to say it was A Great Goal.)

bove I told you I was thin! Doing my best man duties for my friend Bill Stanley (*left*) in 1968.

elow Three years after my debut in Ipswich, I was back for the Testimonial Dinner for Allan unter in 1981. (*Left to right*) fellow comic Keith O'Keefe, Danny Blanchflower, me, Bobby obson, Allan Hunter, John Motson, Ipswich skipper Mick Mills, cartoonist Carl Giles, Terry eill. (Courtesy of the *East Anglian Daily Times*)

Left With Brighton at the Wembley FA Cup Final in 1983. I walked on the pitch with the team and goalkeeper Graham Moseley took this picture of me. Sorry about the trousers!

Left With David Bradford, a Director of European Ferries PLC. He was kind, generous and great company. And he did like a drink. As his PR man I felt I should help him.

Left Doing the Great Goalkeepers' Show with my good friends Gordon Banks (*left*) and Pat Jennings.

Right Cat attacked by dog. During pre-season training at Charlton he was the fittest thing down there!
(Express Newspapers)

Right Teaching top manager and my mate Lennie Lawrence the toe punt. These coaching charts were a great routine invented by a wonderful after-dinner speaker, the late Les Williamson of Old Owens FC.
(Express Newspapers)

Right A real collector's item – me making a save. You can't see my face, but I promise you it is me playing at Selhurst Park for a Supporters XI against the staff. Standing inside my right-hand post is the late Frank Milano. Once, when Palace scored in the first minute, he uttered the immortal words 'only 89 minutes to hang on.' It has passed into legend.

Above Another sport I've mastered. Golf at Moor Park with (*left to right*) Roy Walker, Terry Wogan, an Aer Lingus air hostess and Jimmy Tarbuck. (Courtesy of Mal McNally)

Below At a Lord's Taverners function two of my heroes Lord Colin Cowdrey (*centre*) and Tom Graveney recreate a pose from a famous picture of them entitled, 'And you are?'

Above Sven-Göran Eriksson is clearly overjoyed at meeting Laura (the love of my life) and me. (Copyright Water Rat Doug McKenzie)

Below Delivering my poem 'The Duke and I' watched by (*left to right*) the late John Bromley, Sir Tim Rice and the Duke of Edinburgh. (Copyright Water Rat Doug McKenzie)

Right At a snooker function with Stephen Hendry (*left*) and Ronnie O'Sullivan. It was my dad's favourite picture. He loved snooker. (Donald Stewart Photography)

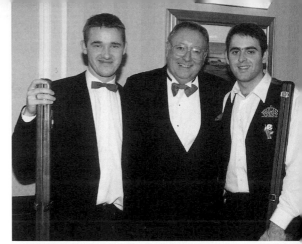

Right With one of my comic heroes and friends, Barry Cryer. (Copyright Water Rat Doug McKenzie)

Right Peter Alliss and I discussing Ronnie Corbett, among others.

...ove I got Catherine Zeta-Jones and Pam Ferris from *Darling Buds of May* to re-name two
...alink ships. Michael Douglas is holding Catherine's umbrella now. (Courtesy of *Dover Express*)

...ove Prince Edward at Lord's wondering why I have more cocktail stirrers in my breast
...cket than anyone else. I am in between (*on my right*) MCC Secretary Roger Knight, and
...tor Frazer Hines. Down at the beginning of the line is actor Robert Powell.

Above Hitting a four at Lord's! I am wearing my yellow and black Old Wilsonians Cricket Club cap which made me look, according to the late Fred Price, like an "out-of-work wasp".

Below Nearly a quarter of a century after our first meeting, Bobby Robson – now Sir Bobby – and I do the Lord's Taverners Christmas lunch raffle in 2002. These days everybody loves him. When I introduced him the audience of over 1,000 people took the roof off.

GOAL CELEBRATIONS

Dear Bob,

My last act as chairman cannot be other than this note of thanks for a brilliant debut, fully deserving the first standing ovation for the guest speaker in my twenty years' experience. You have been the most quoted man in Fleet Street all weekend; work has stopped while sports subs impersonate your performance. And I regard West Ham's victory on Saturday as approval from the highest authority.

Hope you enjoyed it.

Best wishes,

Mike Langley

19. TIME ADDED ON

'Mike Denness – the last Scotsman to captain England. At least, we hope he's the last Scotsman to captain England.'

> Bob 'the Cat' Bevan at every dinner he attends with Mike

In the old days after an FA Cup Final my thoughts went to cricket. Although I was born in Dulwich and went to school just down the road from the Kennington Oval at a time when Surrey were winning their record seven successive county championships, I have always been a Kent supporter. I have no idea why, but there it is.

My ties with the county were strengthened when I played for Old Wilsonians CC against Old Shootershillians in 1964. They had two potential Kent players, Andy Hooper and Graham Johnson. After Johnno had scored 50 in less than half an hour, he smashed one to mid-wicket. Unable to get out of the way, I caught it. After that I followed his career. He was unlucky not to get an England cap, bagging a pair (two ducks, or no-scores, for the uninitiated) in his Test trial. All these years later we still play together, but now on the same side – the Lord's Taverners.

DRINKS BREAK

I was at a lunch with the late and great batsman-wicketkeeper Les Ames, who played in the infamous Bodyline series in Australia. Another late and great Kent batsman-wicketkeeper, Godfrey Evans, was speaking. Godders was unfortunately not on top form that day and we were looking forward to the end. Suddenly he decided to compare the then current touring side with the last one he'd played in. He mentioned both number ones and told a weak joke about each. By the time he got to the number sixes we were almost losing the will to live.

I leant over to Les, by then over 80, and said, 'Les, at times like this you must regret there are eleven players in a side.'

Les replied, 'What bothers me, old boy, is that he's been on four tours.'

Although I'm not very good at it, I like playing cricket, especially on village grounds. I like the atmosphere and the pints of bitter afterwards. I made my debut for the Taverners in 1983, and it could not have been at a better venue – the County Ground at Canterbury. Mike Denness, the former Kent and England captain who also played for Essex, and who is now one of my closest friends, was the skipper. Coming up to tea, he asked me to bowl. I told him that I did not bowl, but he said that everyone had to have a couple of overs. Steve Gritt (former joint manager at Charlton Athletic, Hampshire 2nd XI cricketer and now deputy manager at Millwall) hit the first ball of my second over straight to Mike at mid-off. 'S. Gritt, c. Denness, b. Bevan, 52' – not a bad start to my bowling career. Nobody had ever let me bowl before.

After that Taverners debut I recalled what a friend of mine, John Vickerage, once said: 'When you play for a new side and they ask you what you do, say everything. Say you bat about five, you bowl some useful slow stuff and field extra cover, or wherever you fancy. You then know that you will get a least one reasonable game with them.' I followed John's instructions when another friend, Malcolm McLeod, asked me to go and play a few games for a team called Outwood in Surrey. I got a few wickets nearly every time I bowled. This despite bowling slow stuff that doesn't turn. A lot of cricket is in the mind.

Having scored six goals in a football game once, a hat-trick the next week, and never scored more than two in a game either side of that eight-day period, cricket turned out to be much the same. I have never taken more than four wickets in a game except on two occasions. Playing for a Kent XI against Hextable in 1991, people just kept getting out to me, and I ended up with 7 for 49. Nor were they all caught in the deep by professional athletes. Two were caught behind and three were bowled. I've got the scorecard hanging in the loo. A year later in the same fixture we shot them out for 40 and I took 5 for 21. So we put them in again, and I took 6 for 48. Their batsmen just seemed to have a death wish. But before and since, I have never taken more than four. Funny game, cricket. But it has been a thrill to play with many of my cricketing heroes in the Taverners. I even got West Indian Test player Filo Wallace caught behind once. John Price, former Middlesex and England fast bowler and our square leg umpire, wandered in. 'How many Test wickets is that now, Cat?' he asked. I thought for a moment, then replied, 'One.'

Starting with Graham Johnson, there have been about twenty Kent beneficiaries who have dragged me out for various events, and I have made so many friends and had so much fun with them all. Mike Denness is also known as Haggis and Will – as in Will Denness, which was a name given to him by Aussie Terry Jarman; in the same way Derek 'Deadly' Underwood (another good mate who lives near me) also has to put up with a regular gag. 'People often ask me why he is called Deadly. Is it the brilliance of his bowling? I have to tell them no. It's a name I gave him because if you've ever had to sit next to him over twenty benefit dinners I can tell you it's bloody deadly.'

I have also had great fun travelling the world watching Test cricket, the stories from which could fill another book. Sadly, much as I love Australia, the most irritating place to watch is in Sydney, the reason for which can be explained by the following letter I got published in the *Sydney Morning Herald* in January 2003.

Sir,

I am a comedian from England, and if you will forgive me for saying so, I think you must have a few more running the Sydney Cricket Ground. I can only assume you did not let them anywhere near the organisation of the brilliantly run Olympics.

Four years ago I was out here with the late and great Kent and England wicketkeeping legend Godfrey Evans. On the day when Darren Gough took his historic hat-trick, Godders spoke at a fund-raising breakfast, without payment, and raised several thousand dollars for local charities. As it was a hot day, he decided to pop back to the hotel to slip into something cooler to watch the day's play with us. When he got back, they wouldn't let him in because of the ridiculous no pass-out rule. Not being the sort of bloke to say 'Do you know who I am?' he had to watch the day's play in his hotel bedroom even though he had bought a ticket!

For that game I had been given a members ticket by Nasser Hussein as a thank you for speaking at his benefit dinners. During the five days I became friendly with an Aussie and his two sons, and we have kept in touch. We want to meet for a beer at lunchtime, but we can't. He is in the Members and I am in the Brewongle. I can't get in to see him and he can't get in to see me. He can go outside the ground and get back in, but I can't. It is the only cricket ground in the world I know of that operates like this. Even Lord's, not noted for its flexibility, lets you pass out. It could easily be remedied with tickets, wrist-bands or rubber stamps. It is totally against the friendly spirit of everything else I have encountered in Australia over the years, and I hope the ghost of Godders haunts these jokers until they get their act together.

Yours truly,

Bob 'the Cat' Bevan

Kent, England and, for the moment, the Inter-Continental, Sydney – where, incidentally, they let me back in if I go out

I think it says a lot that I got no reaction.

Of course, the sun Down Under can make you go a bit haywire. It might have been what caused David Gower to get into a light aircraft and buzz the England team when they were out there a decade or so ago. More likely it was his inherent sense of fun. Training is anathema to him. As my friend David Willis, brother of Bob, once said, 'He is the sort of bloke who could work in the City all week and go and play for England at the weekends.' All this was in my mind when I was asked to speak at a Lady Taverners tribute lunch to Gower in the Long Room at Lord's in 2002. They asked if I could do one of my poems, but for weeks I struggled with its composition. Then I went to a memorial service for an old friend, Frank Crozier, and heard a parody on the song 'Miss Otis Regrets'. Although what follows is not a parody as such, it owes a lot to the aforementioned song. I should also explain that the nickname Lubo was given to Gower by Bob Willis – who else? – it is the name of a restaurant in Adelaide with which David fell in love. Goochie is, of course, Graham Gooch, his captain on the tour, and a fitness fanatic.

Mr Gower regrets he's unable to train today, Goochie,
Mr Gower regrets he's unable to train today.
You see, he feels his highly tuned body could get rather abused
And the old tender and delicate hands are so easily bruised,
    Goochie,
So Mr Gower regrets he's unable to train today.

Now Mr Gower regrets he's unable to run today, Goochie,
Mr Gower regrets he's unable to run today.

He finds the quick single can tend to be such a terrible bore
And he feels if God had meant him to run he wouldn't have
    invented the four, Goochie,
So Mr Gower regrets he's unable to run today.

Now Mr Gower regrets he's unable to bowl today, Goochie,
Mr Gower regrets he's unable to bowl today.
For in his arm he says he's feeling such a terribly slight strain,
And as it's the one he uses to lift a glass of the vintage
    champagne, Goochie,
Mr Gower regrets he's unable to bowl today.

Now Mr Gower regrets he's unable to field today, Goochie,
Mr Gower regrets he's unable to field today.
Among all his skills he says his fielding is not terribly strong,
A view he's held since only last night, when he stayed in the
    casino too long, Goochie,
So Mr Gower regrets he's unable to field today.

Now Mr Gower regrets he's unable to bat today, Goochie,
Mr Gower regrets he's unable to bat today.
But he'd quite like to see young Mr Lamb out in the middle again
And he feels that such innings are really best viewed from above
    in a light plane, Goochie,
So Mr Gower regrets he's unable to bat today.

Now Mr Gower regrets he's unable to play today, Goochie,
Mr Gower regrets he's unable to play today.
For after last night it's sad to relate he's not feeling too hale and
    hearty,
But he's asked me to say he'll be perfectly fit to attend the
    after-match party, Goochie,
But Mr Gower regrets he's unable to play today.

Now Mr Bevan regrets he can no longer watch you play, Lubo,
Mr Bevan regrets he can no longer watch you play.
For though to manage you must have been a total pain in the
    arse,
We all know that in your day you exuded absolute class, Lubo,
Yes we all regret we can no longer watch you play, Lubo,
We all regret we can no longer watch you play.

LATE TEST SCORE

Falkland Islands have just beaten South Africa by an innings and 25,000 Rand.

EVERYONE'S MATE

'The only way to have a friend is to be one.'

Ralph Waldo Emerson

I think everyone felt they knew Johnners. Even though he went to Eton, he seemed to transcend all the classes. His obvious sense of joy in everything that happened rubbed off. You couldn't stay miserable if Johnners was on the radio. I grew up listening to him on *In Town Tonight* on the BBC Home Service, so it was a big thrill for me in the late 1970s to meet him for the first time. (No, in this case, I can't find the menu.)

A director of European Ferries, David Bradford, was the father-in-law of the Essex cricketer David Acfield, and for his benefit year I got a three-line whip to speak at the dinner (this was in the days before I earned any money from it) but I didn't care: the other speakers were Johnners and Colin Cowdrey, whom I had also never met. I followed these two legends and sat next to Johnners, whom I found a most charming and amusing companion. I told him during the evening that each Townsend Thoresen car ferry was like a small town: it had a telephone exchange, enough power to light a small community and many hundreds of people working or travelling on board. This would, I suggested, make an ideal venue for one of his famous *Down Your Way* radio programmes. He said it was not up to him but that he would put it to the producer.

A few weeks later his producer Anthony Smith was on the telephone saying they would do not one but two editions. So after a few more weeks we all set off in my car to do a programme in Dover which would end with me being interviewed as we sailed for Calais. I chose as my piece of music Harry Secombe singing the hymn 'Abide with Me', because it was the Cup final hymn. We then did another programme in Calais. In all we spent about three days together and had a great time. Johnners was forever playing tricks on me and was accurately described as an overgrown schoolboy, but it was never anything nasty and he always gave himself away by being unable to stop chuckling whenever he had taken me in.

Once I came on to the circuit we did lots of dinners together, and they were always jolly affairs because that was the atmosphere he created. We even did two Radio 4 *Trivia Test Match* programmes together and I remember one of his terrible jokes.

'During the war a woman went into the butcher's and said, "I'm returning these sausages as one end is all bread."

' "Well, madam," said the butcher, "in these troubled times it's very difficult to make both ends meat." '

I think what I was most proud of was the fact that, if Johnners liked you, you became an 'ers'. I was awarded my version the first time he wrote to me after *Down Your Way*. He started his letter, 'Dear Catters . . .' It was like getting on the honours list.

Half-time

20. WHERE ARE THE REFRESHMENTS?

'The service tonight made the West Indian over rate seem perfectly acceptable.'

Bob 'the Cat' Bevan

Spot a man with gravy stains on his shoulder and you have found an after-dinner speaker. In fact, my own jackets spend more time at the dry cleaner's than they do on my back. So, when I say that I've now been spotted at all the best places around the world, I am not exaggerating.

I've also got to know just about every toastmaster and wine waiter in London. As a result, I get looked after quite well. However, occasionally I am forced to recall Clement Freud's memorable epitaph for wine waiters: 'God finally caught his eye.' Or my own version: 'I'd like to drink a toast to absent friends, coupled with the wine waiter.' In fairness, wine waiters usually manage a smile at such lines, although they often try to draw my attention to other targets. 'You are going to have a go at the chef tonight, sir, aren't you?' They refer to my customary vote of thanks to the temporary chef: 'It's not often you get the soup and the wine at the same temperature.'

I started out, of course, at football dinners, at which you don't need to second-guess the menu – soup, steak and kidney pie, apple pie – but corporate occasions, which I speak at more often these days, often go to the other extreme in terms of food and wine. Consequently, if I'm working every night of the week, I now try to opt for the vegetarian alternative. This is so much easier to do these days. In fact, it often provides a better option, as it will have been freshly prepared.

Of course, there can be disasters. When organising one of the ship launchings for Townsend Thoresen, I once sent a junior public relations executive over to the Netherlands to sample the menu for the 400-guest banquet. Bryan Thompson had requested beef Wellington, and my young colleague returned to report that all was well. Sadly, it was absolutely not at all right on the night. I had wrongly assumed that both the Dutch caterers and the PR man knew what beef

Wellington was. As I looked down in horror at a great lump of pastry inside which there might or might not have been some beef, I could have strangled the journalist on my table who said, in an unnecessarily loud voice, 'Oh good – meat pies.'

Of all the hotels I have performed in, I have never had a bad meal in London's Hilton in Park Lane – except once. The event was a Jewish boxing night for my friend the agent Alan Field. In order to satisfy kosher requirements, the Hilton allowed outside catering and waiting staff for the evening. Clumsy Caterers Ltd were a company from hell: comedian Lennie Bennett and I timed the gap between the arrival of the chicken and the appearance of the accompanying vegetables at twenty minutes. Service took so long that in the end I had to speak while people were still eating. This is every entertainer's nightmare, because the noise from 500 sets of cutlery drowns out your voice. It's known as a 'knife and fork job' in the business.

Just as bad was another Jewish function, this time at one of London's top hotels. A waiter inadvertently told a diner that he was enjoying shrimp sauce (Jewish people don't eat shellfish). In fact, it was tomato, but the damage had been done and the kitchen was suddenly faced with instantly providing over 200 alternative kosher dishes.

Getting the food right is clearly a top priority, but it's all for nothing if the service is bad. And it isn't just the elderly waitress with the trembling hand at the local football club dinner who is at fault. I've had soup in my lap at the Savoy, although, in fairness, they were terribly nice about it and paid my cleaning bill.

Accidents will happen, but there is no excuse for the poor organisation you sometimes encounter at even the highest-starred establishments. My heart sinks whenever I realise that there is only one server allocated to a table of ten. First the plate appears, but even if it's warm on arrival, it isn't by the time the meat turns up. Another wait for the vegetables, by which stage the server will have forgotten where he or she had started in the first place.

Eventually, the potatoes arrive. By the time gravy – now known as 'sauce' in the trade for reasons I've never understood – mustard or horseradish is finally offered around, you feel a microwave should have been provided at each table.

This scenario is no figment of my imagination. It actually happened to me a few years back. Worse still, young, temporary waitresses dangled their untied long hair over – and almost in – the food as they served it. Not just unprofessional, but a case for the local health inspector. What was the function? Appropriately enough, it was a Lady Taverners murder-mystery weekend.

And it's so easy to get it right. The secret is 'double service'. Two waiters are assigned to two tables of ten diners. Waiter A serves the veggies, Waiter B follows with spuds, and the wine waiter brings the gravy and sauces. They then move on for a repeat performance at table two. Easy, isn't it? Nor is it rocket science to have mustard and other sauces on the table. So why don't more establishments do it? Some chefs don't like sauces. They think we should enjoy the flavours they have prepared.

All of this is what I have to put up with. Still, it's a living. Pass the ketchup, Mr Chairman.

21. HERE ARE THE SCORES SO FAR

'We were lucky to get nil.'

Joe Mercer

When Danny Baker left BBC Radio 5's *Six O Six* football phone-in and after a couple of others had had a short run at it, they homed in on me. I expected to be given some training, but I was stuck in front of the nation and just told to get on with it. They had some music on it then, for reasons I never understood, so a bit of production was required.

During the fifth programme of my six-week trial a guy called in and asked me something about the future. I said, 'I don't know, mate. It's my last show next week.' At the debriefing meeting on the Monday they had a bit of a panic as they clearly hadn't realised my time was coming to an end. At the end of the meeting they called asking me to carry on, and the next day I received a very nice letter from the producer saying, 'I hope you realise what a success you've been. Failures don't get asked back.'

CORNER

Here is an item from the *Lloyd's List* diary of 26 February 1993: 'It is always intriguing to hear of old colleagues who have made it in the big time – or the bigger time. One such is Bob "the Cat" Bevan, once of *Lloyd's List* and European Ferries, who went on to find fame and probably fortune as an after-dinner speaker, to which he now adds the appellation "comedian". Bevan, a football fanatic, has also been something of an intermittent broadcaster over the years, and we hear he is now to relieve another sports fan, former Heritage Minister David Mellor, for a spell hosting BBC Radio 5's sports phone-in *Six O Six*. If Bevan, who has appeared on the programme before, is anything like most freelance radio broadcasters, he isn't in it for the money. But he admits it is opening some interesting doors. "I must be the first bloke with one O level to be invited to speak at the Cambridge Union," he told us. Did this mean he was abandoning the after-dinner role? "Not at all. I do a lot of corporate work and take pains to find out about the company and work in some in-jokes everyone will understand. Which two departments are fighting each other, that sort of thing." But why "the

Cat"? He did not deny a former colleague's observations that when he played in goal he was so beatable it seemed to be the natural thing to call him. Lithe he is not . . .'

I had tried to give *Six O Six* some humour, and I encouraged the listeners to join in, rather like Terry Wogan, and you can't fault his format. If you've got a two-hour drive home after the game I think you want a bit of entertainment. I see from my diary in 1998 that Ian Wooldridge, having been laid up for six weeks with the TV and radio, bemoaned in the *Daily Mail* the lack of laughs in sports programmes. I can't see them being there while Bob Shennan runs Radio 5 as I don't think he does humour. They may get good figures, but in my opinion, what else is there to listen to? Do they really think that people want to hear some prat whining on about his midfield or the ref? We all know the answer to that.

When I was on, we had stories about people calling their animals or even children after footballers.

'I've got a dog called Cloughie.'

'Does it bark a lot?'

People called in with bizarre stories, such as St Albans City being denied promotion to the Conference because they had a centuries-old oak tree on the terraces. Then we had silly football scores. The post bag was full for weeks. I'll run a few past you now, and in the following chapters. They may not be award-winning, they may even be groanworthy, but for God's sake, BBC, let's try to have a laugh.

LATEST SCORES

Clyde 0 Bonnie 1

Rochdale 2 Emmerdale 1

(They do get better.)

Second Half

22. FAMILY ENCLOSURE'S BORED – WHERE'S THE BLOODY CONJUROR?

'No one is completely unhappy at the failure of his best friend.'
Groucho Marx

I was speaking from reminder notes at the Footballer of the Year dinner in 1980, quite openly holding them in my hand. Only once had I ever spoken without them. At a Catford Cricket Club function, where I had lots of friends, I decided to memorise my speech. I rehearsed it for weeks at every opportunity. I was trying to emulate my hero Geoff Brown. Geoff played in our league for Old Grammarians and was a big hit at dinners. He had a touch of arrogance in his personality, although ironically he did get very nervous before speaking. His style was magnificent. When he was introduced he would stroll forward, holding a glass of red wine, and address the assembly without notes. With his head slightly tilted back he gave the appearance of looking down his not inconsiderable nose at the audience. I wanted to be Geoff Brown. However, the strain of learning the Catford speech – which, incidentally, was a stormer – sent me back to my notes.

After going down so well at the Café Royal in May, I got a last-minute booking the following Wednesday to speak at a corporate hospitality function after the England v. Argentina friendly. I'd never been to a corporate hospitality function before and had little idea what to expect. When I arrived I was introduced to the compère, scriptwriter, comedian and actor John Junkin. I realised that we were going to be up on a stage, which meant no notes, but I was not unduly perturbed after my triumph a few days earlier. I was determined to do it without my little cards.

We went off to watch the game. It was a great night. Argentina were the world champions but we beat them 3–1 and everyone was in a state of euphoria when they returned. I was to learn subsequently that an audience that has been emotionally drained by defeat or victory can be a difficult one to lift. Not that this phenomenon can be solely blamed on this particular evening.

John Junkin went on and did a few minutes, then he announced me. They had never heard of me and, on balance, were probably not all that pleased to see me. I started badly and got worse. I lost my way and then started jumping from story to story in a totally unconnected way. Not one of them hit the spot. In vain I looked for the conjuror who was due on next, but he had still not arrived. After another couple of disasters I thought, 'Bollocks to this, Junkin's the pro,' and I got him back on. I slipped off to muted and far from widespread applause. I can see John now as he went back on. He paused for a moment, then damned me with faint praise: 'Well, Bob "the Cat" Bevan. Some quite good material there.' He was right – it was the delivery that had been crap. The conjuror arrived and I slunk away. It was quite the worst feeling I can ever recall. If the event had been higher than the ground floor I might have jumped off. I determined never to perform again, but three days later, back with my notes, I stormed a local football club. Fortunately I'd had the bottle to get back in and drive again after the accident.

Many years later, when I was successful and John Junkin was going through a lean spell, we did a Lord's Taverners dinner together in the Midlands. We were among a lot of friends from show business and sport, and I told a group how John had been present at my worst death. Eventually he took me to one side and told me to stop going on about it as it was getting up his nose!

CORNER
An actor playing Widow Twanky in a pantomime died during the interval. At the start of the second half another actor went out in front of the audience and said, 'I'm sorry to tell you that the actor who played Widow Twanky has died during the interval.' As one, the audience yelled back, 'Oh no he hasn't!'

It was at the 1980 Footballer of the Year dinner that I first met Ranjit Anand. He is of Indian descent, but he has never been to India. In fact, he appears to go cold at the thought. He was a friend of many stars, not least Jimmy Tarbuck, and was at the time running a highly successful company called Keith Prowse. They were into theatre ticket booking, travel and corporate hospitality in a big way. When the company folded, Ranj lost everything, even his big house on

Wentworth Golf Course. He had to move his family into his parents' living room, yet today he has fought his way back and now runs a highly successful company selling cheap air flights. But back in 1980 he was at the height of his powers. 'I want to book you,' he said, 'for a year and a day from tonight.' He told me that the following night was a sell-out at the Royal Lancaster Hotel in London, during which they presented the *Sunday People* Merit Awards. In those days that was the only newspaper to give marks out of ten for every player in every match, and also to show goal times against the names of the scorers. Everyone does that now, but then the *People*'s sports editor, Neville Holtham, was setting a trend.

'Tell me,' Ranj added, 'how much do you charge?'

Good question. I had no idea, having only been paid £150 once. In a flash of inspiration I said, 'A pound a head.'

'Christ,' said Ranj, 'there's a lot of people coming.'

'How many?'

'About five hundred.'

'OK,' I said, 'I'll do it for five hundred quid.'

A couple of years ago, when Ranj was back on his feet, I was asked to speak at his 50th birthday party, and I told this story, adding, 'And I've got to say, Ranj, that, as I now get out a bit more, I know that a full ballroom at the Royal Lanc holds about eight hundred people, so I reckon you owe me another three hundred plus interest.' He gave me a wry smile and asked if I was trying to put him out of business again.

As the twelve months from May 1980 rolled round, more details emerged about the 1981 Eve of Cup Final banquet. Jimmy Tarbuck was to be the MC, and Frank Bough (very famous then before scandal wrecked his career) was to do the raffle. The auctioneer would be comedian Lennie Bennett. Top of the bill, and my co-speaker, would be Billy Connolly.

I had clearly arrived, and I thought I'd better get some new material. So I went to my friend Brian Robinson and bought two of his routines. These both involved props – an old football boot and a leg with a sock and a football boot and some blood (red paint) smeared round the top. I'll leave the routines to your imagination, but they are very funny.

I went to the Royal Lancaster with a long-standing and much-mourned girlfriend, Janet Sheridan, who was to die in her early forties.

When we got there we recognised half the audience. Not that we knew them personally – it was like a *Who's Who* of sport and show business in there. The rest were corporate big-hitters; for example, Procter and Gamble had the head buyers from Tesco, Safeway and Sainsbury's on their table. It was a major event, and most of my food stayed on the plate in front of me as I nervously waited to do my spot.

Jimmy Tarbuck finally introduced me, and, thank God, I hit the target from the first gag. After as good a 30 minutes as I've ever done, I sat down to tremendous applause. A break was called, but I hardly heard it. Billy Connolly came over to my cloud nine and said I'd been great.

'Those football routines are fantastic,' he said. 'You'll get requests.'

'I'll get what?' I said.

'You'll get requests. People will want to hear them again and again.'

I'm not sure I believed him, but time has proved him absolutely right.

I'm sad to say that that was the last kind word Billy ever said to me. In fact, it was the last word of any sort. When he stood up he decided to do, among other things, twenty minutes on self-abuse. It was a serious error of judgement to a middle-aged, invited, mixed audience, and he was not well received to say the least. I was gobsmacked. With so many 'faces' there, word went round like wildfire in the business: Billy Connolly had been upstaged by this unknown bloke with a proper job. People who were there still remind me about it over twenty years later.

I, though, at least had it in perspective. This was a one-off bad night for Billy, and I was not about to start entering a talent contest with him. It was the classic situation all pros dread – following the gifted amateur. I had felt proud to be on such a bill with Billy, and was sorry for him. After all, a year before it had happened to me, only worse. Unfortunately, he seemed to blame me for the disaster. Later that evening, when I tried to say goodbye to him, all I got was a grunt.

A couple of weeks later I was doing another job for Ranj at a football international. When we got to our table at the Wembley Conference Centre, opposite us were Billy Connolly and impresario Harvey Goldsmith, who in those days was Billy's manager. Harvey had been at the Eve of Cup Final banquet but clearly didn't recognise me at first. When he did, his face broke into a huge smile and he said, 'Hey! It's the Cat! How are you, Cat? Here, Billy, do you know who this is?' Billy didn't look up. 'Yes,' he said. 'I know who it is.' I've seen him only once since then, at a surprise tribute dinner to Eric Clapton. Billy was brilliant. But still he did not say a word to me.

I had had a phone call from David English, of Bunbury cricket fame, who told me that Eric Clapton was a fan and that he'd been at several of my dinners. I did remember him being at one, but David said Eric was shy and would not have made a fuss. 'Eric thinks he's going to a small dinner party at the Savoy,' David continued, 'but all his friends are putting on a surprise party to celebrate twenty-five years in the music business. It would be great if you could say a few words. Just come along when you can.'

When I got there, I struggled to get in through all the bouncers. They certainly didn't recognise me, and I had to get David to come out. I was a bit out of place. I had a suit on for a start. When I finally got in, it was another eye-popper. They were all there – the Bee Gees, the Rolling Stones, Elton John, Ringo Starr, George Harrison, the list felt like it was endless. I went on after George Martin, Pete Townshend and Bob Hoskins. Barry Humphries and Billy Connolly would follow me. I said I'd first met Eric at a deaf and dumb dinner dance where he was appearing with his famous group the Animals. It's just about my one music joke, and it brought the house down.

Afterwards, George Harrison came up to me, high on drink or whatever but very friendly. He was producing films at that time.

'What are you doing in September?' he asked.

'Not a lot, as far as I can recall. Why?'

'I've just got to get that face on film,' he replied.

I gave him a card, but heard no more. Mind you, I wasn't exactly waiting by the phone.

That Eric Clapton evening was the second time I'd appeared with Barry Humphries. I'd first worked with him at an Old Harrovian rugby dinner. Former England international and coach Roger Uttley, a good friend of mine from Lord's Taverners events, asked me to speak at the dinner to raise funds to send their school team to Australia. One of the Harrovians knew Barry, who was starring in the West End at the time, and he had agreed to come on after finishing his show. I was really looking forward to meeting him. Although I'm not into drag acts, I've always admired his work. Whether you like him or not, I feel he has genius rating, and his range of vocabulary is awesome. When he arrived, still in full Dame Edna costume, I tried to speak to him, but he responded only as Dame Edna. He was not very well presented on the night, nor was he properly lit and he must also have been knackered after his show, which in itself was a tour de force. Nonetheless, it would be fair to say that he struggled, apart from the brilliant opening line, 'It's great to be here working for the underprivileged.' Nor did he win any gold medal at the Eric Clapton dinner, where he appeared as Sir Les Patterson, the Australian Minister for Culture. Again he wouldn't come out of character, so I don't feel as though I've met Barry Humphries yet. Weird.

However, Barry's brilliance was underlined at the Lord's Taverners Christmas lunch in 2001. When he arrived, having agreed to do a favour for Sir Tim Rice, he was visited in his changing room by the Taverners' chief executive, Mark Williams. Having been warned to get there before he changed so that he could actually meet the real Barry, Mark engaged in some small talk until the point when he said, 'It's only a pity Tim couldn't be here.' For once, Barry was struck dumb. Somehow the message about Tim's absence had failed to get through and Barry had written his twenty-minute spot around the great lyricist. It is a sign of his genius, therefore, that he took the stage half an hour later and put in a sensational routine, and it still seemed geared for the occasion. Whenever I have seen him in the West End he has been brilliant, as he was at this Christmas lunch. (Mind you, on this occasion he went first. Following on was William Hague, doing some of the material I'd written for him, and then me!)

Perhaps the worst death I've ever seen could have been career-threatening for me in the days when I had a proper job. As I've explained earlier, one of my jobs at European Ferries was to organise the ship launchings. In 1983 we were in Hamburg and we had booked two top-liners at that time, Clodagh Rogers and Les Dawson, for the surprise cabaret. Chairman Keith Wickenden was not keen on Les, but I talked him into it. To add spice to this particular event, of course, we also had a BBC film crew and a little girl launching the ship for *Jim'll Fix It*.

After a long and tiring day at the launching, we returned to our hotel and the gala banquet. Quite what happened once I had stopped the band playing and asked everyone to take their seats for the cabaret is still shrouded in mystery. All I know is that when I wanted her Clodagh was nowhere to be found, and there was a lengthy hiatus. There was some talk of being trapped in a lift, but I couldn't find out if that was true later. It might have helped if I could have got the band back, but they wouldn't interrupt their long-awaited meal. Eventually Clodagh appeared and did OK. Then we introduced the star of the show. I sat back and relaxed, convinced all would go well now. I was wrong.

I'm sure Les went to his grave not understanding what happened. Try as he might, he couldn't get them to laugh. Even when he did his hilarious bad piano player routine, they wouldn't budge. Then he got 'the runs'. This often happens to lesser performers who, when they are dying a death, start to speed up. This is the beginning of the end. Once you do that, you lose your sense of timing and you might as well pack it in. To see it happen to Les was a nightmare for me as the group PR director, but also some comfort for me as a performer. If it could happen to Les, we were all entitled to the odd black spot.

Next day I saw the chairman. It was not in his nature to do an 'I told you so', but what he did say did little to cheer me up. A major German bank had financed this particular four-ship building project, and Keith had been sitting with the chief executive of the bank who was a particularly humourless and intense character. Not long before Les was due on, the banker had been talking with Keith about the war. 'Mister Vickenden,' he said, 've are very proud of our present, but ve greatly envy your past.' At this point, he tapped the side of his nose to emphasise the point. Soon after that, Les was on. 'My mother-in-law has just come back from holiday,' he said. 'In Poland. She bought herself a new frock. It's a lovely colour. Deep khaki. It'll be nice when she unpicks the swastikas.'

My most bizarre death was almost certainly for a company of foreign exchange dealers from the City. All of them were what we used to call 'yuppies' – more money than brains, totally up themselves. They worked round the clock and played hard. I was booked to entertain them at a Chinese restaurant in Chelsea called Zen.

I knew I was in trouble from the minute I arrived. There were about 200 of them, and almost to a man they had been drinking all day. Hard. I sat at a raised top table with the chief executive, whom I recall was very tall and quite a straight sort of bloke, almost an establishment figure, and totally different from the rest of his colleagues. I thought he might try and get them in order, but he seemed to feel they were all behaving quite normally. As we sat down, we were hit by a barrage of pork balls – something that was to be frequently repeated. Table magicians were struggling round during the meal, and they and the waiters were having a nightmare evening. One of the conjurors I still see from time to time, and we never fail to talk about this evening. He was due to leave after the meal, but he stayed, with a macabre sense of curiosity, to watch me.

During the meal, I said to the CE, 'I don't see a mike around.'

'Didn't you bring your own?' he said.

'After-dinner speakers don't normally come with sound equipment,' I retorted.

'They did last year.'

'Who did you have last year?'

'Ellie Lane,' he said.

'I know Ellie. The blue comedienne. She's got a band. Did she come with the band?'

He confirmed that she did.

'That's why she had sound, then. She's got a bloody band!'

'Anyway, we haven't got one,' he confirmed.

Great. Two hundred people, all totally pissed, impossible to quieten, pork balls flying everywhere, and no mike.

I'm not sure if they heard me being announced, but I stood up anyway and battled against the noise and the pork balls for about fifteen minutes. I might as well not have been there, but eventually something did get their attention. A guy on the table below me fell forward, totally unconscious, and his head lay in the plate in front of him. One of his table immediately whipped out a safety razor and started to shave off the hair on one side of his head. Someone even found – don't ask me from where – a can of shaving foam to facilitate the operation. I did another gag, then gave up and sank into my seat. The CE was not pleased.

'I thought you were going to do more football?' he said.

'More football? They can hardly hear me, I've got no mike, and if I had one they probably wouldn't want to know. And what about that?' I pointed to the man with only half of his hair left.

He regarded it for a moment, then said, 'Very silly of the lad to fall asleep at the table. The boys always do something. Last week we had to take someone to a meeting in Tokyo looking like that. We told them he'd been in a road accident.'

'Fall asleep?' I cried. 'He's unconscious. I'm not sure he shouldn't be in hospital.'

I made my excuses and left. When I got home I called the agent who had booked me, Norman Phillips from the Midlands, and said into his answer machine, 'Norman. Tonight has not been the greatest experience of my career, but it will certainly merit a chapter in my memoirs.'

LATEST SCORES
Bognor Regis 2 Cyrille Regis 3
Aston Villa 3 Aston Semi-Detached 1

'I'M GETTING A LITTLE TESTY NOW'

'Funny is an attitude.'

Flip Wilson

In the 1970s we were still lugging projectors and films to travel agent evenings around the country. One of my jobs was to upgrade the Townsend Thoresen promotional films, and we hired Johnny Morris of *Animal Magic* fame to do one for us. As a result I got him to come and speak at the Old Wilsonians dinner. In this cavernous school hall with no mike, one of his party pieces was to play the 'Sailor's Hornpipe' on his teeth with a fountain pen. It echoed around the room and was note perfect. I asked him how he did it; he said it was all about voice projection. He had trained as an opera singer.

While you're getting over the shock, I'll add that Richard Stilgoe and ventriloquist Roger de Courcey had done the same. Roger has got a wonderful voice, but I can't say the same for Nookie Bear.

Back to the subject. When Johnny's film got a bit dated I had the idea to use a *Dad's Army* type, and although the BBC would not let you use the characters' names we managed to get Arthur Lowe. He loved ships and the sea – he had a small motor vessel himself – and never took a holiday, so he thought it would be relaxing to film for a week on the Felixstowe–Zeebrugge ferry. We hired a film company run by a nice guy called Paul and the actor Martin Benson. He appeared in lots of TV and cinema films, normally playing a villain. He had one of those faces you recognise without knowing the name.

What I did not know at the time, but do now, is that Arthur sacrificed plenty of good parts in order to go into lesser productions that could include his wife, Joan Cooper, in the cast. She was an OK actress, but she wasn't in Arthur's league. We got a script together which basically allowed Arthur to be Captain Mainwaring. Although he thought he was in charge of the holiday, it was really his wife who was pulling all the strings. Unlike Mrs Mainwaring in *Dad's Army*, she would actually appear and be played by Joan.

Filming is a slow and tiring business with lots of hanging around, so I got to know them both pretty well during the week. Arthur was very much like his *Dad's Army* character, but a nice man underneath. I'm sure he was a brilliant grandfather. We had chosen the Felixstowe–Zeebrugge service because it was much quieter. Even so, when he came on board he was besieged by autograph hunters, whom he did not welcome. We set up camp for him in the captain's cabin. Doing my PR bit, I said to Arthur that I would get a load of ship's postcards from the ship, he could sign them, and I would hand them out. He was grateful for this, and, sensing that I was an ally who understood him, we got on famously.

He knew he could make me laugh, and he often slipped in a Mainwaringism. Once, when we were leading him down some very steep, non-public stairs in order to avoid the passengers, he spotted that one of the rubber covers on the edge of the stairs was missing. At sea things get rusty very quickly, and this protector had clearly been missing for some time. As we went down, he put on his best Mainwaring voice and said, 'Get that cleaned by the next time I come on board, will you?' We all nearly fell down the stairs on top of him.

During the trip we had lots of discussions about the other *Dad's Army* characters. Joan said they were all very well cast. John Le Mesurier, for example, who played Sergeant Wilson, was very vague. 'He does some TV advertising work in Australia,' Joan said, 'but whenever he travels someone has to go with him. Otherwise he would get off in Prague.' One day all the cameras broke down for a few hours and we were stuck on a rainy day in a café in Zeebrugge drinking endless cups of coffee. Arthur got a bit frustrated by this and started to drum his fingers on the table. He then uttered the very old-fashioned phrase, 'I'm getting a little testy now.' Joan leant over to me and whispered, 'I told you they were well cast.'

In this promotional film, Arthur falls asleep on the deck and dreams he is the captain. In full uniform, he strolls on to the bridge and says, 'Everything all right, number one?' The script then provided for him to say, 'Call me if the fog thickens.' I felt that we could not have anything negative like that. At this time ships were crashing into one another in the Channel; this was before the introduction of a lane system that all but eliminated such events. 'In my world,' I added to Martin Benson, 'the sun is always shining and the sea is like glass.' A row ensued, with Arthur standing by and understanding my point but not wishing to be drawn in. I stood my ground so Martin challenged me to come up with an alternative.

'Certainly,' I said. 'Call me if the sun goes in.'

Arthur immediately laughed. 'Oh, it's very good, that,' he said. 'I like that.'

I didn't know if he meant it or if he was trying to finish the argument. However, when the film was shown, I was pleased to see that that line always got the biggest laugh.

After that Townsend Thoresen used Arthur at several functions, and he was always good value. When he hit the West End with the *Dad's Army* musical he invited my parents and me round to his dressing room. Unfortunately, the invitation had slipped his mind, and he was rather embarrassed to end up greeting my mother in his vest.

I once went for a meal in Arthur's flat in Little Venice and noticed that on top of the cistern in his bathroom was a pile of the sailor's magazine *Sea Breezes*. 'Good air freshener, that,' I observed. Joan later told me that Arthur pinched that joke and repeated it to everyone who subsequently went round there.

There have been a few books about him in recent years, and it was clear that he and Joan shared a great love. It was on one of the provinical tours he insisted on taking so that Joan could appear with him, in April 1982, that he died suddenly in his dressing room. It was only recently that I heard the somewhat bizarre news that Joan, who has also now passed away, stayed with the production and did not attend his cremation. I have to say that I did find that hard to understand.

23. AWAY TEAM ON TOP

'John Cleese, Evelyn Waugh and the Tottenham back four.'
Lord Simon, when asked what made him laugh

Although the Nat Lofthouse–Bolton event, for which I was booked immediately I sat down at the 1980 Footballer of the Year dinner, would have been my first up north, my first appearance at a Football League club was at Coventry City when Jimmy Hill was still chairman. Also on the bill that night was England rugby international Budge Rogers. Nearly a quarter of a century later, he and I sit side by side on the Board of Trustees of the Lord's Taverners.

After leaving my one-bedroom flat in Bromley, I had moved into a town house in Dalton Close, Orpington. Then, in 1979, I had moved again into a detached house in Lennard Avenue, West Wickham, Kent, just five minutes from the Old Wilsonians ground. As you climb the property ladder, you nearly always overstretch yourself financially. Now, however, after living on floorboards, dinners were helping me to carpet the house and buy new furniture. Walking through the house was a bit like poring over a league table: Oldham – dining-room carpet; Hartlepool – small bedroom; Rochdale – big bedroom; and so on.

I've always had this ambition to speak at every Premiership and Football League club in the land, but I've still got twenty-one left to do. Football clubs are a bit better administered than they used to be, but not much. Most do not even reply to letters, and I have written several times offering my services for next to nothing without even getting an acknowledgement. In case they're reading this book, the chairmen or commercial managers of the following clubs might like to know that I have yet to appear at their dinners:

Boston United
Bristol City
Cardiff City (I've had a fee for a cancellation but no dinner)
Cheltenham Town
Chester City

Darlington
Grimsby Town
Lincoln City
Macclesfield Town
Newcastle United
Notts County
Port Vale
Portsmouth
Rotherham United
Scunthorpe United
Stockport County
Stoke City
Sunderland
Wigan Athletic
Wrexham
Yeovil Town

I have done all the others including some clubs no longer in the league. But my first, at Coventry, was a good night. I felt I was among friends and I went down well. Early in 1981 I headed to Bolton for my first real northern dinner. Nat Lofthouse's friend Tom Finney came along as well to hear me and a comic called Ivor Davis, who had appeared from time to time on the famous ITV series *The Comedians*. I didn't find Ivor the friendliest man in the world, especially when he greeted me by telling me that cockney comics did not go down well up north. Unfortunately I was green enough to believe him, and it put me off a bit. I didn't have a death, but it wasn't exactly a triumph either.

Being a PR man, I didn't just sit back and let my career take off, I assembled a mailing. I got some quotes from three influential people in the game and put them on a cartoon that had been given to me by my colleagues in the office. Bobby Robson wrote: 'After-dinner speaking is a specialised art, just like goalkeeping. I know Bob Bevan is an enthusiastic amateur keeper and I can pay him no higher compliment than to say he is to after-dinner speaking what Gordon Banks was to football. I have heard speakers at functions all over the country, but few have ever received a better response from their audience than Bob. He is the ideal person to ensure the success of any dinner.' John Motson weighed in with this: 'I have heard many speakers at football dinners all over the country while I have been working for *Match of the Day*, but Bob Bevan received a better response from his audience than any football personality from the professional world. I thoroughly recommend his services.' And Jim Rosenthal, who was then on BBC Radio's *Sport on 2*, added: 'I've heard Bob Bevan speak in front of a critical audience of more than 400. Within minutes, they'd warmed to his repartee – he got the standing ovation he deserved at the end. One of the best speakers I've ever heard – guaranteed to enliven any function. Sharp, witty and with a lovely sense of timing. I can't wait to hear him again.'

A few years ago I did a dinner at Ipswich for the departing manager's secretary. She had worked for all the previous incumbents, even I believe Sir Alf Ramsey. Bobby Robson flew in from Eindhoven, where he was coaching for a second spell (and flew out next morning to Tel Aviv for a conference). John Motson agreed to host the evening, and I was the turn. When Motty stood up he referred to the mailing of some twenty years previously, which, to be honest, I had totally forgotten. He said that he had never forgotten it because, although he had done it as a favour, a few days later I sent him and the others a case of wine. I'd forgotten that, too. But I think it was worth it.

Thanks to my mailing I was up and down the country doing dinners for the first three years of the eighties. It was quite tiring as I was still working at European Ferries. I had to leave work mid-afternoon for northern dinners and then get the first train the following morning to reach the office by 9.30. Still, it was good fun, and I was meeting all my heroes. Broadcaster John Inverdale said to me recently, when I was writing this book, that I must have a good memory, and I suppose I do. But all these things have stuck in my mind because I was enjoying it all so much. European Ferries chairman Keith Wickenden was quite happy about me doing it, although I'm not sure about the rest of the company.

CONTROVERSIAL PENALTY

On 31 March three years ago, agent Alan Platt called former footballer, Manchester United manager and after-dinner speaker Wilf McGuinness. He said he had a last-minute job for him for the next day. 'It's only three hundred quid but I don't want any commission and you'll be free by midday. It's at Old Trafford for the Manchester United Disabled Supporters Club, who are having a tug of war followed by a reception, and they want someone to do twenty minutes at about eleven thirty.' Wilf said he was due at Old Trafford to pick up some tickets, so it wouldn't be a problem. Alan faxed a confirmation and Wilf went down the following morning. The receptionist could find no record of the engagement, so Wilf went off looking for a reception in one of the banqueting rooms. He even came across a guy in a wheelchair and asked the bewildered gentleman if he was there for the tug of war. Only then did he realise the date.

I was starting to get noticed during those three years, and the occasional telephone call would come from the newspapers if there had been a goalkeeping clanger. I was asked to write for the first time by the *Daily Telegraph*, who wanted a piece on AFA football. This is what appeared in 1981:

What is the biggest soccer club in the country? Manchester United? Liverpool? National Westminster Bank FC? Right third time. Whatever else the first two claim, they do not field seventeen or eighteen sides every Saturday afternoon, leaving a further twenty luckless souls without a game.

While the professional game soul-searches and worries that its commercial machinery is in need of an overhaul, more people are playing soccer than ever before. Nowhere is this trend more in evidence than in Amateur Football Alliance soccer. From its ranks just before the last war came Ipswich Town – a rise through the various levels of the game which even Cambridge United cannot match.

Today, there are 315 AFA teams fielding 1,120 teams and 12,000 players in an area stretching from Sussex to Derbyshire, with the main concentration in London and the south-east. It is the last amateur bastion of the game where players pay to play and where the stronger clubs play out their Exeter City fantasies in the FA Vase.

Yet even here the dark clouds of 'professionalism' are hinted at among the major banks and insurance companies which inhabit the major competition, the Southern Amateur League. It is denied that career prospects are enhanced by playing for the company side, but many opponents are not convinced.

Wherever AFA football is played, however, sociability is the keynote. Clubs are 'reported' or even dismissed from their ranks if they fail to provide a hot meal and drinks after the match. Unlike the professional game, this hospitality must also be extended to the referee and linesmen.

Communication is strong too. While Fleet Street can no longer produce a classified paper on Saturday evenings, Nat West Bank do so, and, with voluntary labour, cover all their results. Presses roll for the News of the Blues just two hours after the games finish.

Weekly publications abound, such as *Over the Bar* at Old Esthameians and *All the News that's Fit to Print* at the Old Wilsonians. The latter also carries a weekly column on goalkeeping called Cat's Eye.

Gaffes, deliberate or otherwise, are common. If prizes were awarded, Old Actonians would be strongly nominated for reporting that, even though a certain vice president could not attend the annual general meeting, he was with them in spirit.

Perhaps he was. He'd died six years earlier.

———————

LATEST SCORES
Plymouth Argyle 1 Plymouth Gargoyle 2
Exeter 1 Baconmissedhim 2

———————

24. MORE GREAT GOALS

'The toughest thing about success is that you've got to go on being a success.'

Irving Berlin

When the Professional Footballers' Association launched their awards (their Player of the Year is voted for by the players themselves) in 1974, they managed to secure a one-hour programme on the national ITV network. The dinner had to end at ten p.m. at the latest so that the highlights could be skilfully and quickly edited and broadcast 90 minutes later on the Sunday evening of the event.

I remember watching these programmes. They always had two speakers – a noted personality, such as the Speaker of the House of Commons, and someone who would be funny – and one speaker who stood out for me was Canon Reg Smith. He was a fanatical Bury supporter, and he later went on the board and even became chairman for a short time. I can't remember a single one of his lines now, but I do know he was very funny.

They say you have to live the dream, and I fantasised about getting on this slot. But after 1980, anything was possible, and sure enough, in 1981 the call came. I was paid £300 and given a room in the Hilton on Park Lane, where the dinner was to be held. Because of the early finish, there was also an early start. Even so, there was clearly no need for me to arrive at 2.30 p.m. I was nervous. A larger-than-life character called Bob Gardam was producing the programme, and he clearly didn't want me around at that point so I dragged my huge pile of nerves to my room and sat there and worried.

As with all big events, it had hung around me for weeks. On top of it being a big event, it was also my first TV appearance, apart from the occasional news item about Townsend Thoresen. But this was different. You can't die on your arse in a news programme.

I had played football the day before and had ended up in the Plough Inn on Bromley Common. Old Bromleians were our local rivals, and I had many friends there. Knowing I would have problems sleeping, I ended up back at the house of an Old Bromleian called Brian Steer, watching *Match of the Day* and drinking until the early hours. This was somewhat dangerous, as Brian was noted for his eccentric mixed-up drinking contests as skipper of their 4th XI. The most memorable mix I can recall was a sherry and tomato juice. I am pleased to say it wasn't one I had to sink that evening. But Brian was a nice guy, and quite sensible for most of the time. After that Saturday evening he always showed a great interest in what I was getting up to. He felt he had become part of my PFA dinner, and he had. He sensed what I was going through and was a great help to me that evening. I was shattered when he died in his forties, not many years later, from a brain tumour. I wish he was here now to read his name in this book.

REFEREE STOPS GAME

The late Neil Midgley was one of the best officials around. He was once asked how he became a referee. He said, 'Well, I wasn't a bad player and had trials for Preston North End. But then my eyes went . . .'

When I came back downstairs from my hotel room, Bob Gardam seemed more relaxed, but I was told in no uncertain terms that I was not to overrun.

If the FWA's dinner was full of famous faces from our football heritage, this PFA dinner was packed with current-day stars. Most big clubs had their own table packed with players. (Hardly any of them come these days, even if they've won something.) On the top table I was in between George Thomas, the Speaker of the House of Commons, and Jimmy Dickenson of Portsmouth FC. George, later to become Lord Tonypandy, was the first voice to be heard crying 'Order, order!' when Parliament was first broadcast live on radio in 1977. He was great company and a really nice man, but Jimmy was hard work. He was no longer manager of Portsmouth and he was there that evening to make an award to John Trollope of Swindon Town, who had made a record 770 Football League appearances. Jimmy had held the previous record of 764 for years and was not happy about losing it. 'It was the only thing I had left,' he said. I turned back to the Speaker.

Sir Stanley Rous spoke first and was very amusing, as he always was. Then a vicar from Swansea, Don Lewis, stood up. He was OK, but I think he went over the heads of the audience.

I have a video of the programme which was broadcast later that evening, and I was due to be shown after the first advertisement break. As the show came out of the break, Dickie Davies could be seen sitting at a table with Terry Venables, who was at Queens Park Rangers then. 'We've got a chap coming up now who's very funny, isn't he, Terry?' said Dickie. El Tel, whom I had not yet met, agreed that I was, so I can only assume that he too had been at the FWA dinner the year before.

Palace were doomed to relegation that year. Not much of a start for a side that only a few years earlier, under Terry Venables, had been called the 'Team of the Eighties'. Dario Gradi was the latest manager. Not for the first time Palace had had about four managers that year. Although I had written what I was going to do, I had heard what was then a new line at a stag night the previous Friday and had decided to use it. In the clip that was broadcast, I commented, 'I was hoping that Palace might get into Europe this year, but I don't think they will now.' This got a laugh on its own, and I was confident enough to work the audience. 'Do you, then?' Another laugh. 'No, I don't think they will now. Not unless Dario can write a song.' It demonstrates the power of television that over twenty years later people still come up to me and recall that line. I added that Palace had become the first team to be expelled from the Bell's Manager of the Month awards. 'They've been told they've got to have a manager for a month.'

I was still under the impression then that I needed new material every time I got up – a terrible burden if it were true. Consequently I had plenty of new stuff. In those days the ballroom at the Hilton was decorated with some very large and ornate tapestries hanging on the walls. 'I've never spoken in a branch of Allied Carpets before,' I observed, and that remark also went round the nation. On recently re-reading my notes from the dinner, I spotted a gag I have long since forgotten, about my becoming the first-ever goalkeeper to be registered as a charity. I noticed that I also did a joke about Frans Thijssen and £50, but I've no idea what it was. Ipswich was still featuring in my life that night as the Player of the Year was John Wark, his team-mate Frans having been named Footballer of the Year.

It was another great night for me, and now, having become known to the entire football community, there was no going back to the room. I can't remember where I went or what I did, except that I bumped into an Old Bromleians friend, Paul Edwards, who was at that time, by coincidence, captain of Dulwich Hamlet.

BOUNCE-UP

Referee Neil Midgley is alleged once to have called a player over after a nasty foul and asked him his name. The player replied, 'Anton Otulakowski.' Midge paused for a moment before saying, 'Er, well don't do it again.'

I do recall crawling into the office next morning and waiting to see if the phone would ring. It didn't take long. There were dozens of calls congratulating me on my 90 seconds on the box, but by lunchtime my mother had not yet called. Reluctantly, and feeling the need for the hair of the dog and a bit more adulation in El Vino's, I called her. When she answered, she said, 'Oh, hello.' Then, not with much enthusiasm, she added, 'We watched you last night.'

'I should think you bloody did,' I said, feeling more than a little hurt about this lukewarm reaction to the biggest night of my life.

'Were you pleased with yourself?' she said.

Perplexed, I replied that it had seemed to go well.

'Oh, good,' she said. 'Well, your Auntie Win's got the flu . . .' And she trundled on about the family until I left for my wino friends.

It took a week for me to realise what lay behind her reaction. She called me the following Monday. 'We went to Bob's at the weekend,' she said. Bob was her brother, my uncle, the only other member of the family to have a video. With a crowd of relatives they had watched me at the PFA dinner. 'Everyone thought you were very good.' I said that that was nice. After a pause, she then said, somewhat hesitantly, 'Do you . . . do you change your voice when you speak?'

That was it! She was upset that her little boy was common. I was quite a well-spoken little boy when I left Dulwich Hamlet Primary School. Wilson's Grammar School in Camberwell was another world and had I carried on speaking like that I would have got beaten up most mornings. So the aitches started to drop, and I now have this rather strange accent which is not too far from, and is sometimes mistaken for, Australian. I had to tell my mum that I too had noticed that on the recording. I had not been aware of it before, but I definitely do go 'a bit more London' when I'm working.

'It's just a style of delivery,' I assured her, 'and it does seem to work.'

She went off a bit happier, but probably none the wiser. I think I went to El Vino's.

The day after the PFA dinner, it was handy that I had my dinner jacket in the office because I received a call from Ken Wolstenholme. When he was not saying 'They think it's all over', he used to run the Anglo-American Sporting Club. They held boxing dinners in the Hilton, and I had been the 'last bell ringer' on a couple of occasions. By law, boxing has to start no later than nine p.m., so the dinner is rushed through, a comic rings the last bell with a fifteen-minute slot, and he can then clear off if he's not into boxing. For this appearance they used to give you the princely sum of £75 and then ask you to sign for it. With tax levels as they were it was hardly worth doing, but in those days getting plenty of exposure was everything. Ken had been let down for a boxing dinner he was running that night for the Furniture Trade Removals Association. Geoff Hurst was the guest of honour, but they needed the last bell to be rung. Complete with a new dress shirt, I was back in the Hilton the night after my triumph.

People often ask if I get bored sitting through dinners. I always tell them that it's better than working. In fact, having been a journalist, I find most people and their many ways of earning a living interesting. Everyone has their little wrinkles and their funny moments. This night would be the exception. As usual, the last bell ringer was seated right on the end of the top table; he either talks to the bloke on his right or gazes at the stairs leading from the platform.

When I first sat down, an Italian waiter came up those stairs and leant over me. 'You was very good last night, sir,' he said. I thanked him. 'We love the line about the temporary chef. We all run in and tell him. It was very good.' I thanked him again. 'You do it again tonight, sir, and we go get him to listen.' Fearing the likelihood of a temperamental white-hatted, knife-wielding assassin racing through the door, I told my new fan that I was not sure if I was going to use it tonight.

By now, my companion had joined the table: he was the secretary. After introducing ourselves we had a silent few minutes through the prawn cocktail until he said, 'Do you go fishing or anything like that?' I said that I didn't. 'Neither do I,' he said. While I was pondering why on earth anyone would commence a conversation with something he knew nothing about, he came in again.

'Do you go racing at all?'

'No.'

'No. Neither do I.'

It was unbelievable. As soon as I could, I went and sat with Geoff Hurst, and then went home. I don't like boxing much either.

LATEST SCORES

Dundee 0 Eccles 1

Port Vale 2 Yard of Ale 1

'DO YOU THINK YOU'LL CATCH THE COIN?'

'I am a part of all that I have met.'

Lord Tennyson

When Bobby Moore died and Upton Park was awash with flowers, I recall one card from a supporter. It said, 'I wanted to be like you.' For those of us lucky enough to have been one of his friends, this was a very telling remark. We all wanted to be endowed with not just his football ability, which was enormous, but his personality. His charm, his modesty, and above all his good manners. He oozed class in just about everything he did.

He was one of many people I met for the first time at that Footballer of the Year dinner in 1980. He was also there on the Billy Connolly night a year later. Then, when I was in Hong Kong on my own over the New Year in 1982, I heard he was there. I found out where he was staying and called him. He was still with his first wife Tina then and we met in a bar run by a former Rangers player whose name now escapes me. From then on we saw each other quite frequently at various functions and became friends. Although I didn't realise it at the time, he was in Hong Kong to talk about taking over a local team as manager. When he did so, I was commissioned to write a piece about him for the British Caledonian in-flight magazine.

We met for lunch in the Wig and Pen Club in Fleet Street, and he told me of many interesting events in his life. Some, such as wiping his hands on a cloth just before he shook hands with the Queen at the World Cup final in 1966, are now widely known and indicative of his good manners. 'The first thing I saw as I climbed the steps were the Queen's white gloves,' he recalled, 'and I thought I would make them dirty.' Extraordinary that at the greatest moment of his sporting life he should think like that.

Not so well known is the tale about his debut for West Ham. His guide, mentor and maybe his best friend was Malcolm Allison. An innovative and much-respected coach, Allison was the man who started the idea of cutting down the size and weight of boots and playing strip. Moore gave him much of the credit for his development and was desperate to learn. As a schoolboy he had achieved no representative honours; all his youth team-mates were internationals.

On the first Tuesday evening of the 1958/59 season, in the year of the Munich air crash, the Hammers were at home to Manchester United. It was between Moore and Allison as to who would get the number six shirt. If Bobby got in, it would be his debut; if Malcolm played, it would be his first ever game in the old First Division. It went to Moore. Allison was transferred to Charlton and never played in the top division. Bobby felt bad about that until the day he died.

That Tuesday evening Bobby got the bus – yes, the bus – from his home in Dagenham. He had to change buses to get to Upton Park, but, he recalled, 'I hadn't reckoned on the size of the crowd so I had to let two buses go. When I got to the ground they had closed the gates and wouldn't let me in!' He did convince them eventually that he was playing, but the episode shows both the changing social times and the good manners of Bobby Moore, who really should have jumped the queue when he changed buses. During the interview, Bobby recalled, 'On the evening I marked Ernie Taylor, and we won 3–2. But the next week I was brought down to earth when I was selected again and had to mark Jimmy Quigley. He gave me a real roasting at Nottingham Forest. I remember going out at half-time and a wag in the crowd shouting, "Play on their number six – he's their real weakness." It really brought me down to earth. I not only didn't get in the next week, I was lucky to be allowed on the train home. That season I played only about six times in the first team. I think in my heart of hearts I had hoped they would pick Malcolm. He had come back from tuberculosis with one lung missing. But he was in his late twenties and these two things combined made it very difficult for him to come back.'

After 1981 I was an invited guest at Crystal Palace – and I'm ashamed to say I haven't stood on the terraces, or sat in the seats that are now secured there, ever since, although these days I do insist on buying my season ticket. In late 1981, when the Old Wilsonians didn't have a game, the then Palace club secretary Alan Leather sat me next to Bobby at a home match. I'm sure he thought it would be quite amusing to have the world's worst goalkeeper next to our biggest football hero. I decided that I couldn't possibly talk football with Bobby (this was before our interview), so I sat there uncharacteristically quiet. After ten minutes he turned to me and said, 'What do you make of it so far, Cat?' Now, I can't remember what I replied, but years later he assured me that I'd said, 'It's a bit bloody cold, isn't it?'

That led to the development of what is probably my best football routine. At least Alan Simpson says so, so that's good enough for me. By the following Tuesday the comic possibilities of this legendary figure calling me 'Cat' and asking for my view of the game had hit me. Thereafter, whenever Bobby was in the room I would do the routine.

'He turned to me and said, "Pardon me, Cat."

'I said, "What is it now?"

'He said, "I'm sorry to bother you, Cat, but I was wondering, how long have you actually played the game?"

'I said, "Well, Mooro, I've only been a keeper for seven or eight years. Prior to that I was a hard tackling wing-half. Not unlike yourself, but a touch more creative."'

There then follows a whole list of goals I have conceded and how they went in. I'm still not quite sure if he minded me digging him out like that, but if he did, he certainly would never have told me.

Despite his good manners, he still had a very sharp and dry sense of humour. Once he knew you he would feel able to take the mickey, but never in a cruel way. Whenever we met he would say, 'Play Saturday?' Is this a leg-pull? I thought at first. But he assured me he understood that everyone's game was important to them no matter what level they played at, and he really meant it. Mind you, he might have secretly regretted it when he was regaled with the doings of the Old Wilsonians 6th XI in some detail during many meetings.

One night we were at a party on a boat on the Thames hosted by Ranjit Anand. It was a Friday, so he had to alter his normal enquiry.

'Playing tomorrow?'

'I'm captain.'

'I see. Do you think you'll catch the coin?'

But his greatest line came in 1988. By this time he was working in the corporate hospitality arm of Blue Arrow (owned by the former Tottenham director Tony Berry). Through this company, Bobby was getting me plenty of work. One Monday morning I got a telephone call in my office from Richard Keys, the Sky football presenter who was at this time still on the TV-am breakfast show. He asked me what I was doing on Sunday. Nothing, I told him. He said there was a celebrity match prior to the Sherpa Van Trophy final at Wembley; would I like to play in goal? Needless to say, he didn't have to ask twice.

This competition was for the then Third and Fourth Division clubs. The final was to be between Burnley and Wolves – two giant clubs that had inexplicably slipped into Division Four. But they still had massive support, and 80,000 packed Wembley that day. Our game was to be between ex-players of both clubs, sprinkled with a few guests from the media and show business, but they would all be people who could actually play. Old Wolves had ex-players such as John Richards, Willie Carr, Steve Kindon and goalkeeper Gary Pierce, along with commentator Alan Parry and Richard Keys himself. I would be in goal for Old Burnley; our team included Ray Pointer, Paul Fletcher and guest Nobby Stiles. The managers were Ron Atkinson and Lawrie McMenemy, although Ron, who could never resist a game, and probably still can't, insisted on getting changed and playing for them. Nor was it one of those soppy games across the pitch: it was fifteen minutes each way on the full pitch. We came out of the tunnel in the proper way, too.

All week I couldn't sleep. I was like a kid again. When Bobby called me about a job a few days later I barely let him say hello.

'Mooro!' I yelled. 'Guess where I'm playing Sunday?'

'Go on.'

'I'm playing at Wembley!'

'Oh yes,' he said. 'Are you in that celebrity game before the Sherpa Van?'

'I am. How do you know about that?'

'Well,' he replied, 'I'm playing as a guest for Old Wolves.'

'Oh,' I said. 'I'm in goal for Old Burnley.'

'That's great. I'm ever so pleased.'

'That's very nice of you, Mooro.'

'Well,' he said, 'I've never scored at Wembley.'

The day was unbelievable. I had walked on the Wembley pitch at the Brighton cup final in 1983, but never to play. You expect the pitch to be the biggest ever, but of course it's – or, sadly, it was – just a normal maximum size with a big stand around it. I walked out wearing the regulation glasses, but I still wanted to play well even though, as a comic figure, it wouldn't matter if I didn't. In fact, that would be what was expected. Perhaps that was why I wasn't too nervous.

Surprisingly, although the noise is massive when you walk out, once you start playing and concentrating, you hardly notice it. Within seconds of the start one of the Wolves forwards let one go from the edge of the area. It's the best thing that can happen to a goalkeeper, to get into the action straight away. Without thinking I threw myself to my left and it smashed against the post and was cleared for a corner. I had actually touched it. With a fingertip. But I was the only one in the ground who knew. I certainly didn't change the direction of the ball. I was sorry it hadn't been six inches closer as it would have been a fantastic save. But my moment was to come.

After we had taken a 1–0 lead, Richard Keys, who is quite a useful player, came through on his own. I came out and spread myself as he shot, the ball bounced off me, and we went straight up the other end and scored again. As he came running back over the halfway line Nobby Stiles, teeth out and looking as competitive and fearsome as ever, even in this game, was yelling at me. The crowd noise was massive after our goal so I couldn't hear him. I kept yelling 'What?' back at him as he got closer and closer. It was not until he was a few feet away that I could make his words out.

'I said, good save.'

I've never felt so proud. But I have wondered ever since how players and coaches can hear one another during a game.

Later, Bobby got into the area with the ball but shot weakly, and I collected it. I still wonder whether he did it deliberately, but he denied it. 'I was knackered,' he said. I'm not so sure. As we left the pitch he put his arm around me. 'Tell you what,' he said, 'many better goalkeepers than you have never played here. And a lot more have never had a clean sheet.' A magic moment you wish you could have bottled. Sadly, I haven't even got a video of the game. TV-am lost it. Can you believe it? But Ron and Lawrie will vouch for it. In fact, they spent most of the rest of the afternoon wandering around the Wembley restaurant saying, in very loud voices, 'It was the goalkeeper who made all the difference.'

I have, however, got a video of the following year, when I played for Old Port Vale against Old Torquay United. I let in four very quickly and got substituted. I've only watched it once.

As with most commercial ventures in Bobby's life, Blue Arrow soon came to an end. We continued to meet at dinners and I got him some sporting lunches with me at various venues up and down the country. We would travel together on the train, and I used to say to him, 'You never mention the World Cup when you speak. Jack Charlton does it all the time. It's not boasting. It's what everyone wants to hear about.' He would listen politely, usually without commenting. But he never changed.

He trusted everyone, and was frequently let down. Consequently he had several financial worries, with which he never bothered his friends. But he was soon to have even bigger problems.

I can recall the game well. It was Crystal Palace against Oldham in the Premier League, and it was memorable for Oldham manager Joe Royle getting upset with a photographer and throwing a bucket of water over him. Bobby was, by then, commentating with Jonathan Pearce on Capital Gold. The press box was up at the back of the stand, just behind and to my right in the directors' box. As usual, I called out to him and we waved. 'You all right?' he mouthed. I gave him the thumbs up and he gave it back.

A few days later, I called him at home. His second wife Stephanie answered. 'I'm afraid he's in Harley Street Hospital,' she said. Assuming it was something minor, I said that I was doing a dinner up north the next day and would call in and see him en route to my train. 'Bob,' she said, 'you can't. They're only letting close family in, and last night even that was stopped.' I was stunned, but I didn't like to ask what was wrong.

I sent a card the next day and dropped him a line. Two weeks later, he called. He said he had just come out of hospital and was catching up on his messages. He told me that after he had waved to me at the Palace v. Oldham game he had been driving home and had picked up a message from Stephanie. He'd called her, and she'd said that a letter had come from the hospital. 'She didn't need to say any more. I just said, "When and how long?"' He said he was getting stronger every day, and we chatted away. At no point did he ever mention the word cancer. He didn't have to.

The last time I saw Bobby was one cold, wet night Palace beat Chelsea in a League Cup match. I went to my car after the game but realised I had left my umbrella in the vice-president's room. As I was walking back across the dark car park a voice called out to me. It was a bloke wearing an apparently oversized cap, and I couldn't see who it was.

'Who's that?'

'Mooro.'

I asked him how he was, and he said he was fine. We had a chat, but not for long because of the weather.

On the Saturday, when I was presenting BBC Radio 5's *Six O Six* show, I talked about this meeting and took the mickey out of his hat. A few days later I was told why he was wearing it: his trademark blond hair was suffering from the chemotherapy. I called to apologise, but I only spoke to Stephanie who told me not to be silly as Mooro would understand.

I can recall the day he died, two days before my birthday in February 1993. I had been told that he was pretty ill so I wrote him a 'cheer up' letter over the weekend and posted it on the Monday. On the Tuesday I was walking back to our flat in Fulham from the tube station to change for a dinner I was speaking at in Kensington. My mobile rang. It was Tom Pendry, now Lord Pendry and the former shadow Sports Minister who I feel was so disgracefully overlooked by Blair when he came to power. He asked if I'd heard the news. I said I hadn't. 'Your pal's died,' he said. I didn't twig until he mentioned Bobby's name.

It was one of the few times I have shed a tear for someone unrelated to me. I went back to the flat and Laura gave me a hug. She knew how much he meant to me. I got changed, but I was early. I wanted to be with someone in football, so I left and went to Terry Venables' Scribes Club, which was next door to where I was working. There was one other guy in there and Nick the barman. I asked Nick if Terry was due in and he said he wasn't. The other guy wanted to talk, but I didn't. I sat there for ten minutes staring into my wine. Then, as if by magic, Terry walked in. We had a long chat about Mooro and it seemed to help. I still reckon Mooro sent him in.

I did the dinner and went home.

The response to Moore's death the next day was amazing. Some newspapers carried more than a dozen pages, and Upton Park was inundated with flowers. Only the Football Association let everyone down by refusing to put a statue of him up at Wembley. What a great ambassador he would have made had they used him.

Bobby was not just a model player, he was a terrific guy. I heard of only two occasions when he lost his cool, and these were both second hand. Once when I was doing a dinner, the guy I was sitting next to said that the most difficult bloke he ever met was Bobby Moore. I was flabbergasted. Later it turned out he was a bailiff. The second time was when he was out drinking with his Fulham team-mates near the end of his career. Somebody made a snide reference to the bracelet incident before the Mexican World Cup when he was arrested and held in Bogotá, Colombia, after being wrongly accused of stealing some jewellery. Apparently Mooro totally lost it and had to be dragged off the bloke.

I certainly never asked him about the bracelet, and he probably would not have gone into it had I done so. But I do recall him mentioning it once, and it again shows his dry sense of humour. It was at a Footballer of the Year dinner when he presented the trophy to Kenny Dalglish. The *Mail on Sunday* soccer writer Bob Cass made a brilliant speech, giving journalists several useful phrases to be used during the forthcoming World Cup in Spain, among them 'Atención, hombre loco', which was translated as 'Look out, here comes Jeff Powell [the *Mail* soccer writer]'. When Bob had finished and the presentation was announced, Mooro rose to present the trophy to Kenny. Mooro wasn't expected to speak, so everyone was stunned when he grabbed the microphone.

'I've got one other useful Spanish phrase for the World Cup,' he said. 'Bracelet gonno.'

The place erupted.

He may be gonno, but he'll never be forgotten. Mooro, we all wanted to be like you.

25. IS THAT PLAYER A TURKEY?

'The object of cricket is to hit the ball to one of the fielders. If you fail to do so you have to run up and down as a penance.'
    An Aussie 'helping' an American woman to understand cricket.

Armed with the information above, the American woman sat down and watched a game quite happily for a whole afternoon. In fact, to the uninitiated, the explanation is not without a certain logic. An Aussie mate, Barry Priem, whom I met in Brisbane in 1986, related this tale to me. We stayed in touch until he was tragically knocked down and killed by a car as he walked home from a party a few months after I last saw him in his home city in 1999. He was a nice bloke, and may have been pissed when he was killed. Let's hope so. RIP, mate.

Football has always been my first love but cricket comes up not far behind. I can't pretend that I understand it as well as football, and my cricket material is somewhat lessened by this fact, although I am getting better. My relationship with cricket can be compared to Franglais, that amusing mix of French and English invented by Miles Kington in the old *Punch* magazine. I've written a few Franglais articles myself in travel trade magazines from time to time. The point I'm making is that you can't write Franglais if you don't have at least a little knowledge of French. So it is with cricket and me. I love the sociability of cricket and the fact that the crowds still turn up to watch the opposition almost as much as their own team, and give generous applause to achievements on both sides. I actually wrote this chapter while watching the 2003 Ashes series in Australia.

Here I pause to pass on to you a piece of material given to me by an Aussie the other day when he heard I was also visiting their near neighbours, New Zealand. The Aussies joke about the Kiwis rather in the same way we have joked about the Irish for many years, and the Aussies are a good deal less politically correct than we are. I remember on my first visit Down Under listening to a radio phone-in programme which was full of racial stuff about Aborigines, and included a guy calling in and saying, ''Ere, Bruce, what do you call a Kiwi in a suit?

The defendant!' Seventeen years ago it was the first time I'd heard that gag. Anyway, this Aussie asked me if I knew the three most common lies in New Zealand. I confessed that I did not. 'Well, number one is "My father played for the All Blacks." Number two is "There is no Maori blood in my family." And number three is "It's all right, officer, I was just helping this sheep over the fence."'

Despite my admitted lack of knowledge, I am now as friendly with members of the cricket world as I am with those of the football world. Even my Petal was impressed at a party in Sydney when Richie Benaud came up to say hello to me. I like Richie a lot. He is a cricket workaholic. He produces endless material in the form of books and articles, and appears to commentate almost daily for twelve months in a year. He lives for half of the year in Australia and the rest of the time in Europe. He is likeable and very approachable, though people are sometimes put off by the fact that he doesn't smile a great deal. I know he likes my stuff and enjoys it because he has told me, and I know he means it. But this enjoyment doesn't seem to reach his face. When I'm working, it bugs me if I see someone not laughing with the others, and I tend to look at them often to see whether I've finally cracked them. It bugged me with Richie until I came to know him.

Snooker ace Alex 'Hurricane' Higgins was another case in point. At a Glenn Hoddle golf testimonial dinner he was just yards away from me, but he didn't crack once, even though everyone else was falling about. Afterwards, as we weed side by side, he started telling me jokes. So he must have enjoyed it, he just didn't show it.

It was in 1982 that I received a telephone call from one Captain Anthony Swainson (Royal Navy retd), the secretary of the famous cricket charity the Lord's Taverners. It was to prove almost as life changing as the Footballer of the Year dinner two years earlier. I insert the 'almost' because without that 1980 dinner the 1982 call would almost certainly not have happened. Then again, on reflection, it might have affected my future life even more . . . but enough of this navel gazing. Let's move on.

Let me tell you a little about Tony Swainson. He is an honest man to the point of bluntness, but he is also a kind and thoughtful person. Most important of all, he is not star-struck, and I can tell you, as I am now a trustee of the charity, that has not always been the case with some of his successors. As such, I believe he was certainly the best in his position in my time. A story that illustrates his blunt honesty occurred during Tim Rice's first term as president, in the days before the famous lyricist had been knighted. Tim is a great chap, totally without airs and graces and able to laugh at himself, which is refreshing in the egocentric world of show business. In view of what follows, this is just as well. He said to Tony, 'I've got a great cabaret lined up for the annual ball.' Tony looked doubtfully at his long-haired, almost bohemian president and asked who it was. 'David Essex,' Tim replied excitedly, and awaited the expected praise for pulling such a big name. He was to be disappointed. Tony was not impressed, and said he was far from sure about Essex's suitability. Tim persisted and promised Tony he would be fine and a big draw. After a lengthy conversation, Tony finally gave in. 'OK,' he said, 'as long as he doesn't sing "A Winter's Tale".'

'Don't you like that song?' asked Tim.

'No, I don't. It's bloody awful.'

'Er, Tony, you do know I wrote that song?'

Tony paused, perhaps slightly taken aback but not prepared to admit it. Eventually, he said, 'No, I didn't know you'd written it.' He paused again. 'But I still think it's bloody awful.'

Who can fail to warm to a man like that? Certainly not Tim, who tells the story against himself. But Tim comes out on top because not only did he get David Essex to sing the song as his second number, he also planted someone to request it as an encore later.

Tony asked me if I would be prepared to speak at the Lord's Taverners Spring Lunch, which would be held, like the Footballer of the Year dinner, in London's Café Royal. Although I was by that stage a good deal more confident in my ability, it became clear during the build-up that this was one of the significant events in London each year.

As usual before a major event, my mind was occupied for most of my waking hours. But I still had the proper job, and that stopped me dwelling on the lunch too much. In fact I was quite busy when the day came, and I left my office in Fleet Street a little later than I had planned. I knew that Ronnie Corbett, the Taverners' president that year, would not be attending, and that he would be replaced by one of my heroes, Harry Secombe. My fellow speakers were to be broadcaster Ted Moult and novelist and former MP Jeffrey Archer. Sadly, Ted shot himself in the study of his Derbyshire farm at a time when, as his widow Maria confided to me later, he was clearly not himself. When he was himself he was a jolly and engaging chap. He had come to fame as a contestant in the long-running radio programme *Brain of Britain*. Most people think he won it; in fact he came second, but he was so much fun on the programme that he was invited on to others, and he soon became a celebrity. At the time of our lunch he was appearing in a television advertisement for Everest double glazing which showed Ted dropping a white feather in front of a newly fitted window. As it floated gently down without deviation either to the left or the right, Ted explained why there was a complete lack of draught.

When I left my office and hailed a cab I still had two errands to perform, as I explained to the cabbie.

'I want to go to the Café Royal, but on the way I would like to go to Fleet Street to collect my new glasses and then on to any butcher's in Smithfield.'

'What do you want to go to Smithfield for, mate?' asked the cabbie as we pulled away.

'Well, I'm speaking at this highly important lunch, and as one of the other speakers is Ted Moult I want to drop a feather for a highly amusing joke.'

We pulled up at a butcher's, and I went in and asked for some turkey feathers.

'What do you want them for, mate?'

'Well, I'm speaking at this highly important lunch, and as one of the other speakers is Ted Moult I want to drop a feather for a highly amusing joke.'

Having listened carefully to me, he then told me he hadn't got any. We went elsewhere and tried again.

'What do you want them for, mate?'

'Well, I'm speaking at this highly important lunch, and as one of the other speakers is Ted Moult I want to drop a feather for a highly amusing joke.'

He hadn't got any either; nor had the third butcher we tried. By the time I eventually got hold of some I was quite late: I arrived just as they were going into lunch. At least I had my pocketful of feathers. I also had a cricket bat prop for a routine I had bought from Brian Robinson.

SHOOTS WIDE

When David Gower was captain of England, one of his bowlers asked
him, 'Do you want Gatting a little wider?'

'No,' Gower replied. 'Any wider and he'll burst.'

This lunch marked my first meeting with Ian Botham. He was the
Lord's Taverners Cricketer of the Year, and he'd turned up to receive
his award. He must have been the last one to do so because we don't
give it out now.

Ted Moult went first and did a gag about Everest. I was looking
forward to getting my feathers out as he had played into my hands. I
thought my joke was, after all, highly amusing. Archer went next and
spoke fairly well. Then he told a completely unfunny joke at the end
of which he mentioned Everest and dropped a few feathers. The
bastard!

I was sitting next to Harry Secombe. What a joy he was when my
turn came! Every time I got a laugh there would be a pause, he would
give that famous giggle again, and the audience would be off once
more. I probably had to scrap half my material. No wonder everyone
thought I'd gone well. When I sat down he enveloped me in a big bear
hug – and broke my new glasses! Years later, when I spoke at a tribute
dinner to him, I told the story. At the end I reached into my pocket
and gave him an invoice for my glasses.

It is only recently that I was shown the proposal form for my
Taverners membership. Harry had sponsored me, and on it he had
written, 'This man is magic – we must get him in the charity.'

LATEST SCORES

Inter Milan 1 Outa Rome 3

Leicester 0 Piggott 1

26. AS A GOALKEEPER, YOU MAKE A BLOODY GOOD CRICKETER!

'What this episode reveals, I fear, is the sad decline in the standards of the English barmaid.'

> E.W. Swanton, when asked whether he, as a custodian of cricket values, felt that Mike Gatting's alleged romantic fling with a barmaid revealed that standards had slipped

Soon after that lunch I started to play for the Tavs, and I've been lucky enough to do so around the world. I've played for them in Hong Kong, Florida, La Manga, Los Angeles and Kenya. I've bowled a wicket maiden on the Equator – something of which not many people can boast. Although it has to be said that in my case most people are more surprised by the wicket maiden part.

SHARP TACKLE

In my first game of the 2003 season for Bells Yew Green away to Outwood, it might be fair to say that my fielding was not yet into its usual mid-season sharpness. Our captain, Mark Beard, who as club treasurer is not generally noted for his humour, said to me, 'I've found out how to hide you in the field.'

'How?' I enquired.

'I'm bringing you on to bowl.'

In Florida in 1991, I got as close as I'll probably ever get to a hat-trick. Having taken a wicket, I awaited the arrival of the next man. In Taverners cricket you are not allowed to be out first ball, but this sporting gesture had clearly not been conveyed to the Floridian umpire. When the batsman hit his first ball straight to John Emburey, for some inexplicable reason he caught it when he should have dropped it. The batsman was halfway back to the pavilion before we persuaded the umpire to give a no-ball. The batsman returned, and promptly skied his second ball. Somewhere underneath it, though not too close, was author Leslie Thomas. He will, I'm sure, forgive me for saying that he has never been the sharpest fielder in the game. On top of this, he was at the time breaking in two new plastic hips. He kept waddling in, getting closer to the ball, and suddenly he fell forward and caught it. At this the batsman had to go for what I decided to call a Cat-trick. That trip was also memorable because I met Laura. We've hardly been apart since.

Our Hong Kong game came at the start of the first Gulf War in 1991. We were given tickets by Cathay Pacific's top man, Rod Eddington, who is now boss of British Airways. When the troubles started, all direct flights to Hong Kong were suddenly full, while those that touched down in Bahrain were virtually empty. We fielded an interesting team, just the bare eleven plus a lady manager. We had four current (then, at least) players – a very young Mark Ramprakash, Mike Roseberry, Mark Nicholas and John Emburey – and four ex-players: M.J.K. Smith (captain), Farokh Engineer, Butch White and Neil Durden-Smith. In case you don't recognise the last name, Neil is Judith Chalmers' husband and once played for Combined Services. He was a last-minute replacement, but I'm not sure for whom. Making up the numbers were three show business representatives: Tim Rice, Bill Wiggins (the man who became famous for squiring Joan Collins), and me. We were given a choice of which flight to go on, so we obviously went for the Bahrain option. It was a good move. We had the whole of the first-class cabin to ourselves both ways, and as we took off we made a toast. 'Here's to Saddam Hussein. We've always liked him'. We might not say that now.

A couple of years ago I met Rod Eddington again. He said straight away, 'I remember you and that wok joke.' I had done the cabaret at a ball out in Hong Kong, and he had remembered one of the gags I'd told there. Quasimodo comes home from work and Esmeralda's got the wok out. He says, 'Oh good, Esmeralda. I love Chinese food.' She says, 'Don't be a prat. I'm ironing your shirt.'

We had a great time in Hong Kong, as we did in La Manga. I had been in Portugal for a week with a friend who has the unfortunate name of Gerry Adams. We'd shared a room, which was a disaster. He would go straight to sleep and snore. I would eventually get off, but he would wake me at about three a.m. to tell me I was snoring. Then he would go straight back to sleep and snore. I flew back to Heathrow and then went straight up to Liverpool to speak at a farewell lunch for former Liverpool and Wales player Ian Rush, who was off to Italy.

Then I went back to Heathrow and joined up with the Taverners for the La Manga weekend. When we arrived at the complex I was looking forward to some decent and much-needed uninterrupted sleep, but was shattered to learn that we were again sharing. The fact that my 'roomie' was to be Geoff Hurst did not cheer me up. Ten years earlier I would have died for such a chance. I explained my previous week to Geoff, and he then proceeded to go over the top. 'I'm a great roomie,' he said. 'I'll get Martin Peters to fax you a reference . . .' On and on he went. Then he started running my bath and laying my towels out. Eventually I had to tell him to piss off. As it happened, neither of us ever got to bed before five, and neither of us ever made it to breakfast.

Los Angeles was a great experience too. I couldn't believe how many games of cricket were being played on the park there. For our last game, skipper Mike Denness promoted me well above my abilities to bat at number three. I looked in the book to see who was opening and found it was Brian Close and Chris Broad. I put my pads on, but I felt I would easily get through the Sunday edition of the *Los Angeles Times* before being called upon. As I settled into my seat I heard the sound of crashing timber. Some ex-pat fast bowler had taken Closey's middle stump out.

I walked nervously out past our square leg umpire, John Price ('Sport' to his friends).

'Christ, Sport,' I said, 'what chance have I got?'

'You should be all right, Cat,' he replied, ' 'cause you don't play down the line.'

I survived the rest of the over and then drilled a single. As I got to the non-striker's end, I remarked, 'Well, Sport, I've outscored Closey.'

'If you're planning to tell him, Cat,' he said, 'I should keep your box on.'

I scored eight before being caught at extra cover. And I didn't bother to tell Closey.

But the most memorable moment on any of my Taverners tours, was in Kenya. If you've never been on a safari in Kenya, I should tell you that you view the game from minibuses painted in zebra colours. In these vehicles the roof goes up and you can stand to watch the animals. The minute someone in one bus spots something interesting, they all gather round. It is hard to take a picture without getting a zebra bus in shot.

Part of our cabaret on tour was the brilliant double act of Richard Stilgoe and Peter Skellern. Peter had to miss our last show, so Richard wrote a sketch for the two of us to do. We were to play two elephants. I read it, and I have to admit I had my doubts. But the written word brought to life is another matter. 'Trust me, Cat,' said Richard. 'It will go well.' We performed it, and he was absolutely right. He has given me permission to reproduce it for your delight. In case it is not obvious, the straws are our trunks.

MC: These two elephants go into this waterhole . . .

Richard and Cat walk on with bottles of wine and straws. They suck.

Richard: Morning, Kenneth.
Cat: Morning, Daniel.

They have another suck.

Richard: Remember what we saw yesterday?
Cat: Nope. Not with my memory.
Richard: Neither do I.

And another suck.

Richard: Ssh. Look over there.
Cat: Where?
Richard: There. Beyond the bushes.
Cat: Oh yes. It's a Nissan.
Richard: No it's not. Look at the markings. It's a Micato's Toyota.
Cat: Are you sure?
Richard: 'Course I am. It's in the book. White body, three long dark patches on the sides.
Cat: There are two of them.
Richard: Look, they're putting their roofs up.
Cat: That shows they're pleased.
Richard: They're making that clicking noise.
Cat: That's not them. That's Pentaxes.
Richard: Pentaxes?
Cat: Little black things that live on their back.
Richard: Are they a pair?
Cat: Yeah. The female's the one in front.

Richard: How do you know?

Cat: Vanity mirror and velour upholstery.

Richard: Look!

Cat: What?

Richard: They're mating. The one at the back's driven into the back of the one in front.

They watch.

Richard: The young are born quickly, aren't they? They're all getting out.

Cat: They don't look nothing like the parents, do they?

Richard: They don't half fight.

Cat: I feel privileged to watch this.

Richard: It must have made a big difference for them having these Toyota reserves.

Cat: Yeah. They used to roam wild on the roads charging at each other.

Richard: They don't eat each other?

Cat: They do. When one of 'em dies they break it up and use it for spares.

Richard: Barbaric.

Cat: Uncivilised.

Richard: Disgusting. Here, we've been here ages. It's the giraffe's turn. Do you want a wash?

Cat: Good idea.

Exit, squirting each other with straws.

LATEST SCORES

Wrexham 1 Mendsam 2

Frankfurt 1 Chipolata 2

---

27. COULD THIS BE A RECORD?

'A goalkeeper is a goalkeeper because he can't play football.'

Ruud Gullit

When I started to earn money, I thought I had better get myself an agent.

In the 1970s – for once I haven't got the programme or the menu – I ran an evening for Townsend Thoresen's top travel agents at the old Talk of the Town restaurant/cabaret venue in London's Leicester Square. Marketing director Bryan Thompson wanted some suggestions for the star. We'd had Faith Brown the previous year when she was a big name. I always wanted Tommy Cooper, but Bryan was the one bloke in the world who didn't find him funny. No wonder I didn't always get on with him. The new double act of Lennie (Bennett) and Jerry (Stevens) had just started on TV. Based on the premise that our acts were booked at least in part for their fame as well as their ability, I suggested the 'curly-haired one', Lennie, as I thought he was a good comic, even if the show itself wasn't pulling up too many trees. We decided to book him, so I contacted his agent, Alan Field. Of all the agents I've met, I've always thought Alan came across as the straightest, and we have been great friends ever since. That night Lennie went down really well. In fact, I have never seen him go better. After my 1980 triumph, about which Alan, as a Spurs supporter, was well aware, I asked him if he would represent me.

After a couple of years I discovered that after-dinner speakers do not have dedicated agents. Instead, they work through a series of brokers, which is not ideal but is the only system at the moment. Most of them are straight, and it is useful from a booker's point of view because a replacement can be found in the event of sudden illness. However, I have come across one or two who have added 50 per cent – in one outrageous case, 100 per cent – to my fee. This means that these people are advertising me at a far higher fee than I would wish, but there is nothing that can be done about it. So if you do want to book a speaker, ask how much commission has been added. It should be taken out of their fee. After a year or two all my bookings seemed to be coming direct and not via Alan. When I told him that I felt it was best if we ended the agreement, he was, as usual, very decent about it, and it didn't stop him coming back to me with any opportunities he came across.

Alan was starting to become friendly with Laurence Marks and Maurice Gran, whose series *Shine on Harvey Moon* was going down well on TV at the time. Now, of course, they are famous for so many more, *Birds of a Feather* among them. These two Jewish guys are unusual in that they support Arsenal rather than Spurs. In fact, they are as fanatical about football as I am, and they were to be very helpful to me over the next few years.

One night I appeared at a Jewish function in north London and had to pick the evening up after a conjuror had died a death. In the audience was Ernest Maxim. He produced a lot of the *Morecambe and Wise* shows and was a brilliant choreographer as well. Among his many classics is the two boys' famous 'Singing in the Rain' routine. He came to see me after my show and said I was one of the funniest comics he'd ever seen. I was knocked out. Could this be my big break? He said he would send his brother Jerry, who was an agent, to watch me. Jerry came to Ealing Golf Club, but it didn't go well for me. I thought I'd blown it, but knowing the business, Jerry said it had been a terrible audience and that he would come again. He did, and this time I went well. He said they would get me a summer season in Great Yarmouth and wanted me to wear a pinstripe suit and a bowler hat. I'm always ready to try anything once, but I struggled to understand that. They also said they would put me on at Blazers nightclub in Watford and get some producers to come and see me.

I talked at length about this to Laurence, Maurice and Alan. They all said they didn't think it was right for me. They also worried about me going on at Blazers. 'You've got to be careful,' Alan cautioned, 'that you don't kill what you've got.' Then they took me to watch Jimmy Tarbuck at Blazers. The audience was largely coachloads of women from the water board and Jimmy was doing some of his 'bloomers gags'. 'Is this really you?' the three of them asked me. 'And you'll be stuck in digs in Yarmouth all summer. You'll hate it.' I decided they were right. I remained hugely flattered that someone of Ernest Maxim's pedigree had taken such an interest in me, but I decided to carry on along the path I had set.

Alan suggested a long-playing record (remember them?) of football jokes, and got in touch with a friend of his who ran Red Bus Records. Their representatives came up to Birmingham on 1 March 1982 (yes, I've got the menu) to watch me do the testimonial for the West Bromwich Albion centre-half John Wile. We met to discuss the script. I decided I would use some of my stuff but not a lot as I was worried about killing the live act. This material would be on the A side, and Laurence and Maurice would write something for the B side.

In my act at this time I was introducing silly fictitious players and names into the Old Wilsonians 7th XI. One was Ashley Easden, our centre-half and captain, whom I claimed was our only international 'because two years ago, in France, he had two of his teeth capped'. Ashley was a real person, a great big lumbering guy who was such a gentle giant that I can't ever remember him making a tackle. I chose Ashley because of his funny name. Whoever heard of a footballer called Ashley? (Apologies to Ashley Cole are in order here, I think.) Two others we created. Justin Fashanu was starring for Norwich City at the time, so I invented a black striker Justin Frontofhim, a centre-forward who 'couldn't hit a pig's arse with a handful of wheat'. Then we needed a manager. Dario seemed a funny name, as did Michael Caine's real surname, so Dario Micklewhite was born.

Prior to the 1982 World Cup in Spain, England went to play a friendly in Bilbao at a time when the Basque separatists were causing a lot of problems, so Laurence and Maurice wrote a letter (it's always a good comic device to read out a letter in a flat monotone voice) in which Dario is writing to me from a cave in the mountains. He had applied for the new England job when Ron Greenwood left and been told that he had got it. But it turned out they only took him along because they wanted an expendable person in case the Basques tried to kidnap someone. There is one especially good line in it where the doorman at the FA (who we claimed was the former Arsenal and QPR centre-half Terry Mancini) won't let Dario in for his interview. Dario says, 'So I dropped my left shoulder, sent him the wrong way, and went past him. Not a new experience for Terry.' Terry Mancini told me several years later that he loved that too.

Lots of famous football people were asked for quotes for the cover of the album, which in homage to the film *One Flew Over the Cuckoo's Nest* we called *One Flew Over the Bar*. I think the best was from

Chelsea centre-half Micky Droy: 'You're almost as funny as an FA tribunal.'

THROW-IN

Extract from Laurence Marks' book *A Fan for All Seasons*: 'It is a fun evening [the Footballer of the Year dinner in 1999], and the high point is meeting up again with Bob "the Cat" Bevan, a very old friend of Maurice and mine. Bob is one of the most popular after-dinner speakers on the soccer circuit, and what must be twelve years ago [it was actually seventeen years] we wrote some material for him for an album to be released at the time of the 1986 [1982, actually] World Cup finals.

'Immediately we meet, Bob starts rattling off topical jokes. One of the finest of the night was "I think this Robbie Fowler's been hard done by when he was suspended by the FA. I've been watching a video of his goal celebration after scoring against Everton [when he went on his hands and knees and started sniffing the white line] and it's pretty clear that the whole of his nose wasn't over the line – although Geoff Hurst said it was!"'

Incidentally, my mate Bobby Robson got the England job that year, and in my scrapbook I found the following letter he sent after I wrote to congratulate him.

Dear Bob,

From one Bob to another, many thanks indeed for your congratulatory letter on my appointment as the next England manager. I realise what an honour it is, and what a close decision it was between Dario Micklewhite and myself, but then he didn't know that you have to play cricket with Bert Millichip in order to get the job!

However, now that I am in command, the argument can no longer be between Shilts or Clemence, but that Bevan plays and the other two stand by. Look out for my first selection.

Kind regards, and best wishes,
Bobby Robson

He never picked me, the swine. Do you think I could sue?

I have always hated canned laughter, but reluctantly agreed to some for the LP, and we recorded it in a studio with a few friends. On it you can hear some of the biggest over-acting (in laughter terms) coming from my mate Roger Kitter. You have seen him in *'Allo, 'Allo*, starring with Jim Davidson, and much more. But I have to be honest: I can listen to the tape of the FWA dinner in 1980, but I have never been able to bring myself to listen to the album all the way through. Clearly it was a good deal better than I thought because for years Adrian Juste played clips from it on Radio 2. My OW team-mates were forever turning up at games saying, 'You were on the radio on the way here.' It didn't stop them giving me stick though.

OFFSIDE

I was in Toronto on a business trip a couple of years after I made the LP. With a colleague, I passed a record store claiming to be the world's biggest, to be the home of every record. We went in and asked for *One Flew Over the Bar* by Bob 'the Cat' Bevan. I told him it was on the Red Bus Record label, number LP1002. He went away and, after a long time, came back to admit that they had not got it, but could order it.

'OK,' I said.

'What's it called again? *One Flew Over the Bus*?'

I patiently spelt it all out again. I wonder if it's in yet?

I think it might have been New Year's Day 1988, but I could be wrong, when I sank into my British Airways seat en route to South Africa. I was suffering, having been to my mate Lennie Lawrence's New Year's Eve party. The hangover was also masking the fact that I was going down with the flu. I put on my headphones and had a very strange experience. My voice was coming out of them. It took me some time to work it out. Had I put my Walkman on by mistake? No, even I don't go around listening to myself on tape. Eventually, legendary American Comedian Bob Newhart came on. I opened up the in-flight magazine and found that my LP was on the BA comedy channel. By coincidence, my headphones had been tuned into it. It seemed amazing that I should be there alongside Bill Cosby, Ben Elton and many other big names. Quite what the Americans thought of it I can't imagine, but it must have gone down well because I would be on BA twice more until it became too out of date even for them. It included a line about Terry Neill being manager of Arsenal – that's how old it was. In the early 1980s, Arsenal were known as being boring. There were loads of nil-nil draws. At that time I needed a football pitch for a publicity shot so I called Terry one morning soon after the end of the season and asked him if the posts were still up. He said, 'They haven't been up all season. We haven't needed 'em.' Not a bad line.

We recorded the LP after I had finished work on the evening of 19 December 1982. I remember the date for the saddest of reasons. On my way home I switched on the car radio for the news and heard that one of our freighters, *European Gateway*, had capsized off Felixstowe after a collision and six people had died. In the days before mobile telephones, my number two, Paul Ellis, had been lumbered with all the press calls, as I found out when I called him on my arrival home at 1.30 a.m. As I was often out and he was a family man, he frequently got the short straw on such occasions. Perhaps the man upstairs had decided that I'd done my stuff with the Basle air crash.

'I'LL TELL 'EM YOU'RE THE DUKE OF KENT'

PHILLIP AND QUEEN IN BRAWL AT PALACE

> Sports headline about a match at Crystal Palace
> featuring Gerry Queen and Ian Phillip

My first encounter with a royal was back in 1979. Townsend Thoresen had a new terminal to open at Felixstowe. It was decided that we would ask Princess Anne to do the honours. To our surprise, she agreed, even though the date was just six weeks away.

Charged with organising this event, I was put in touch with her private secretary, a Major Nigel Lawson (no, not that one). I was due to meet him at Buckingham Palace one freezing, snowy winter's morning. I was feeling rough with a heavy cold and might have sneaked a day off but for this important meeting. At the allotted time I hailed a cab outside my Fleet Street office.

'Where to, mate?'

I contrasted his heavy London accent with a rather posh one. 'Buckingham Palace, please.'

'Whereabouts, mate? Out the front or wot?'

'No,' I replied, becoming even more pompous, 'just go to the gate and we'll take it from there.'

Due to the weather the journey was slow and he was a chatty driver. It turned out that he played for Mill Hill Village, a team in our league, and we worked out that we must have played against each other. By now my accent had reverted to the dropped aitches and we had become mates.

When we arrived at the palace it was coming up to the Changing of the Guard and the railings were packed with tourists – largely, as far as we could see, Japanese. In those days vehicles were still allowed through the gates, so we drove up, gave my name to the policeman and pulled into the courtyard in front of one of the big doors, in full view of the crowd. As I got out I looked back at the Japs peering through the railings.

'Look at that lot,' said my new friend. 'I bet they all wonder who you are.'

'I suppose they do,' I said.

'Tell you what,' he said. 'When I drive out I'll tell 'em you're the Duke of Kent.'

Major Lawson was seated behind an extraordinary desk of multi-coloured wood. You didn't need to be told it was African. As an icebreaker, I asked about it. He told me it had been given to the Princess by some African potentate and that she believed in trying to use at least some of the thousands of gifts given to the royals each year. This led to a conversation that is now of particular significance, given the collapsed trial of Princess Diana's butler Paul Burell and the subsequent investigation into Prince Charles's office about the selling off of gifts. It hadn't occurred to me before that over the years the royal family must have accumulated mountains of strange presents.

'I suppose you have a sale every so often?' I ventured.

Major Lawson looked at me over his glasses with some disdain and explained that they couldn't possibly sell them off. They had to be catalogued and produced at the right moment in case one of the donors arrived for a visit. Rather like hiding one girlfriend's picture when another came round, I thought, but decided not to say it. 'Sometimes,' he continued, 'they ask to borrow the gift back for an exhibition.' I was getting the picture. Imagine that happening and Her Majesty having to say they'd sent it to the jumble.

'So what happens to them all?' I asked.

There are, in fact, warehouses all over the place holding all of it. Its cumulative value could probably clear Third World debt.

THROW-IN

Here's a topical gag I wrote at the time of the Paul Burrell story and Princess Anne being taken to court after her dog attacked some Asian kids: 'When Princess Anne went to court everyone expected the dog to be put down, as would happen in most such cases. The judge was just pulling on his black cap when he had a call from the palace. Apparently, the Queen had suddenly remembered that she'd had a meeting with the dog and had said it would be all right if it attacked a few kids.'

It's extraordinary how the arrival of a royal gets everyone moving. Extra little decoration touches, which the PR man had suggested for the new building but which had been ruled out by budgets, were suddenly now affordable. Moreover, even the most confident executive found himself getting nervous about what to say and how to behave. For once, even our chairman, Keith Wickenden, was looking to me for guidance.

Major Lawson had loaned me a book, which was a great help, and I had to admire the thoroughness of their PR set-up. It even told you what to do when travelling in a lift with royal personages. Apparently, you should let them get in first, then you should manoeuvre yourself into a position that allowed them to get out first. However, if the lift is so small as to make this impossible, it is acceptable for those blocking the royal passage to get out first and then stand back. It was all there, in print.

Before the day, security had to be checked out. Inspector Jim Beaton was the Princess's man and I met him at Felixstowe one morning. He had been with her when someone had tried to kidnap her in The Mall. He had been shot for his pains, as had a journalist, Brian McConnell, who'd been passing by and had gone to help. By coincidence, Brian was a drinking pal of mine in El Vino's. After the Felixstowe event was all over, the three of us met several times for lunch, and although Jim was discreet, he did give us some insight into the lives of the royals. And, after our event had been declared a success, he told us that that would help if we ever approached them again. 'Like any other family, they all sit round, have a chat and tell one another about good dos and bad ones,' he said.

But back to Felixstowe, checking for possible security risks and, most important of all, locating suitable places for the royal to visit a toilet when required. Suddenly the budgets were torn up again and every loo in the vicinity was emulsioned. After half an hour the place was full of uniformed officers, most of them wearing gold braid. Every senior policeman in the area had arrived to greet the royal rozzer and get in on the act. As they hung around, I suddenly realised I was supposed to entertain them to lunch. When we got to a local hotel no fewer than eleven of us sat down to what turned out to be a long lunch. Burglars must have been very active that day. Jim has now retired and lives in Yorkshire, but I spoke to him not long ago, and without any prompting from me he recalled the day I got stung for all these lunches.

Before long, the big day arrived. Several hundred guests were drinking coffee and jabbering away in the lounge of the new terminal when the big car swept up in front of the building. The Princess got out, wearing a very attractive green outfit, and the chairman greeted her and led her into the building. As she entered, the noise stopped instantly. Nobody so much as coughed. It was quite spooky, and I realised for the first time what an impact the royals made. In show business they call it 'star quality', and Anne certainly had it.

At that time she was getting plenty of stick in the press, for being both brusque and a bit horsey. So it came as a surprise to see that she was not especially tall and very attractive and feminine. It also turned out that she was a good sport.

Keith was always an unguided missile. He could be a PR man's nightmare. He would never prepare speeches so I was unable to provide the press with the transcripts they were always asking for. That day, too, he would be speaking off the cuff. It had turned out that the new terminal was the site of his station when he was in the RAF, so it was quite clearly something for someone to go back and buy up their old barracks. In fact, we'd got a story about it into the *Daily Telegraph*. As Keith stepped forward towards the plaque, he announced to a stunned audience, 'The last time I attended an unveiling ceremony on this spot an airman had fixed a picture of a lady in a state of undress on the plaque underneath the curtain. She was revealed to us all when the Air Vice Marshal performed the ceremony.' If he was hoping for a big laugh, he didn't get it. There were a few chuckles, but many more anxious glances towards the Princess. She gave a rather thin smile before a chastened Keith asked her to perform the ceremony. She went to the mike. 'I would like to thank Mr Wickenden for this kind invitation,' she said, before turning to him with a much warmer smile and adding, 'I must say I now view this ceremony with even more nervousness than I did before.' It might not have been her funniest-ever line, but a relieved audience roared. Keith relaxed, and for the rest of the day everyone, including her, was in a great mood.

The mood wasn't even broken when she was getting in and out of a car in pouring rain in order to greet dockers who had lined up to meet her. The local managing director had suggested that, as it was so wet, she should stay in the car. 'But aren't these people all waiting to meet me?' she asked. On being told that they were, she insisted that she would get out at every stop. There weren't many anti-royals around by the time she left.

In the late 1980s I had a three- or four-year relationship with a lady called Sally Woodward. Her father was Sir William Pillar, the Governor of Jersey. (I called him Sir Bill.) Sadly, both are no longer with us. He was a great chap who had risen from being a Royal Navy engineer to the rank of admiral. It's quite unusual for an engineer to climb this high. At one point he was Fourth Sea Lord and also head of the Centre for Military Studies – a very high-powered training centre that attracted future chief constables and similar senior figures in defence from all over the world as well as the United Kingdom.

THROW-IN

One of those tales you just hope is true. During the war, so the story goes, an admiral was caught in a compromising position on New Year's Eve in St James's Park with a lady of ill repute. When it was reported to Churchill, he allegedly said, 'Now let me get this straight. Seventy-five years old, five degrees of frost – it makes you proud to be British.'

One of Sir Bill's 'students' was John Stalker, the former deputy chief constable of Manchester, who was sent to Northern Ireland to report on the 'shoot to kill' policy. When Stalker came back with a politically sensitive report, he was linked with another man who had alleged criminal contacts. In the end they were exonerated from any wrongdoing, but not before Stalker's career had been ended and the friend ruined. Sir Bill spoke highly of Stalker and said that he had not the slightest doubt that he had been truthful and honourable throughout.

Sir Bill, being the Queen's representative on Jersey, was like a minor, temporary royal, so when Sally and I went to Government House for Christmas one year it was an interesting insight for me into what life was like for them. A butler didn't go as far as squeezing my toothpaste but he did clean my shoes, bring me tea in the morning and run my bath. You didn't even get up to pull the curtains as dusk fell. A maid arrived to do it for you.

Sir Bill and his wife – 'Lady P' I called her; I couldn't bring myself to call her Ursula – had hosted extended visits by most of the royals and seen them at close quarters for a longer period than most. He told me that he liked Prince Charles, and that he thought Sarah Ferguson was great fun, but he had not taken to Prince Andrew. He also felt that for all Andrew's publicity about flying in the Falklands, where to be fair he had put his life on the line, Charles was the better pilot because he was more prepared to listen to and learn from his instructors.

It was most unlike Sir Bill to speak ill of anyone, but I put it to the back of my mind when I was asked to speak at a charity lunch with Andrew at the Café Royal for the National Sporting Club. My friend David Willis introduced me to him on the day. Andrew fixed me with a fairly blank stare. 'So what do you do, where and why?' he said. It was an odd sentence that might have been friendly had it been said with any humour, but it wasn't. During the lunch he was opposite me on a large oval-top table that seated about twenty. For the meal he was quite jolly. At one point he asked me if I was going to do any blue stuff. I told him that that wasn't my style, and that even if it was it would not be fair to him as everyone would look at him for his reaction. He ignored my courteous point and told a rather off-colour story. After the speeches he got up and went without saying goodbye to any of us.

How different was his brother Edward. He was president of the Lord's Taverners for two years and turned up at quite a few functions. I thought he was a nice man, and rather shy. As it was pre-Sophie, I also thought he was rather a lonely figure. Once, during a lunch at the pre-Wimbledon tennis tournament at the Queen's Club, I noticed he was left standing on his own. Laura was at the time the Lady Taverners chairman and I felt that, as a trustee and her partner, I should do my duty. But what do you talk to the royal family about? You can't say 'How's your mum?' or 'Been up the Palace lately? They're not playing too well, are they?' Still, knowing that there was a real tennis court there and that it was his favourite game, I wandered over and asked him if he had played there. He became quite animated and took me into the court to tell me in some detail how the game was played. I was none the wiser afterwards – it's very complicated – but at least he was doing all the talking and I didn't have to think much. He also attended the Lady Taverners Ball and made an impromptu and very funny speech that included a reference to God, 'although you would know her as the Queen'. I feel sad that he gets so much stick as under it all he is a really nice bloke.

His father is certainly the best value of the lot. I know he makes the odd gaffe, but I genuinely think he's only trying to be friendly. To break the ice. At over 80 years of age political correctness seems to have come too late for him.

FREE-KICK
'I was wondering who the hell he was talking about' – the Duke of Edinburgh, after listening to a list of his own achievements on receiving an honorary doctorate.

My first encounter with the Duke of Edinburgh was at a 1985 Variety Club lunch in his honour at which I was to speak with Frank Carson and Frankie Howerd. It was a nerve-racking day for me. Apart from it being my debut speaking in front of a royal, I had also just broken up with my then girlfriend Gaby. She was sixteen years younger than me and had clearly got through the older man syndrome. We still loved each other but it was time to move on, and it was upsetting for both of us. Although she hated these occasions, I had accepted on behalf of both of us before the split and she gamely insisted on keeping the date. It might have been better if she hadn't.

Frank Carson was down to go first. I wasn't too bothered as I had worked with him in Canada once when he didn't do so well. Looking back, I think it was because he was trying some new material. However, at this lunch he was sensational. He brought the house down, which made Frankie Howerd, who was on next, even more nervous than usual.

Frankie's first line was his best. The toastmaster said, 'And now, Mr Frankie Howerd.' In a prearranged ploy, Frankie did not get up; instead, he beckoned the toastmaster towards him. The toastmaster leant over him, then returned to the mike and said, 'And now, Mr Frankie Howerd OBE.' Frankie stood up and said, 'That's better. I may not be as funny but I'm better class.' After that he wasn't that funny and died a death.

My turn. Nervous, emotional and having to pick up a flat audience. I did OK, just about, but I definitely got the silver medal rather than the gold I was hoping for. Still, as he left, the Duke of Edinburgh went round behind me and said, 'Cheerio – very good,' which I greatly appreciated.

Afterwards, Gaby and I went for a walk. It was upsetting to see each other again, and we parted after a few more tears. We have never met since. I do know she is married with two children, and I hope she is happy and fulfilled.

The Duke was to feature quite often at events I attended, not least because he is the patron and twelfth man of the Lord's Taverners. Thirteen years after that Variety Club lunch, for instance, Laura and I were invited to a garden party at Buckingham Palace. We got into all the gear – top hat, tails, the lot. We also had a message to make ourselves known to an equerry who would introduce us to the Duke. Only one other Taverner was invited: Ken Lawrence, the former chairman.

I looked, if I may say so, pretty sharp, and we got a cab through the pouring rain. Fortunately, it had stopped by the time we joined the queue outside the palace. It's quicker by the side entrances, but we wanted to go through the front. It's all very well organised, although you have to be patient. It's a nice touch that when you eventually get to the door an elderly Chelsea Pensioner takes your ticket.

We got called to one side in the Bow Room and hung around there. Ken Lawrence and his wife joined us, then the first of many equerries came to tell us what was happening. He was a jolly chap with a ready smile, but when Courtauld, the temporary equerry who had written to Laura, appeared, he seemed rather pompous and talked down to us as we got our instructions about being led out in single file. Mind you, it was a plus, as by now several thousand were lined up to await the Queen. We got a few glances, as befits the chosen few. I had to stop Laura from thumbing her nose.

We then got positioned in little groups to await the Duke. We stood in the same place for about an hour and watched with some amusement as the equerries poked the odd person out of the way with their umbrellas as their particular royal was moved down among the groups. When the Duke appeared, resplendent in a very long silk top hat which made him look a good deal taller than he is, he clearly had no idea who any of us were or what we did. I didn't, of course, expect him to remember me, but I told him I had done the *Six O Six* phone-in on Radio 5 and had frequently been on *Auntie's Sporting Bloomers* with Terry Wogan, but he said he must have missed them. 'I'm always out when these things are on.' I thought Ken might be distraught at his non-recognition, but he took it well.

All in all we had a smashing afternoon. After the Duke wandered off, we went for a walk round the lake. The gardens are huge; the whole site is some 40 acres. I asked if a mallard was the Duck of Edinburgh, and someone who overheard me suggested my head ought to be put on a spike. We spotted Tom (now Lord) Pendry, Lord St John Stevas, the Lord Chancellor and actor Geoffrey Palmer. The whole thing was very British and riddled with class.

First there was the mob.

Then there was us lot who got singled out to be chatted to by a royal.

Then there was the royal tea tent, away from which the crowds are kept at a distance of about 75 yards.

PLAY STOPPED – INDIAN ON THE PITCH

In my local village cricket team is an Indian newsagent called Sunil Patel. He had been invited to a Buckingham Palace garden party the week before us in recognition of his work on behalf of the Indian community. I was to reflect on the extremes in my life the night after the garden party as I lay on the straw mats in the back of Sunil's delivery van. Along with a whole crowd of club members, I was on my way to the East End of London for our annual curry in the now quite famous Lahore Kebab House. It's nothing like the normal kebab house, just a basic Pakistani restaurant with excellent food. After a few beers in a pub we headed off for our meal, armed with a slab of beer (the Lahore Kebab House is unlicensed). We ate like kings for a tenner, and the beer whip was a fiver. Sunil and I reflected on the change in circumstances: the day before – in his case, eight days before – at Buckingham Palace, then rolling around in the back of a van. As I arrived home I wondered what Prince Philip had got up to that evening.

After trying the tea – which I have to say was rather good, with tiny sandwiches, nice cakes, ice creams and, a new discovery for me, iced coffee, which was wonderful – we went to gawp at the royal tent. There was the Queen, Prince Charles, Princess Alexandra and the dear old Queen Mum. She wobbled off to her car to great applause. She was only 98 then. The day ended as it had begun with the National Anthem, and we all trooped out. A great institution, and in some ways I felt I had been to something very British. For all the mickey-taking about such things, I doubt there was anyone who regretted being there. Even Tony Blair – only in a lounge suit, I noticed – was beaming as he left with Cherie.

We met Richard Stilgoe on the way out and went off to Langan's to have a glass of champagne. Laura and I stayed on for dinner, and to pose in our finery. Sadly, we saw hardly anyone we knew.

Despite his understandable failure to recognise me, in my book the Duke has always been quite jolly to talk to and he genuinely seems to enjoy Taverners events. In recent years I have come to the conclusion that what he probably really likes is a night out with the blokes.

In 1999, when the Taverners had their 50th anniversary, they held a dinner in his honour at the Savoy. It was black tie and men only. About 300 attended, and the speakers were told they had to 'roast the Duke' (in this context the expression 'to roast' means 'to give some stick to'). Now, this is not easy. At the Royal Variety Show these days they seem to go all the way with poor taste and lavatorial humour, but I think that shows a complete lack of respect to the royals who turn up and probably hate the evening even more as a result. It also shows a lack of professionalism on the artists' part.

At this Taverners dinner the other speakers were to be the late John Bromley (former Head of Sport at ITV, known to me as Brommers), Sir David Frost, Robert Powell (the president), Sir Tim Rice, Barry Cryer and myself. Desperate to find something new, I agonised over what I was going to do. A poem crossed my mind, but still the angle wouldn't come. I woke up at about three one morning and couldn't get back to sleep. It was then it came to me. For all the times I had met him, he still hadn't got the foggiest idea who I was. I got up and wrote the poem there and then, and added a couple of verses in the days to come, one at the suggestion of my mate Robbo. He also came up with the Palace line.

As Barry Cryer often went into verse, I thought I had better ring and tell him of my plans. I read the poem to him, he thought it was great, and he thanked me for calling him. On the day Barry caught flu and had to drop out, so as it turned out I was the only roaster as Brommers and the others chickened out of taking the piss.

There is a major problem with writing something original for a special occasion: you only get one chance to use it, and if it's a poem, you need an escape route if it starts to die. So I was nervous when I stood up; when I sat down, I can be heard saying quite clearly on the video, 'Thank God for that.' I'm pleased to say it went well. The full script is as follows:

When I was given my brief for this evening by our chief executive, Mark Williams, he told me we were roasting the twelfth man, which is all a bit difficult really, and many of you may feel I look a bit out of place on this top table. You may also feel that our guest of honour and I have little in common. Well, you'd be wrong. I mean, only last Saturday I was up the Palace. We beat Tranmere 3–2.

I first met the twelfth man (he is Patron and Twelfth Man of the Taverners) seventeen years ago, and I've met him about a dozen times since. Now it would be fair to say that all those meetings have been far more memorable for me than they appear to have been for him. So, with this in mind, I've written this song. Well, it would have been a song, but the music hasn't turned up. Lloyd Webber and deadlines are not twin brothers. Do you find that, Tim? Always lets you down. So now it's a poem, and I've called it, with apologies to Rodgers and Hammerstein, and Tim Rice – and, by the time I've finished, probably everyone else in the room – 'The Duke and I'.

I'd like to test our twelfth man's memory.
We first met back in 1983 [actually 1985, but that doesn't
   rhyme!].
He knew Frankie Howerd and Frank Carson,
He'd even heard of Nicholas Parsons,
But he didn't recognise me.

The Variety Club is another good cause,
I spoke in his honour and drew some applause,
And as he started to go
He did say 'Cheerio',
But I don't think he knew who I was.

I went to Windsor, which is a bit of a hike –
Too far to go on me bike.
I commentated after tea,
Then, as he walked by me,
I heard him say, 'Who's that bloke on the mike?'

Soon after, though I was full of flu,
I struggled out to another Taverners do.
I bided my time
As he walked down the line.
He looked at me and said, 'Who are you?'

Last year at a garden party
I said, 'You must remember me.
Six O Six on Radio 5,
With Wogan on live?'
He said, 'I'm sorry, I never watch TV.'

I said, 'At the risk of being a bore,
I've just been on Radio 4.'
He said, 'I've thought long and well
But you just don't ring a bell.
Perhaps I should get out a bit more?'

Well, he's been a Tav for all our lifespan,
So he's got 50 years in the can.
I said to my lady, 'To us he's been vital,
And it's an honourable title,'
Then I found out I'd been her twelfth man.

It's thanks to him the Tavs have never been on the skids.
At auctions he's led us to make silly bids,
For when he's turned up at a dinner
He's been a real winner,
And he's even sent round the kids.

A Greek friend last week I had to rebuke.
I said, 'His popularity isn't a fluke.
And while we might give in
On the marbles of Elgin,
We'd like to hang on to the Duke.'

Well, I'm so glad we've all had this chat
And my little poem has not fallen too flat.
I hope, sir, that you are glad you came,
And just remember the name:
It's Bob Bevan – but you can call me Cat.

There's a postscript:

So as I come to the end of my shift
And into the night we all drift,
I know, sir, you've got the use of a car
And, as neither of us live far,
I suppose there's no chance . . .

You have to be fair to the Duke. He had no prior knowledge of who was going to say what, but he came back with something for each of the speakers. In my case it was, 'Incidentally, if you want a lift home I ought to tell you I came in a metro cab. You won't know what one of those is . . . no, I didn't think so.' He also told a quite risqué story about a new gents toilet in the Garrick Club. 'Everyone was getting a bit concerned about the old-fashioned troughs, so it was decided that they would install one of the then modern stalls, all enamel and porcelain. When it was fitted it was decided that the oldest member in the club should be given the honour of inaugurating it. So we all went down to the gents to watch this "ceremony".

'When he'd finished, we said, "Well, what do you make of it, then?"
' "I don't know," he replied. "It makes your cock look a bit shabby." '

During the summer of 2000 I went to Windsor to play cricket for the Taverners in the presence of the Duke. Chris Tarrant was due to be the auctioneer, but he dropped out at short notice so I was asked to stand in and was moved to the Duke's table. I knew he had enjoyed the evening at the Savoy, and especially the poem, so I waited to see if he referred to it. Although he was only three seats away on the round table and we chatted away quite happily, he gave no indication that he knew me.

To date, the penultimate time I was with him was in March 2002 at a Water Rats dinner at our pub in King's Cross. There were just 70 of us in the room so it was an even more informal evening than the Savoy. Once again he appeared to love it all. Along with the Bachelors, a banjo player called Steve Galler, comic Johnnie Casson and the amazing dancers the Clark Brothers, I was in the cabaret and I rewrote some of the poem and did a few new gags as well. Before that, during the meal, several of the company had stood up and done a gag or two, including the Duke. He came up with two good stories.

He told of a time in the late 1940s soon after he was married. 'The Queen, then Princess Elizabeth, and I paid a visit to the United States at around the time when Winston Churchill had won the election to get back into power. Harry Truman was US President and his mother, who was a bit gaga, was installed in a flat at the top of the White House. Out of courtesy, we went up to see her.

'She said to the Queen, "It's very nice to see you, my dear, and I'm so pleased that your father has been re-elected."

'The Queen replied, "Well, that's very kind of you, but in fact it wasn't my father, it was Winston Churchill."

'Whereupon Truman's mother turned to me and said, "Oh, congratulations!" As there was no point in trying to explain further, we thanked her and left.'

He also told of a time when he was trying to promote electric-powered vehicles. 'I had one I used to use to go round London in. It was a big green thing with no windows and looked rather like a van. I wasn't driving it, and every time I went to the Savoy those chaps outside in top hats would always try and wave us on. They looked a bit sheepish when I clambered out.'

At the end of the evening, the King Rat, scriptwriter and entertainer Keith Simmons, came up with a good wheeze. He said that he and his wife had been to a Buckingham Palace garden party and had taken a picture of the lake – something which strictly speaking you are not supposed to do. He said, 'I've had this framed and I thought you might like it, sir. As you are about to hold a couple of pop concerts it may be the last time you see the gardens in good nick!' He then went on to thank the Duke for coming. 'And in this special year of the Queen's Golden Jubilee I hope when you go home, sir, you will give Her Majesty our love.' The Duke was straight back in, phrasing his words so that we would be in no doubt as to what he meant. 'I certainly will,' he said, 'but not tonight!'

I'm told he can be a bit tricky and a bit moody, but I have to say that in more than a dozen meetings he has always been great value.

At the end of 2002, the Toastmasters decided to hold a lunch in honour of the Queen's Golden Jubilee, and the Duke consented to pitch up after it was agreed that the bulk of the money would go to Commonwealth servicemen's charities (the rest would go to the Grand Order of Water Rats for providing the entertainment). Three speakers were approached – Barry Cryer, Roger de Courcey with Nookie Bear, and me – and we were due to 'roast' Roy Hudd. However, as Roy was filming for *Coronation Street*, Jim Davidson stepped in. This made the material easier, not least because of Jim's four marriages. I said that I had last spoken at the annual reunion dinner of Jim's ex-wives. 'This was held in the Great Room of the Grosvenor House [the audience got this quicker than I'd expected, and there was a big laugh]. He took me down the line introducing me to them all. He has pet names for each of them. For example, he calls one of them "Marinade" because she left him overnight.'

Before the lunch, the Duke came into the reception and we shook hands.

'I'm pleased to see you're wearing your [Water Rat] emblem, sir,' I said. 'I have sometimes caught you without it.'

'I can't always remember these things,' he said. And then came the defining moment. 'Anyway,' he added, 'you speaking today?'

28. WE COULD GET TO THE FINAL

QUESTIONABLE DECISION
What have the following teams got in common: Blackburn Olympic, Bradford City, Bury, Coventry City, Ipswich Town, Old Carthusians, the Wanderers and Wimbledon?

You will remember that Keith Wickenden once bought an airline without telling the rest of his board. Nice man though he was, doing PR for him was not a bed of roses. Because I was always trying to be cautious about what he said, he often failed to contact me when he should have done. He had a rather protective secretary, Margaret Neville, who managed to make herself unpopular with many of the other directors. She could be difficult at work, but she was a good-looking girl with a great figure. She was also good fun, as I discovered when we had a fling for a few months and nobody ever found out.

One day I arrived in the office to a barrage of telephone calls from the City pages of the national papers. They were asking about a story in *Lloyd's List*. I wouldn't speak to anyone until I had seen it. I picked up my old newspaper to find that Keith had given someone an interview and had said we would be building new ships to the value of £100 million. Twenty years ago, that was an amazing figure, not least for a company that had grown from five ships to twenty in about ten years. Nobody else knew about it, and as the City hates major expenditure, it drove the shares down. Moreover, any price-sensitive information such as this must be declared in advance to the Stock Exchange. Keith denied that he'd said it, but when I spoke to the journalist, whom I knew well, he said, 'Honestly, Bob. He did say it. I'll bring round my notes.' I told him he didn't need to, but that unfortunately it would have to be denied, so I hoped it wouldn't cause him any problems with his editor. I had no doubt that Keith *had* said it.

Keith was such a kind man that had he realised the implications for the journalist he might have been more careful. In fact, he certainly would have been. But he seemed sometimes to treat the company's money as though it were his own entrepreneurial kitty. Ever since he'd become chairman he'd been like a kid in a sweetshop. He could never get over the public image he had built up. He even put money into airships, which clearly did not please Ken Siddle, even though he steadfastly refused to admit it to me. I should say that faced with these eventualities I was very much in Ken's corner, but I had observed plenty of PR men who'd taken sides in such corporate divisions, chosen the wrong one and perished. I managed to steer a sufficiently middle course to avoid such problems.

Airships were one of those ideas that were always being put forward, but usually by mad professor-type people, so once again the share price dipped. Another investment that left us cold was when Keith decided to partially back a bid for the new ITV franchise in the south. In fact, a guy called James Gatward who was running the application was actually given space in Keith's office. It was felt that they had no chance, but against all the odds they did win the franchise, and I was left to deal with the publicity for TVS on Boxing Day, of all days, when it was announced. TVS eventually got into a bit of trouble by spending too much on old films, but at least this was one of Keith's investments that did pay off, if only temporarily.

Keith's biggest jump was into property at a time when the market was quite volatile. Two surveyors came to him for backing, Paul Norman and Irving Scholar, the latter a real Spurs fan even when he was penniless and who was later to become chairman of his favourite team. Sadly, Scholar's tenure was not an ultimately successful one, and I was surprised that he later got involved with Nottingham Forest, although that too ended after a short time. Keith agreed to back them, and they called their company Townsend Thoresen Properties. This, too, was against all our wishes as it played havoc with the branding of the car ferry division.

It did get us off the hook once, however. The one bad year the ferries had was when the nationalised Sealink started a price war. For a private company to get involved in such a fight is a disaster. Ultimately, Sealink had a bottomless pit; we did not. TT Properties came to the rescue by making a £15 million profit on one building in Holborn. Eventually, though, Paul and Irving cashed in their chips and left for Monte Carlo to keep a respectful distance from the taxman. Thus encouraged, however, Keith got involved in property in Denver and Atlanta, which would ultimately spell the end for the European Ferries group.

But there was one investment that was to give me one of the greatest experiences of my life. Keith had become deputy chairman of Brighton and Hove Albion. Chairman at the time was the late Mike Bamber, a self-made millionaire who – as Lord Runcie said of the legendary cricket writer E.W. (Jim) Swanton, at his memorial service – was not a man plagued by self-doubt. Keith did not invest any of the company money in the football club, but Mike was instrumental in his buying the La Manga Golf complex in Spain. An American called Greg Peters had found this site and decided that he could build luxurious villas around the two golf courses and sell them to Hollywood stars. In the event, only Debbie Reynolds bought one.

Yet again the board was unhappy, not least Ken. We were in the middle of a dispute with the ferry crews, who wanted another £10,000 a year for cleaning an ashtray or something. The personnel people were plunged into these difficult negotiations and pleading poverty was not easy when the press were carrying stories about us paying £6 million for a couple of Spanish golf courses. Not that Mike Bamber cared. He thought I was being negative. Ken had to mark Keith's card. In fact, the board was so disgruntled with Keith's latest move that La Manga stood idle for two years. Eventually, Ken asked me to go and look at it and make a report on what might be done with it. He chose me rather than Bryan Thompson because he didn't trust him not to stay down there and play golf for a week. At that stage I was a non-golfer. Some people think I still am.

I recall sitting on the balcony of the original clubhouse. Perched as it is on the side of a hill, you can look down to La Manga itself, or, as it is known, 'the Strip'. This is an isthmus of land on which a whole range of apartments, bars and restaurants can be found. It might sound good, but it is best viewed only from a distance. At this stage the course trees had not yet matured, and you could see all 36 holes. At ten a.m. there was not a soul on any of them. Nor was there anyone in the clubhouse, apart from the guy cooking my breakfast and the maid serving it. I flew back to England, told Ken that it really needed a property man and a golfer to look it over, and ducked out of the row.

Later on we decided to build a cricket ground there and, to launch it, I got Seve Ballesteros down to the Oval and into some cricket whites. After spending about twenty minutes trying to get him to hold the bat correctly, we got some good pictures. In fact, we made the front page of *The Times*. Mike and Keith had hired Seve as our tournament professional. For a huge fee he had to give us four days a year. He seemed to spend two of these being taken by Mike to his own club, which hardly helped Ken's enthusiasm for the project.

La Manga leaked money until it finally got sorted. To start with, a pro–celebrity tournament would be filmed and shown around the world. Unfortunately, in trying to get the courses back into good order, someone managed to water the greens with sea-water. They turned brown, and in order to fool the viewing public we had some of the world's finest golfers putting on greens that had been painted that colour for the cameras.

Despite our differences of opinion, I remained on good terms with Keith and Mike, although sometimes I wonder how. I'm glad I did, though. Had I not done so I would not have received a call from Keith in May 1983.

Brighton had risen to the dizzy heights of the old First Division for the first time in their history. Sadly, they were now heading out of it. Yet, against all the odds they had made it to the FA Cup final. My cousin Roger and his family are even more fanatical about Brighton than I am about Palace. Roger was working in South Africa at the time, but he flew in on the morning of the semi-final against Sheffield Wednesday and flew back in the evening. He said he knew they wouldn't win, but he just had to see them in the semis for what he assumed would be their one and only time. He is still right about that. What he got wrong was that they won. He came back for the final with the wife and three kids. It was the first time we had met for years. In fact, on the last occasion we were so young we probably played Subbuteo together.

Keith told me that Brighton manager Jimmy Melia had decided to hire a comedian to relax and amuse the team. He asked the players who they wanted, and, having watched me at the PFA dinner, they decided on me. It was a tradition for one of the Cup final teams to stay at the Selsdon Park Hotel near Croydon, which was only two or three miles from my house. So on Friday afternoon I headed off to join the squad.

Quite what was expected of me I had no idea. Nor did anyone else, it seemed, not least Jimmy. But they were a good bunch of lads and I already knew the captain, Steve Foster (Fozzie), a larger-than-life character with that distinctive headband. Whether you thought he was a good player or not – and there were those that didn't (I was not among them) – it was indisputable that he was an excellent leader. Everybody looked up to him and were quite happy to go along with what he said on almost any subject. Sadly, he was suspended for the final.

After I checked in, we all had dinner together. I did feel a bit like a stranger at the feast, but this was one of only two awkward moments. Mike Bamber asked me to stand up and do a few gags, which I did, even though the atmosphere was not quite right at that moment. I think we were all relieved when I sat down. After that, however, they all went out of their way to make me feel part of the squad, and we have still got a great bond between us. This despite me being a Palace supporter and pointedly wearing their colours whenever we meet. There are still great reunions twenty years on.

Mike then presented us all with carriage clocks as a memento of the occasion. I think he had got them cheap from Allders of Croydon, where Fozzie's stepfather, Peter Saunders, was the store director. In typical football dressing-room style, someone mentioned that Pete and I looked alike, and this has led to me being called Pete and him Cat whenever we are together in the same room, even now. It didn't help when we turned up wearing similar outfits, quite by chance, on more than one occasion. It became almost spooky. Pete suggested that one day we should go into the store and get into identical clothes, including boxers, and turn up for one of the reunions. We've not done it yet, but we must one day.

You will gather from this that the guys seemed pretty relaxed. I had had no previous experience of being close to a team before such a big game, so it wasn't until later on that I realised what a unique experience this was.

After dinner, we went to play in a snooker tournament. I got drawn against the goalkeeper, Graham Moseley, who was obviously the butt of many of my gags. Mose turned out to be no better at snooker than me, and after ten minutes neither of us had potted a ball. Someone said that was because neither of us could bear to see a ball hit the net. When the players went to bed at about ten p.m., Fozzie and I stayed up drinking. I was surprised that he was not more disappointed about missing the final, but typically he was taking it in his stride.

The following morning there was a little light training – not for me, of course. Then we all got on board the coach and headed for a nearby school field from where we were going to be flown to Wembley in a British Caledonian helicopter. I have to admit it, this was a marvellous publicity coup, and it was Mike Bamber's idea. I had never been in a helicopter before, and the view as we flew over Wembley was unbelievable. Almost as unbelievable as Jimmy Melia asking me to stand up and do a turn on the coach as we drove in from the landing field to Wembley. As we hit Wembley Way, I wished the lads all the best and said I was sure they preferred to soak up the atmosphere than listen to me. Tony Grealish, skippering in Fozzie's absence, said later that the lads hadn't wanted to be rude to me, but my doing a turn on the coach was the last thing they'd wanted, and they were grateful to me for sensing their mood and letting them enjoy the atmosphere going down Wembley Way.

I was still with them in the dressing room, and then they asked me to do the traditional walk out on to the pitch with them. It was an amazing experience as we walked out of the tunnel and the wall of noise hit us. As I had had a fair amount of publicity myself, at one point the crowd even chanted 'Bob the Cat'. On the pitch I met Steve Coppell, who had been chairman of the PFA when I did the dinner in 1981. All the Manchester United lads were strolling around on familiar territory. They had seen it all before. Brighton, in contrast, were treating it as a day out. Some of them walked out with cameras, and Mose took a picture of me standing in the goalmouth with the crowd behind me. I was beginning to feel like a game myself. After this, I left them to it and went to my seat in the stand. Some of the lads tried to get me on to the bench with the coaching staff, but Jimmy quite rightly drew the line at that.

Most of the country were feeling for Fozzie. When he led the side out, Tony Grealish was wearing a bright white headband. Entirely his own idea, and a clever two fingers to the FA. By now it goes without saying that I was rooting for Brighton. Even though I knew I'd done nothing towards their success, the papers were full of the value of using humour for motivational purposes. If Brighton won, I could have made a mint.

BADLY TIMED TACKLE

In *The Times*, Stuart Jones wrote, 'Logically, Brighton's claim to the FA Cup is almost laughable. No wonder they have hired a comedian, Bob Bevan, to accompany them on their journey to Wembley Stadium. He might be advised to join them on their flight back to the south coast tonight as well. They might appreciate a few jokes by then.'

After fourteen minutes Gordon Smith scored, and Brighton led at half-time. Could they do it? Ten minutes after half-time Frank Stapleton equalised, and when Ray Wilkins curled in a shot over Mose's head I feared the worst. But three minutes from time Gary Stevens, who had had an excellent game in the back four, popped up to equalise. Sadly for Gordon Smith, nobody now recalls how he gave Brighton the lead, or that he had a great career for Rangers, or that he went on to Manchester City after leaving Brighton and was their top goalscorer the following year. Even a Brighton fanzine is entitled *And Smith Must Score*. Mick Robinson broke clear and squared the ball to Gordon. On a poor pitch – when we walked on it, the water came up over part of our shoes – the ball bobbled as Gordon hit it. Man Utd goalkeeper Gary Bailey spread himself, as all we top keepers do. The ball was nearly through his legs, but caught the inside of his thigh. Extra-time provided no more goals, and the game went to a replay.

Back in the dressing room, the lads were in high spirits. They had played really well, and they knew it. We left the stadium, went back to the chopper and flew direct to Brighton where we were due at a celebration banquet and ball, at which I was to do the cabaret with comic impersonator and now brother Water Rat Johnny More. When we landed at Brighton there were massive crowds to greet us, and the police had a job holding them back. Even though they were friendly, it was quite scary, and I decided that an unfriendly mob must be terrifying. I walked from my hotel to the hall where the banquet was to take place and again came across big crowds outside. I got another 'Bob the Cat' chant as I went in.

FREE-KICK

Gordon Smith was lying on a beach in Malaysia when a little kid came up to him.

'Are you Gordon Smith?' he asked.

Gordon said he was.

The kid said, 'Aren't you the bloke who missed that goal in the Cup final?'

Gordon reckoned the kid couldn't have been born until after 1983.

Next morning, there was some bad news. I had had so much publicity that, on Saturday afternoon, it was clear I was out and my house had been burgled. I lived on a corner, and the guy opposite had disturbed the robbers as they were loading stuff into a van. I drove back home and found that the TVs and videos had gone but not much else. My suits were piled in the hall, ready to be loaded next. I cleared up and went back down to Brighton for a dinner. I arrived late and sat down in between Mick Robinson and Gordon Smith, resplendent in my new white dinner jacket. Mick looked at it and said, 'Is that the only thing they left? Obviously burglars of taste.'

During the week I went racing at a televised meeting at Epsom with my friend, Fred Price. As by now I reported only to Ken Siddle and Keith Wickenden, I insisted on logging my holidays with the company secretary, Ted Overington. Ken and Keith said it was unnecessary, but I'm glad I did it. On arrival at Epsom, Brough Scott came up and asked if I would do a spot on television between races. I agreed, and managed to get in a few plugs for Townsend Thoresen during the interview. I also slipped in the following gag: 'One of the Irish players said it was a bit cold in this helicopter and could we turn the fan off?' Obviously my new-found fame was causing some jealousy among certain colleagues, and it had clearly got too much for one of them as the next morning, Ken called to say that someone had reported that I had slagged off the company on television the day before; he had also asked if I was ever in my office. I asked who had raised it, but Ken would not say. I suggested that the person concerned have the guts to call me and I would put him straight. Again, he refused. He said he thought it would be best to get hold of a transcript of the broadcast. I said I could get one, but I was disappointed with him for even asking. I told him so in a covering note I sent with the transcript, adding that if he checked with Ted he would find that I had taken a day's holiday. Needless to say, the transcript completely exonerated me, but I'd still like to know who the rat was. However, I'm sure the culprit made a terminal career move for putting Ken in that position. I certainly hope so.

We reconvened at the Selsdon Park Hotel on Wednesday evening for the Thursday replay. I took part in some five-a-sides the next day, much to the team's amusement. There were no selection problems as Chris Ramsey – a quick, black right-back who was given the name Yifter after a famous Ethiopian athlete of the time who was known as 'Yifter the Shifter' – had been injured during the final and was unfit for the replay. Therefore Steve Foster came back into a reshuffled defence.

Looking back, the atmosphere was different from the first game. This time the lads were nervous. We went through the same routine with the helicopter, but in the game Brighton were never at the races and were easily beaten 4–0. It was the biggest margin of victory in an FA Cup final since Bury beat Derby County 6–0 in 1903, which is still the record highest score. But Brighton's is still the biggest defeat ever in a Wembley final.

Fozzie came into the dressing room after the game and threw down his headband. 'What were their crowd singing?' he said. ' "Stevie Foster, Stevie Foster, what a difference you have made?" They were right, weren't they?' When he came out of the shower he was back to his old self, going round the lads telling them to get their heads up. As we left in the coach he actually got them singing, and to their credit they all joined in. Then I piped up, and surely Brighton were the only Cup final team in history ever to go down Wembley Way singing 'Old Wilsonians, Old Wilsonians, we'll support you ever more.'

DECISION EXPLAINED

They are all unbeaten in FA Cup finals. Mind you, each played in the final only once, except for Bury, who played twice, and the Wanderers, who made a staggering five appearances.

On the helicopter I was sitting next to Mose. As we looked down on the magnificent sight of the now empty but still floodlit Wembley, he said sadly, 'Worst defeat ever at Wembley, then.' There was nothing I could think of to say. Then he picked himself up. 'Still, look at that. It's been some experience, this.' Mose is one player I've lost touch with since, but I hope he still looks back on that 1983 FA Cup final in that positive way. It certainly was some experience, that.

LATEST SCORES
Hamburg 2 Hot Dog 1
Everton 1 Polo 2

250

29. DICK MILLINGTON GOES FOR A DRAW

'The art of journalism is to invent a story and lower the truth slowly towards it.'

Peter Ustinov

Around the time of the 1983 FA Cup Final, when I was getting the most publicity of my life, I was asked to write some funny pieces about goalkeeping. At the same time I got to know a cartoonist called Dick Millington. I had created a Junior Sailors Club as a sales tool for Townsend Thoresen, and we had hired a couple, Robin and Ann Tucek, to produce the kids' magazine. They had, in turn, hired Dick to draw a cartoon character called Captain Clot, who was loosely disguised as a Sealink skipper.

I had an idea to produce a cartoon strip based on my Cat character, and, rather like the legendary Peanuts strip which started with the loser Charlie Brown, I thought we could add a few additional characters. Apart from Dario Micklewhite and Justin Frontofhim, we added Cyril Smooth. There is one player in every team who comes off without a speck of dirt on him or a hair out of place, no matter how muddy the pitch or how dirty the game, and Cyril was that man. Another character was based on the fearsome Millwall and Rangers midfielder Terry Hurlock. Then there was the club's drainage expert, a mole who appeared in the back of my goal and gave lofty opinions on the game that were far above the heads of any of the team.

I took the idea to *Daily Express* sports editor Ken Lawrence, and he liked it. However, there were a few problems with it. Resident sports cartoonist Roy Ullyett was not best pleased for a start. He already had an occasional goalie character who wore glasses. On the plus side, I had a nice card from the legendary Carl Giles, another Ipswich supporter, who wrote that it was good to see a strip on the back page again. Ken unfortunately decided to start it in May, at the end of the football season. The first cartoon was a good one. We used a joke I was already doing about the captain saying to me at half-time, 'I'd like a word with you about the second half.' I reply, 'What about it?' and he says, 'Would you like a wall for the kick-off?' After that I was featured doing other sports, and I think the strip lost its way. With more experience I would have dug my heels in, but if you get a cartoon on the back page of a national newspaper you don't argue too much. When Larry Lamb took over as editor a few months later, he dropped it. I still think that if we'd started in the August we might well have had a hit on our hands.

This is how the arrival of the Cat was greeted in the *Daily Express* on Friday, 13 May 1983:

Brighton's FA Cup hopes crashed dramatically last night when they discovered that their secret weapon is cup-tied. Bob 'the Cat' Bevan revealed that he has already played this season in the Amateur Football Alliance Cup for 6th XIs and below.

Bob, better known as an after-dinner speaker, has been signed up by Brighton to join the squad next Friday to ease their nerves before their final fling against Manchester United the following day.

But 38-year-old bespectacled Bevan – who claims to have access to the Brian Clough diaries [this was at the time of the Hitler diaries] – admits he still has hopes of appearing for the Seagulls at Wembley.

'If Ted Croker turns a blind eye, I might make it,' says Bevan, whose hapless exploits for the Old Wilsonians FC at Hayes, Kent, have delighted guests at soccer dinners throughout the country. 'I shall be dropping fivers around Brighton's team hotel, and when Graham Moseley bends down to pick one up I might accidentally step on his hand.'

But what about reserve keeper Perry Digweed?

'He's just a well-known gardening correspondent, isn't he?'

Bob's sporting adventures – he once let in fourteen at the Old Wilsonians 'Superbowl' – have been captured by artist Dick Millington and will appear every Saturday from tomorrow in your *Express*.

And he has devised some coaching charts for Brighton 'to show them the dying art of the toe punt'. Jimmy Melia needs some help with the free-kicks.

On the day of the final, I wrote this piece to go with the cartoon:

Advice for Gary [Bailey] from the Cat
'Cat,' said Jimmy Melia, 'come and amuse the lads during our cup final build-up.'

I shall be only too pleased to pass on to the lads my experience as Old Wilsonians 6th XI custodian. I shall, of course, be advising Graham Moseley (Mose to me) not to leave his line. After all, we keepers (Mose, Baylo and me) get enough stick when the ball goes over it, so why take the risk?

As for Jimmy Case (Caso to me), I shall be suggesting that he reverts to toe punting to increase the power of his free-kicks. Ashley Easden, our centre-half and captain, is one of the finest exponents of this in the game today, as can be seen from the large bandage he wears on his big toe every Saturday night.

Despite the serious level at which we 6th XI players perform, even we can be involved in some bizarre incidents. Like the time when our substitute forgot his tie-ups. Having no knife, he used a cigarette lighter to burn an old lace in half, then got changed, put his tracksuit on and came out to watch the game. Five minutes later the game was stopped to tend to the smoke pouring from his legs.

Another true story occurred only three weeks ago. In a prestigious home friendly against Nat West Bank 13th XI, one of our players was quite seriously injured. An ambulance was called and we left him on the side and played on. Ten minutes later another of our players went down with bad cramp. As we bent over to help him, the ambulance roared through the gate, raced past the guy lying on the side and nearly added a heart attack to knotted muscles as it pulled up alongside the wrong casualty.

Only last October I sat in the dressing room before our first-round AFA 6th XI cup-tie. I was resting in between tying up my left boot and my right boot – the doctor has told me not to lace up one immediately after the other – when a young player in the corner piped up.

'Pardon me, Cat, but is this the first round?'

I bit my lip. A tear rolled down my cheek. I tried to catch it, but missed.

'Yes, son,' I said sadly. 'We only play in first rounds.'

LATEST SCORES
Real Madrid 7 Synthetic Madrid 2
Dumbarton 0 Smartbarton 4

30. WHAT'S THAT IN THE SKY?

Statler: That was some programme. I'd only have changed one thing.
Waldorf: What's that?
Statler: The channel.

The Muppets

Before and after the Brighton cup final in 1983 I was spotted by TVS, independently of their part-ownership by European Ferries. I got called in to do a New Year's Day programme in 1982 with Lawrie McMenemy and George Best. In the chair was Fred Dineage. Not surprisingly, George didn't show, so Lawrie and I did what was almost an hour between us reviewing the year and talking about the highlights of Brighton's latest game. It all went down very well, and I was asked back several times for the evening magazine programme, always with Fred. We hit it off really well, and this came over on the screen. Fred is certainly the best presenter/chat show host I've worked with, followed by Terry Wogan.

It was some years before I finally met George Best. There were two more occasions when he failed to appear, but we eventually met in Belfast on an Ulster TV show called *Kelly's People*. George was recently divorced from Angie, so this must have been in the late 1980s. He had been all over the papers after Angie had disclosed that George had not been turning up at the weekend to take out his son, Calum. I liked George immediately. He is a pleasant, articulate, intelligent man. Sadly, he has the disease. On our first meeting he told me that if he went out for a drink on Fridays there was every chance he wouldn't come round until the following Tuesday. He said, 'Calum is now old enough to know a little bit about what's going on. So when I called to apologise he said to me, "Was it because you were drunk, Daddy?" It went through me like a knife. If anything's going to stop me drinking, it will be him.' Later on we all went out, and he tucked in again. Today, even after his liver transplant, he still seems to go off the rails.

FREE-KICK

'Bob "the Cat" Bevan has done for goalkeeping what Dr Crippen did for medicine' – the late Ted Croker, former FA secretary, writing a message for the cover of my LP.

After several good shows, I also wrote a small sketch prior to the Brighton cup final.

Graham Moseley was shown letting in goals, so I came on to the pitch, looking awful in my glasses and faded jersey. I told him to stand to one side, look and learn. Then Jimmy Case, of the Exocet shot, placed the ball on the spot. I said, 'Do your worst, Caso.' Jimmy ran up and smashed it in the top corner. I was then shown standing stock still, facing forward and saying, 'Ready when you are, Caso.'

TVS decided that there was more mileage in me, and, not long after I left European Ferries, I had a call from the deputy sports editor, Vic Wakeling. If you recognise the name, it's because he is now the boss of Sky Sports. He came up to buy me lunch and said they wanted to put a sporting chat show on with plenty of humour, and they wanted me to co-host it with Fred Dineage. To our eternal regret, Fred did not want to do it on top of his evening show.

Frankly, it was a bit of a shambles. It was an entertainment show put on by sports people. Vic and I still often say how damaging it might have been to our careers but, luckily, we've both survived it. We would drive down on a Friday morning and write the script. It would be recorded as live at about 8.30. We would then watch it go out at 10.30, have a chat, and drive home. It was a long day. Instead of Fred, they got hold of an impersonator called Aidan J. Harvey who was appearing in Bournemouth with Jimmy Tarbuck for the summer. He was a good act, but he lasted only for a few of the 36 shows we were booked for. He was not a presenter, and he was even more nervous about it than me. Nor did it help that the audience was almost always old ladies from the local British Legion; any joke about Halifax Town gate receipts was lost on them. Only on one night did we have a good atmosphere. A Sunday football team was in the studio and they were good value for me to bounce off. That night we were fifteen years ahead of our time with a kind of *Fantasy Football League* show. I recall saying to Vic that we should get those sort of people in every week, but he said we couldn't. Not long after that Greg Dyke took over the company and killed the show. He was right. He might have saved all our careers.

LATEST SCORES
AC Milan 3 DC Milan 0
Kilmarnock 6 Burymarnock 0

'I PLAYED THE SHETLANDS TWICE'

*'Freud said humour was the economy of psychic energy, but, as I've said
before, the trouble with Freud is he never played second house at the
Glasgow Empire.'*

Ken Dodd, 1978

In 1998 I got to work with one of the living legends of show business.
I'd been to watch him at Bromley earlier in the year, and he was
brilliant. He'd brought his tax case into his act: 'Income tax was
invented two hundred years ago at tuppence in the pound. My
trouble was I thought it still was . . . I've had problems, but nothing
compared to the trapeze artist with loose bowels.' Other gags included
the surreal 'Do you know that if you put your teeth in back to front
you can make a Rolo last a fortnight?', and 'I played the Shetlands
twice. They didn't believe it the first time.' He is renowned for going
on all night. At Bromley he did five hours! 'Do you give in?' he would
say. 'When you get home your family will have grown up.' 'Look
under your seats, you'll find a will form.' 'My first agent died at a
hundred. Actually, he was ninety. He kept ten per cent for himself.'
According to one newspaper report Ken thought Ted Ray was the
funniest stand-up ever, but he claims, amazingly, that he modelled
himself on Arthur Askey whom he thought was unbelievably fast and
inventive.

I travelled to Manchester for the St George's Day club lunch. Doddy
arrived very late, apparently as normal. He seemed a very nice guy,
and with his energy and unchanged looks it was hard to believe he
was 70. Mind you, he did look like he'd just stepped out of the Oxfam
shop. He had with him a battered red plastic basket in which were
loads of cards, all of them scribbled on. Some were held together with
plastic bulldog clips. It was all very weird, but who was I to query the
great man's methods?

I did my half hour and, although I couldn't look round to see if he
was laughing, I was proud to hear him saying to the guy next to him,

'He's very good.' With 550 in the audience it's much easier to go well, and they were certainly quiet and listening. Always a buzz, that. I said something nice about Ken to the effect that nobody was more English than Doddy, and what a thrill it was for someone like me to work with him. To anyone who tries to make people laugh, he is a hero. I said that my dad, who at the time still thought I should have a proper job, was quite impressed when he heard I was working with Ken Dodd. He thought maybe I'd made it. I think I have.

When Ken stood up, he must have done nearly 90 minutes. A lot of it was old material, and after each one-liner he threw another card away. He was so obviously reading a lot of it, which he clearly wouldn't do on stage. Occasionally he would leave the notes and go into a routine, before going back. At one point there were a few people talking, but he ploughed on through them. 'There's a technical term for this. It's called struggling,' he said. And he was very flattering to me: he kept saying 'when the comedian was on earlier'.

When you looked at it, it was an amazing performance. If you had to find criticism it was that he went on far too long and he covered areas I'd already done. Like the wine, Lord Irvine and George Michael, who had just been arrested in a Californian toilet. Mind you, his George Michael gag was better than mine: 'He went in to spend a penny and came out with two coppers.' Other memorable lines included 'William Hague has said he's not taking us into Europe, and clearly he's persuaded Alex Ferguson to go along with that'; 'What's the similarity between a three-point plug and Man Utd? They're both bloody useless in Europe'; 'I went into the kitchen here and, do you know, there isn't a single bluebottle in there. They're all married with kids'; and 'I said to the chef, "What do you do about salmonella?" He said, "I fry it in a little butter."'

I thought about it on the train home. He'd received a standing ovation – more for who he is and for the length of his act than the quality of it, I felt. Yet he browbeats you into laughing at him, he's got loads of warmth, and he isn't afraid to try new stuff. He had clearly written down material for the day and had given it some thought, but the fact that he was reading so much of it seemed to take the edge off his performance. Still, he's a great comedian. One journalist who was there remarked, 'When he goes, that's it. There's nobody like him left.' That's got to be true.

Most of all, I was pleased to find him such a nice man, and so complimentary. He asked for my card, then enquired, surprisingly, if I knew Terry Seabrook. I said I did but hadn't seen him for years (I have since as he's a brother Water Rat). Terry is a magician/comic who does an act similar to Wayne Dobson's. In fact I have wondered whether he was a large influence on Wayne.

I got Ken to sign my menu. He wrote, 'You're wonderful and TATTiphilarious. My admiration, Ken Dodd.' I'll always treasure it.

31. TIME FOR A SUBSTITUTION

'I'm never bored or anomic. As for suicide, I would commit murder first.
You see, I'm all I have.'

Gore Vidal

Saturday, 8 July 1983 was a lovely hot summer's day. I was skippering
the Old Wilsonians Cricket Club 3rd XI somewhere in Kent. My father
fancied an afternoon out, so I collected him en route and we had a
pleasant day followed by a few beers. I dropped him off around nine
and headed home to collect a steak for a barbecue I had been invited
to.

By then I had an answerphone, if not a mobile. There were loads
of messages on it. I thought twice about listening to them there and
then, but out of interest pressed the button to hear the first one. It
was a guy from the *Sunday Express* who wanted to talk to me about
the death of Mr Wickenden. My first thought was that they were doing
a follow-up on Roland, but a second message told me the worst. That
morning, Keith had gone for a spin in his little plane and had crashed
by the A27 at Shoreham airport. Once again, Paul Ellis had been
lumbered with all the press calls, but this was a story that would run
for days, if not weeks.

Years later, I bumped into our parliamentary agent, Joe Durkin, on
a domestic flight. He had been convinced that Keith had committed
suicide, and nothing would dissuade him from that view. Certainly the
company had been heading for the rocks because of its US property
interests, but I remain unconvinced. Calculated suicide, as opposed to
mentally disturbed suicide, is a selfish act, leaving others to pick up
the pieces, and Keith was not a selfish man. I cannot think that he
would do such a thing to his wife and four sons, one of whom was
handicapped. It has to be said, however, that Joe is not on his own in
thinking this way, and certainly the inquest did not strike me as totally
straightforward. It was held on a Thursday, and the coroner opened
by saying that he hoped to conclude it in a day because if that were
not achieved they would have to wait until Tuesday to reconvene. I
recall thinking that justice should not be controlled by a cooking

timer. I was also amazed to see that the family had hired a famous and high-powered barrister, Fenton Bresler.

It seems that while Keith had spent a fortune on some state-of-the-art radio equipment, he had bought a reconditioned engine at a knockdown price. It was just the sort of thing Keith would do (before telling us all how sharp he'd been). Within this engine was a small part that had corroded; had he bought a more up-to-date engine the part in question would have been made of plastic.

Bresler was a good operator. I remember him verbally knocking some chap all round the room until he seemed to almost totally change his evidence. Even so, there was an undercurrent of doubt running through it all, and when the coroner, quite late in the day, turned to the jury and suggested accidental death, their first inclination was to ask to go out and discuss it. This would certainly have brought us all back the following Tuesday, so the coroner put them under some pressure to decide against going out. They whispered in a huddle, and agreed. As I left the court, one of Keith's relatives winked at me.

I had been thinking of leaving the company for a couple of years. My mother had died in 1982, which they say is a watershed in any man's life. You realise, perhaps for the first time, that nothing lasts for ever. I had also been in a senior job at a young age, and it was clear that I was not going to go any further. I might have gone earlier, but I had been sitting in the back of a car with Keith one evening about two years before he died when he started talking to me about a parliamentary pensions committee he was sitting on. Pensions were not portable then, but Keith said they would be shortly. Not for the first time he had got it wrong, and I'd hung on for nothing.

With Keith gone, a new chairman had to be found, so the main board met to elect one. This was a company that had resisted proper PR, but Ken Siddle would at least listen and take some advice. I pointed out that we had no proper photographs of the main board, something they had always refused, and that we ought to prepare statements for approval, assuming that each of the directors had a chance of coming out on top. So before the meeting I took a photographer along and we took pictures of them all. By this time we had added a merchant bank, Singer and Friedlander, to our group. Their chairman was a man called Tony Solomons. He was not someone I took to, and I think the feeling was mutual. Tony clearly thought he had a chance and was extremely impatient during the photo sessions. We all knew better. He had no chance. We thought it would be Ken, although Geoff Parker, the man who used to buy the fags for the Dover ships and was now the hugely successful boss of the port of Felixstowe, was a dark horse. This was probably because he was excellent with the media while Ken was not. Ken chain-smoked, drank too much and was very nervous, but he loved the company, and when he became chairman I was very pleased for him.

A month later I went off to Eindhoven where we were sponsoring a pre-season football tournament. Apart from the home side PSV, taking part were FC Bruges, Real Zaragoza and Nottingham Forest, managed by Brian Clough. I had met Brian before and had found him a very nice guy. He sometimes had a bit too much to drink, and he did put on this act that we all know so well, but he was a decent bloke, and he proved it on this trip – to my embarrassment.

I had organised a competition in *Shoot!* magazine for a kid and his dad to come over for the tournament as our guests. Also with us was David Bradford, one of our non-executive main board directors, and his son Michael. 'Brad' was great fun. A little man with one eye (lost in the war), he was a stockbroker who loved life and lived it to the full. No matter what he said or did to people, everyone loved him because he was so kind, generous and funny. Nottingham Forest played badly in the tournament. They lost their first game to PSV and then lost to the Spaniards, who were a poor side, two days later. I had promised to get this kid the Forest autographs, so I walked into the dressing room after the second game. Brian said, 'I'll take it from you, Bob, and get it back to you. First of all there's going to be some harsh words spoken in here.' You could see the players slump in their seats at this. I was quite glad to be out of the way. I went back to one of the hospitality rooms where I joined Brad in sampling a new Indonesian liqueur he had discovered. Later, the Forest assistant manager found me. 'Brian's held the coach up for nearly an hour to get this back to you, and I couldn't find you anywhere,' he said. I had totally forgotten the kid's autograph book. I didn't go and say goodbye to Cloughie. I think I might have got a few harsh words too.

Later that night, after an Indonesian meal, I was sitting with the two Brads – father and son – in the hotel having yet another nightcap. I remember thinking that I really liked these blokes, with whom I'd been friends for fourteen years, but that the time seemed right to leave. I had saved up £20,000 from my speaking fees to start up on my own, so I decided to sleep on it and make sure that it wasn't the Indonesian liqueur talking.

We drove home on the Monday and I resigned on the Tuesday. Ken was not best pleased. If anyone needed a PR man he did, but I had been telling him for years that I had no proper contract, that I could go and work for Sealink the following day if I wanted to, and that I only had to give a month's notice. It was careless on his part as I was privy to many of the company's secrets. For example, we had been banned from collaborating with our competitors on fares but we had got round that by meeting with the overseas divisions of Sealink, who in the days before the European Community were not under the jurisdiction of our government. Ken asked if I would stay on for a few extra months, and I said I would as long as I was off the PAYE. Over the next few weeks he couldn't make up his mind whether or not to promote Paul Ellis, which went down like a lead balloon with Paul. Ken even called me at seven a.m. one morning, at a most inconvenient time for both me and a young lady, to further discuss the issue. By November he had made up his mind to give Paul the job, and he said I could go when I wanted.

'Before you do,' he added, 'I'd just like you to write me a letter confirming you won't go and work for Sealink.'

I couldn't see why I should. 'Are you going to make it worth my while?' I asked. He wasn't. 'Well then, Ken, I don't know what's going to happen to me. Clearly my credibility would take a hit if I went there after slagging them off for fourteen years, but if I'm starving, who knows?'

We were heading into our first ever row.

'No one's ever done that before,' Ken pointed out.

'Done what? I just said I almost certainly won't go there, but if you want some new clauses in an agreement you'll need to pay for it, like you should have done years ago.'

Years later, at Brad's funeral, a subsidiary company director told me that I had done him and a dozen others a big favour. He said, 'When you left, we all got service contracts.' Even so, I was sad to part on bad terms with Ken as I had a lot of time for him as a human being.

Once, when Bryan Thompson had got himself involved in a show business promotion that was going wrong, he tried to unload it on to me. Ken spotted what he was doing before I did and called me from home before he left for a holiday in Kenya to let me know and advise me to take care. On another occasion, when Phil Holt had returned from the French Government Tourist Office to run the overseas side of Townsend Thoresen, I had another problem. One thing I had always hated about the job was the politics as I normally like to play a straight bat. As I saw it, Holt could never get over the fact that he used to be in charge of PR and tried to get rid of the member of staff I used to deal with overseas PR. I refused. I had the utmost confidence in Jane Lawrence and, after Bryan, to whom Holt reported, also got knocked back by me the matter was taken to Ken. The four of us met, and I pulled no punches about my opinion of Holt to his face. Ken listened to it all, then gave his verdict. 'On the basis that Phil Holt is more important to the company than Jane Lawrence, she will have to be moved.' As I slumped in my seat, I saw Holt start to grin. Ken must have seen it too because for the first and only time in our fourteen years together I saw a flash of temper. Looking directly at Holt, he added, 'But I don't want to hear any more about this again. Ever. If any one of you raises this with me again, you're out.' I think we all sat there stunned as he left. This was not like Ken. Bryan wanted me to stay for a drink, but I couldn't bear to be in the same room as Holt and drove home.

Next morning, as I pondered how to break the news to Jane, I had an inspiration. I would not dare go near Ken again, but neither would the other two. So I did nothing. Holt never raised it again. Two weeks later Thompson snapped at me about the situation and asked when I was going to get rid of her, and I told him I wasn't. I suggested he might mention it to Ken. She was still in her job when I left.

Once I'd resigned, I was to be grateful within months. I always gave people an example of the differences between the two previous chairmen at AGMs. Both Wickendens were brilliant. Roland, if asked how many rivets there were in the hull of one of his ships, would give you an answer. If you then went and counted them you would find his answer totally correct. Keith, when asked the same question, would give you an answer you'd find to be totally wrong. On returning to Keith, he would, using his politician's skills, convince you that he was actually right, or that you had misunderstood his answer. For his first AGM, however, Ken Siddle had an absolute disaster. It said so in the press. A couple of years later he was replaced by Geoff Parker. I had not been in touch with him since I left, but I called him at home and commiserated with him. To my amazement, after a brief chat he actually went back to moaning about how Les Dawson had died on his arse at that launching all those years before. I began to wish I hadn't called him. I never got to speak to him again. Like his colleagues, he was to die young. He was only 53.

As the US property division of European Ferries foundered, P&O moved in. There was no love lost between European Ferries and P&O. When we took over Normandy Ferries from P&O we treated some nice people quite badly. Now the roles were reversed. During Thursday, 6 March 1986, they took an axe to much of Townsend Thoresen's middle management at Dover. That evening I was sitting at home contemplating an evening in the Plough Inn when my phone rang. It was the *Guardian*. National newspapers are not much good at keeping their contact books up to date, so I was not surprised, even three years on, to hear he was calling about the ferries. 'One of your boats has capsized, mate,' he said. I resisted the desire to correct him (it's *ships*) and said I hadn't got any boats, and that he should call Paul Ellis, whose home number I remember to this day.

I did not set too much store by this call until suddenly *The Times*, the *Telegraph* and the *Mail* all rang in quick succession. I turned on the television and watched in horror as the Zeebrugge disaster unfolded. As the days passed I heard of many ex-colleagues who had died, and there was even an Old Wilsonian footballer among those lost on board the *Herald of Free Enterprise*. It was a ship whose launching I had organised, I had been on it many times, and that day is still heart-breaking to recall, even more so considering the tragedy could so easily have been avoided.

There was a lot of misinformation about ships running around in harbour with their bow or stern doors open. In calm, enclosed water there is no danger associated with this; it helps to clear the fumes from the car deck. Once in the open sea, as speed picks up, a bow wave is created and water can then get on to the car deck. Once that happens, if it continues, these vessels can go down like a stone. Forget the lifeboats. You wouldn't have time. It would have made sense to have watertight doors which automatically closed in the event of any ingress of water. This would isolate the problem and at least keep the ship stable for longer, if nothing else. Although there was talk of this happening, it would have been prohibitively expensive for existing ships. With such sophisticated navigation equipment it is now unlikely to happen again, but human error can still play a part. Human error was what caused Zeebrugge. A seaman failed to shut the bow door and the captain did not know about it. Had it not been a calm night and had the *Herald* not fallen on to a sandbank, I doubt anyone would have survived.

Some of the technical people were dragged into court, but the case collapsed. There was, however, one telling piece of evidence. For some reason, Ken Siddle despised the captains. He once, in my hearing, called them parasites. I could not have disagreed more, but this lack of respect may have drifted down to the senior staff in Dover. When the captains asked for a warning light to be fitted on the bridge to indicate if the doors were open, this was ridiculed. In court, a sarcastic memo on the subject was produced, and its author broke down in tears. At this time I recalled an incident involving company cars. In the days when a second wing mirror was an extra we were refused them, even though it is essential for safety if you are on the Continent on your own with a right-hand-drive vehicle, as we often were. I told my people to buy one and put it down as something else on their expenses. I may be wrong, but it has always nagged at me that if they had been prepared to spend a few hundred quid per vessel fitting warning lights, Zeebrugge would never have happened.

IF ONLY SHE'D PLAYED HER CARDS RIGHT

'Mistakes are part of the dues one pays for a full life.'

Sophia Loren

Ironically, and it must have made Ken Siddle spin in his grave, I did end up with Sealink as one of my clients when I started my consultancy, although this was long after P&O had gobbled up Townsend Thoresen. In 1991 Sealink decided to rename two ships and wanted me to run a launching event at Dover rather like the ones I used to organise for their competitors, though on a much smaller scale. We thought that a female double act would go down well, such as Jennifer Saunders and Dawn French, but in the end we hit on two actresses from the then-recent TV series *Darling Buds of May*: Pam Ferris, who played Ma, and Catherine Zeta-Jones.

Monday was the day of the event, and Catherine arrived the night before to join us in the Holiday Inn, Dover. How she must long for those days now. Pam arrived the following morning and, in order to get the maximum out of the two girls, we arranged for them to be driven around the Dover shopping area in an open-top vintage car. I went with them. Then it was off to the ships, the naming ceremony and a grand lunch with all Sealink's top customers. Pam and Catherine could not have been more friendly and helpful throughout the day. The girls from my office particularly liked Catherine. 'She was great fun at dinner on the Sunday night,' said Eileen Peal, my secretary over many years. 'She was just like one of the girls.'

I too had arrived on the Sunday night, but I'd been on a very boozy weekend in Paris and felt so rough that I went straight to bed. Had that not been the case, I would certainly have joined them. And had I done so, Michael Douglas – a man much older than me – would, I think we can safely assume, have remained a lonely divorcee.

32. FRESH LEGS

'I was asked what I thought about the recession. I thought about it and decided not to take part.'

Sam Walton, founder of Wal-mart

It's a big step, going out on your own. No pay cheque comes in and you suddenly realise how many outgoings you have. Some friends of mine, including my football partner Robert Newey, ran a publishing company in Fleet Street and they agreed to let me use their address. In fact, Robert gave me the bottom drawer of his desk. He still seems quite proud of the fact that that drawer was my first office. Largely, though, I worked from home, which as an only child I thought would be fine as I had always been happy with my own company. To my surprise, I did not feel comfortable, even though my old flame Margaret Neville, having been unceremoniously kicked out of European Ferries after Keith died, came to work with me for a time. It took me a few weeks to realise that I missed my colleagues. We had always got on well and had a laugh. Each morning I would walk in and say 'Morning, team' in a none too serious way, but even this silliness was a bit of unsophisticated bonding. Something I didn't realise at the time. When I left, they gave me a most wonderful glass ship in a bottle on which was inscribed 'To Bob, With Best Wishes and Affection from Your Team'. It still has pride of place in my office.

Having made this momentous decision, I nearly got sucked back in again. Word soon got round that a successful PR man was on the move, and that he'd jumped rather than been pushed. I received a call from one Albert Hall (there's a name you can't forget), a psychologist who worked for Asda. They were unhappy about their set-up and interviewed me with a view to my becoming their head of PR. I was sorely tempted, but they wanted me in Leeds and I didn't fancy it. Albert said I would be a senior player and there was a company private plane I would be entitled to use. I felt that one of their problems was that they had no PR operation in London, where all the media were. They asked me to do a corporate PR plan for them, which I did for a very nice fee, and they agreed that they needed a base in London. But they still wanted their top man in Leeds. Having previously agonised over taking the independent path I turned it down and have no regrets.

Instead, I started my own PR company, Bevan PR, as a safety net in case the speaking didn't take off. Ironically, for the next ten years its success would slow down my entertaining. We had some big names, including KLM Royal Dutch Airlines, ITT Sheraton (for most of the world except the USA) and the builders' merchants Harcros. We also had Dan-Air Scheduled Services. In line with my usual debut luck, on our first morning as their PR consultants one of their pilots landed at the wrong airport in Belfast.

After renting a room from my accountant, I bought a small building in Penge, south London, and later, when we outgrew it, I bought another in Beckenham, Kent. We grew to have up to twenty people working for us and were listed in one survey as being among the top 50 PR companies in Europe, although to be honest I don't think we were anywhere near that – 70th in the UK would have been nearer the mark. I once turned down an offer for the company which perhaps I should have taken. We had turned over £850,000 during one year in the early 1990s, which was quite good for a PR company, but I wanted to hit the million. We never did.

OFFSIDE

When we worked for Sheraton Hotels, we used to be involved in their guest satisfaction programme. One rule was that the staff had to be sure to speak to the guests before the guests had a chance to speak to them. One of the top brass, Bob Collier, who was visiting a hotel, went for an early-morning run. When he came back, a young African bellhop called urgently across the reception area in an almost panic-stricken voice, 'Mr Collier! Mr Collier!'

Bob was both startled and alarmed. 'What's the matter?' he said, feeling quite anxious.

The bellhop came racing across to him and said, 'Good morning.'

Back when we were starting to build up, I heard that my old boss Gordon Wharton had left *Travel News*. I needed some help, certainly someone who could write well. I also felt I owed him for all that he had taught me. He had a few problems at the time, but was not too open about his situation. Everyone has their pride. By this time he had learnt to drive, and he owned a small Fiat sports car, but for the nine months since he'd left *Travel News* it had been stuck by the roadside. Gordon came to do some freelance work and then joined the company. I made him a director. I also got a friend who owns a garage to sort his car out – it turned out to be only a few minor problems, and Gordon paid it off out of his salary over the next few months. Our old colleague Dennis Holman, now retired, lived nearby, and the three of us went out one night. I later learnt that Gordon had told him that, apart from when they started *Travel News*, this was the happiest he'd been in his working career. I was very pleased, but it was not to last.

One morning he turned up very pissed, having got back from a travel exhibition in Berlin. I was upset. I was in no position to criticise someone for having a drink, but I was concerned about our image in the industry. He was representing Bevan PR now, and I did not want clients or potential clients to see him in this state.

We got over it and continued to grow. Towards the end of 1988 I bought the bigger building in Beckenham, and we were due to move in over the New Year. Then I had some health problems. In the late autumn I had to have a piles operation – not to be recommended to anyone. Having got over that, at our Christmas party I ate some mussels, among other things, and also had a lot to drink. I was dropped off home and then some friends called to ask if I fancied going to watch Bromley that evening. They picked me up, but I was unwell at the game and they brought me home early. I assumed it was the mussels. At this point I was living alone, and I had a very poor night with severe stomach pains. Some sixth sense told me all was not well, so at seven a.m. I called the doctor. As usual he was not keen to come out, and he asked if I couldn't wait until surgery. Having found I couldn't, he arrived an hour later, but having picked up the wrong notes he had to turn round and go back to his office. When he reappeared, he took one look at me and dialled 999. I had acute appendicitis. When they got me to hospital, Ian Higton, the surgeon who had operated on the other side of me a few months earlier, was on duty. He was quite jokey, but for once I wasn't. 'I can't wait for you to knock me out,' I told him. Later I learnt that another 45 minutes at home on my own and I wouldn't have survived. Thus does our life hang by a thread.

I was due to be away in Australia and the Middle East for one and a half months from the second week of 1989 so I went back to work too early. We were in new premises and more and more business was coming in. I came back to the office with a colleague, having just been unexpectedly appointed to handle Kenning Car Rentals. Having wondered on the train journey how we were going to fit it in, we were then faced with another problem.

Another client, a very nice man called Tony Clarke of Official Airline Guides, had been due to have a meeting with Gordon that morning. He called to ask where he was. 'I thought he was with you?' I replied. He hadn't shown. I called his flat and there was no answer. Then I called his girlfriend, Dorothy, who worked on the *Business Traveller* magazine. They had separate flats at that time. We both believed he had been drinking again and she was a little exasperated. She said she would go round to his flat that evening. I went off to do a dinner and got home about 1.30 to a very tearful lady on the answerphone. I called her. Dorothy told me that Gordon had left a note and disappeared. The car had gone too, and so had some clothes. I calmed her down, saying that if he was going to commit suicide he would not have taken some clean shirts. For a few days we wondered where he was, and Dorothy was busy on the phone. Then she called some Spanish friends and, while they were talking, the Spanish lady said, 'Guess who's just walked in?'

Obviously Gordon had to resign, and although he wrote me an apologetic letter we have not been in touch since. Although we couldn't work together, I certainly didn't want to end our friendship, but I suppose his pride got the better of him.

Even these events had their amusing side, though. When he'd left for Spain, Gordon, obviously not thinking clearly, had left his car in Heathrow's short-term car park. By the time he came to remove it the fees were more than the value of the car. Still, coming on top of my health problems, the stress of all this was getting to me, and my colleagues insisted that I honour my trip to Australia and the Middle East. They reminded me that even I was not indispensable and they were proved right. The company was still there when I got back.

In the late 1980s Tony Bennett, the much-praised P&O PR man, came to join us. I had got to know him over the years and had approached him on a few occasions about working for us. At one point he was working for Polly Peck, the business that collapsed amid scandal in 1990, although they seemed quite respectable when he was there. When that ended he went to one or two other major companies but things didn't work out, so he called me one day and said he was interested. I thought I would be able to hand over the running of the company to him and concentrate on entertaining.

I started to think I had made a mistake in the first few days when I saw a memo he had written referring to 'my staff'. I had never used that phrase, even though I owned the place. My staff were never 'my staff', they were always 'my colleagues', and I was immediately worried about the appointment. Although we survived together for about a year and he did some good work for us on crisis management, Tony was not popular, and I never felt able to take my hands off the tiller as much as I would have wished.

Then fate took a hand. The UK pulled out of the Exchange Rate Mechanism, the recession hit, and I eventually had to close down the company. It was like losing a child. Even so, everyone was paid, and some of my colleagues took some of the smaller clients with them. While it was clearly sad for everyone – and one or two of my colleagues took it worse than others – it was out of my hands. PR is always the first to suffer in a downturn.

So from 1993 I was a full-time entertainer – and landlord. I still had the buildings to let out.

LATEST SCORES
Tottenham 1 Tottenpork 2
Benfica 1 Billfica 2

----

33. WHICH WAY ARE CRYSTAL PALACE KICKING?

'Nookie Bear is a Palace supporter, but we wouldn't trust him to run the club.'

Palace fan confronting former chairman Mark Goldberg

'Which way are Crystal Palace kicking?' a former girlfriend once asked me about ten minutes into a game against Derby County. She was not a football fan, but given the standard of play up to that point it was not an unreasonable question.

I have been wondering where Palace have been going since 1 March 1958, the day I first saw them play. (How do I know the date? Do you really need to ask by now?) We were at home to Aldershot in Division Three (South) and we drew 1–1. Our goal was scored by George Cooper, a striker we'd snapped up from Brierly Hill Athletic.

To tell you all about my love affair with this club would fill another book. Let me just say it has been a roller-coaster ride, and if CPFC were a woman I would have kicked her out long ago. Sadly, as any true football supporter will tell you, you are stuck with them for life. Palace have had financial troubles from which we've recovered only to plunge into them again. We've had more chairmen than you could shake a stick at. We've had some great players, too, like Johnny Byrne, Don Rogers, John Jackson, Mark Bright, Ian Wright and Nigel Martyn. And we've had a few that needed different-coloured laces in each boot so they could work out which foot to kick with. For 25 years I watched Palace infrequently as I was busy playing, but I would be there whenever I was not playing. I watched in despair as they missed the cut when Divisions Three South and North were amalgamated, and slipped into the Fourth Division. Then I watched them climb the divisions and hit the top flight for the first time ever at the end of the 1969/70 season. They only had to get a home win against Fulham, who were already relegated, to go into the First Division. What happened? After twenty minutes we were 2–0 down. Thankfully, in the end we won 3–2. We've been up and down ever since. We've had cup semi-finals galore and lost them all. That is until the 1989/90 season.

I had started that season by going training with Charlton for a week for an article in the *Daily Express*. It tested my 44-year-old body as I chose the week of a heatwave. This is what happened:

As a lifelong Crystal Palace supporter (I told you we were the Team of the Eighties) I've always had a soft spot for Charlton – it's a swamp just outside Woolwich. I saw my first ever professional game at Charlton in 1956, five years before I was snapped up by the Old Wilsonians FC. Charlton went down soon after and languished in the lower regions until Lennie Lawrence arrived to do his Houdini act. It has been said that if Lennie had been captain of the *Titanic* it would never have gone down. [Brian Richardson would use that joke years later.]

These days Charlton share Crystal Palace's Selhurst Park and draw the third largest crowd, after Palace themselves and Sainsbury's. So I felt it was something of a missionary visit when Lennie invited me to train with the lads, muttering something about how I should be able to make anyone look good.

Training at the Old Wilsonians largely consists of going to the annual general meeting and trying to remember the right-back's name, but at a First Division club it's deadly serious.

They do running and things!

I did a twelve-minute run and greatly impressed right-back John Humphrey. I pointed out that I used to be good at the cross-country. 'I suppose you had to be,' he said. 'No buses and trains in those days.' Humph nearly joined QPR recently. 'I was halfway out when the tunnel collapsed.' He is now known as Lifer at Charlton after Lennie said he wanted him to end his career there. Kiss of death if ever I heard one.

Lifer is the comedian of the team, and he wanted to know from Garth Crooks why, when other people play Monopoly and Scrabble, [Garth] had a Martin Luther King game in the back of his car. He had, too! But I was very hurt when, during an eight-a-side game, Lifer complained that our side had two goalkeepers . . . and me. So the new reserve keeper was moved out. He's called Mike Salmon, and this season he might need to leap like one.

I had a bad effect on Peter Shirtliff, who welcomed me to training as the captain. After a week with me he left to join

Sheffield Wednesday. Lennie said he might use the money to buy three Fulham supporters.

In fact, what with Shirty and Steve Gritt (now Walsall) also training there, not to mention Garth Crooks not training ('Ever thought of going full time?' said Lifer one morning), it is hard to see how Lennie ever got a team together to tour Sweden.

All week it was running and exercises, warming up, warming down and warming up again. Where was the coaching? I asked coach Mike Flanagan. No instructions on performing the toe-punt, and clearly the back-heel is being coached out of the game.

At the end of the week I suggested to chairman Roger Alwen that he sack Lennie and appoint whoever trains the youth team manager's collie. 'I gave it a "free" once,' said Lennie, 'but it keeps coming back.' Pity the midfield doesn't. In my view the dog is the fittest thing down there. And not the worst at ball control, either.

It's such a homely club, Charlton, that on the day I left the chairman's wife, Heather, was doing the flower beds. She was being watched by a whippet. Either that or it was the collie with its coat off.

One thing's for sure. All week it was bloody hot.

DIRECT FREE-KICK

Lennie said to me one day, 'You like Charlton, don't you?' I confirmed that I did. 'I've watched you at the games, and you like us to do well, don't you?' Again I confirmed that he was correct. 'And I've watched you at Palace games,' he added.

I was slightly taken aback. 'Really?' I said.

'Yes,' he said, 'and I realise that, although you like Charlton, it's Palace that gives you a lump in your trousers.'

Palace started that 1989/90 season normally – struggling in the First Division. I remember working late in my office listening to the Capital Gold commentary when we played Liverpool at Anfield. My ears were assailed as goal after goal went in. We lost 9–0, and I penned the following piece for the *Daily Express*:

I am writing to you from a bunker somewhere in south London. With me are Lord Lucan, Salman Rushdie, Shergar and the

Crystal Palace goalkeeper Perry Suckling. I'd rather be at home, but people keep leaving messages on my answerphone – largely consisting of the Eagles chant followed by a lot of laughter. Even last night, as I tried to watch my *Dad's Army* video, the phone kept ringing. It was mainly Charlton supporters trying to get out of the ground-sharing agreement.

At times like this you clutch at straws. How must Wigan be feeling having just agreed to play both legs of their Littlewoods Cup tie at Anfield, or Wimbledon, who lost to us last weekend and failed to score? I should also draw your attention to the fact that we are above Wimbledon in the table and have a better goal record than Sheffield Wednesday (3–13 to 1–14).

One lesser journal has already asked me if I plan to withdraw my sponsorship of my mate Perry for the season, but my emphatic answer is 'No!' This is not misplaced loyalty, more that I have already paid the money. No, my main task is to take the pressure off Perry in his hour of need.

I'm testing him with the little good-natured jokes he can expect. Like how he tried to get on the team bus and it went underneath him. How he put his head in his hands and missed. I've pointed out that even I played in a team that lost 18–3 once. Mind you, I wasn't playing goal. None of this seems to have brightened him up. I've said that everyone will soon forget it – in about 30 years or so.

So all is not lost. After all, we are the Team of the Eighties. Perry? No, that's not how many I think you'll let in this month. Perry, Perry! Where are you going? Perry . . .

It's not always the goalkeeper's fault when you let in nine. In fact, when I could bring myself to watch the video, I don't think he could have stopped any of them. Perhaps I was judging him by my standards? Palace manager Steve Coppell obviously didn't see it my way and signed Nigel Martyn from Bristol Rovers for £1 million. Once again in the *Express*, I sent him this open letter – obviously heavily tongue in cheek:

Dear Nige,

What have you done? There you were, sitting quietly in the
Bristol dressing room after repelling the odd Third Division
attack, delivering an occasional antique for Gerry Francis, when
suddenly you sign for the only team in the country that's let in
more than the West German government [the Berlin Wall had
just come down]. Perhaps you were dazzled by the colour of Ron
Noades' hair? It went like that when the ninth goal hit the back of
the net at Anfield.

Have you checked your contract? If you get it out of the
drawer, taking care not to drop it, you'll probably find a couple of
noughts have faded in the special ink Ron uses. Ron just doesn't
spend that sort of money. I saw Perry Suckling using a spanner to
get 50p out of his hand only a couple of weeks ago. In fact, it was
only a day later when the men in white coats came and carried
Perry off to the funny farm. I can hear his plaintive cries now.
'Four in a wall, four in a wall!' he bleated as they dragged him
away.

Perhaps, Nige, you are part of a master plan? As we've got more
goalkeepers than centre-halves, perhaps we're going to play more
than one? You look a fit lad, Nige. Perhaps you could go rush
goalie in front of Perry when he comes out. Geddit? When he
comes out? Forget it, Nige.

Of course, it's not all bad, Nige. I mean, you get to meet a lot
more forwards than you're used to. Quite nice lads, some of
them. That Lineker has got an O level, you know, and Gascoigne
must be taking his eleven-plus, judging from his display on
Saturday. His mouth was busier than you'll be in the next few
weeks. Another plus is that down at Palace all clean sheets start at
four, so you could do quite well next week.

Well, good luck, old son. I must close now as I'm trying to find
the number of Ken Dodd's solicitor. Ron reckons, if all else fails,
he should be able to stop us going down.

OFFSIDE
'Bob "the Cat" Bevan – the finest goalkeeper never to play for England. I
hope' – Frank Bough on my LP cover

And then things did change. Palace started to play better and had a run in the FA Cup. Fortunately we avoided a First Division team throughout the first four rounds. After winning at home against Huddersfield and Portsmouth we got another home draw in the fifth round. Who did we draw? Rochdale. Into the quarter-finals. Surely now we will meet a proper side? We were drawn away to Fourth Division Cambridge United. My friend Robert Newey and I saw all the games and awaited the semi-final draw. We were punished for our earlier luck: Liverpool at Villa Park. Worse still, we had no Ian Wright, who had broken his leg.

GOAL-KICK

When Robert Newey's son David was small and too young to come to a game, he made the assumption that as his dad went to football with a goalkeeper called Bob, I actually played for Crystal Palace. When he came on his first visit to Selhurst Park and saw me keep goal for a supporters' team against the staff, for which we wore the club colours, it strengthened his belief. We did nothing to dissuade him.

One morning he came down to breakfast and Robert said, 'David, guess what? Palace have just signed a goalkeeper for a million pounds.'

His eyes filled with tears, and he choked out, 'What's happened to Bob?'

He's taller than both of us now and beats us up if we tell the story.

Robert, his wife Glyn, my late girlfriend Sally and I travelled up and had great seats. Right in the front row of the upper stand, on the halfway line. My mate Lennie Lawrence said afterwards that it wasn't the best football match he'd ever seen, but it was the most exciting. I have certainly never been in an atmosphere like it. We were sponsored by Virgin then and they had come up with the idea of handing out red and blue balloons. When the lads came out, everyone at our end let them go. It was an amazing sight. I get emotional just writing about it.

Understandably, nobody gave us a chance, but I always go to every game with an open mind. On their day just about any team can beat anyone else. It's what makes football such a great game. You don't get giant-killing in any other sport like you do in football.

It was a poor first half, and it was no surprise when Liverpool went one up. At the start of the second half I noted that we had run out at a sprint. 'Steve's wound them up well,' I said to Robert. Deputy manager Alan Smith told me later that Steve had been very quiet. He had said, 'We're only one down. Keep it tight at the back. Don't do anything silly and see if we can nick a goal later on.'

From the kick-off, right-back John Pemberton went charging down the wing, smashed it over, and Mark Bright scored. Steve was still coming out of the tunnel, and when he heard the roar his first reaction was 'Oh, Christ. What's Pembo done now?' Then Gary O'Reilly scored from a free-kick. We were in dreamland. Then Steve McMahon equalised and John Barnes scored from a penalty. Back to the nightmare, but not for long. Andy Gray nodded in another equaliser. Extra-time, and each side had chances. Then, near the end, Alan Pardew headed our winner.

All hell broke loose at the final whistle. When we finally let the players go they threw chairman Ron Noades in the bath, fully suited. Former player John Salako told me later that the kit man, Spike, was sitting on the skip crying his eyes out. He'd been a Palace supporter all his life and he never thought he would see Palace in an FA Cup final. Up in the stands I was crying too, for the same reasons as Spike. Sally couldn't stand it. She said, 'I'm going to talk to Robert. He's much more sensible.' But he was crying too.

We drove back down the motorway listening to the other game between Manchester United and Oldham. That went to 3–3, and we were worried that it might overshadow our game. Stupid, really. Nothing would ever beat that day. I'm moist-eyed now just thinking about it.

For the next few weeks the atmosphere around the ground was amazing. I drove up there during the day once and there was a milk float doing its rounds completely covered with red and blue balloons.

I received a telephone call from a TV researcher on *Wogan*, Tom Webber. Terry had a daily live chat show in those days, and we had met several times through the Lord's Taverners. Would I appear on *Wogan* with Bobby Charlton? I certainly would. A few days later Tom and I discussed what material I would use so that Terry could feed me a few lines. I told him I normally took the mickey. He said he knew; he had seen me before. When I asked him where, he said it was at the PFA dinner. 'Have you not seen me since?' I asked. He hadn't. 'Do you realise how long ago that was? It's nine years!' Never underestimate the power of the television. This contact was to last for another nine years as I made four further appearances on *Auntie's Sporting Bloomers*.

On the night of my *Wogan* debut I walked on wearing a huge Palace rosette and a scarf. We went through the set pieces and I threw in a joke at Sally's expense. 'I was in tears after we beat Liverpool, and the girlfriend turned to me and said, "Sometimes I think you love Crystal Palace more than you love me." I said, "I love Wimbledon more than I love you."' It was scary doing it live on national TV, especially when Terry fed me a line I didn't recognise. I froze, but he spotted it straight away and carried on talking, so you would never know on the video. Then Bobby, who knew my act by heart by now, asked me about playing on Wimbledon Common Extension. I was forced to do the 'so slippery we had a job to turn round at half-time' line. This was new to Terry, and on the tape you can see him falling back into his chair, corpsing.

Next day, as I walked round Wembley, everyone recognised me. Loads of autographs. This was fame at last! Sally and my dad walked a few paces behind just to watch the reaction I was getting.

Everyone thought it was a great final. Manchester United's goal-keeper, Jim Leighton, was having a bad time and was lucky to be in the side. He was at fault when Gary O'Reilly gave us the lead after nineteen minutes. Bryan Robson equalised, and then Mark Hughes put them ahead after 65 minutes. Ian Wright had not played for months, but he was on the bench. Steve Coppell put him on, and almost immediately Wrighty scored. We went mad.

Now it was extra-time, and two minutes in Wrighty scored again. We went even madder, but as we sat down I said to Robert, 'We've scored too early.' He called me a miserable bastard, but, sadly, I was right. Normally a goal gives a team a lift, but we were out on our feet. It was no surprise when Mark Hughes equalised seven minutes from the end.

We were awful in the replay. We played badly, and tried to kick them off the park. We lost 1–0. It was disappointing, but at least now I would always be famous. Or would I? I called Sally the following Monday. I said that I had been up to London Bridge and back on the train. No autographs. Not even a double take. The dream was over.

Next season we came third in the First Division and, but for the Heysel disaster after which English teams were banned from Europe, who knows where we might have been now. As it is, we're lucky we're still here. Ron Noades did not want to sell the club, but if someone keeps piling millions on the table, as Mark Goldberg did, who can blame Ron for picking it up? Especially as Noades kept the ground. Goldberg's actions defy description, and I don't want to sully these pages further with his name. I didn't like him the first time I met him, and after his ill-judged actions nearly destroyed our club, my thoughts are now unprintable. We truly have been lucky to survive.

When I was on *Six O Six*, a Doncaster supporter called me and said that he was hopeful that his team would at least go into the Conference. 'If they folded, Bob, I don't know what I'd do. Who would I support?' David Mellor, who moved from Fulham to Chelsea, might not have understood the emotions he was expressing, but I did. A few years after I took that call I would experience the same fears.

LATEST SCORES
Motherwell 2 Fatherdead 3
Peterborough 3 Fredborough 4

THE BRYLCREEM BOY

'Not that I recall.'

Allegedly said by Michael Jackson in court when asked
if he ever suffered from memory lapses

When Denis Compton died in 1998, the newspapers were full of tributes to a man who was probably our greatest ever batsman. I met him 30 years ago on one of my frequent visits to El Vino's in Fleet Street. When I met him I immediately found him a likeable and friendly man. It was hard to believe that I was in the company of a legend. In *The Times*, the great cricket writer R.C. Robertson-Glasgow had written, 'Denis has a genius, but if he knows, he doesn't care.' It summed him up.

There were many stories about his forgetfulness. Once, in El Vino's, he said to me that he had called in at Gerrards Cross Cricket Club the previous evening 'for a quick one on the way home'. He'd found them all in dinner jackets. 'What's on here tonight?' he'd asked. They'd told him it was their centenary dinner, reminded him that he was the guest speaker, and packed him off home to change.

The papers also wrote of his great friendship with legendary Australian cricketer Keith Miller. Apparently they'd spoken on the phone every Sunday morning. This brought back a memory that will stay as a picture in my mind for ever.

It was January 1995 and I was in Adelaide for the Fourth Test. Michael Parkinson and I had spoken the night before at a Sundowner, a pre-dinner party which is common in Australia, for the Lord's Taverners. The next day we were in the 90-degree sunshine enjoying some hospitality in a tented area. Behind me was a mobile home wherein Keith Miller was entertaining his cronies. Oz may claim to be a classless society, but Keith was royalty to them. Suddenly, Compo appeared, straight from the plane and looking, in his grey suit and tie, rather inappropriately dressed for the heat. After the usual greetings I, along with an Aussie Taverner, helped him up the steps. I turned back to see his familiar bow legs, supported by sticks, and I heard the warm greeting from his old friend. For reasons I still find hard to explain, tears welled up in my eyes. Perhaps I was moved by the sight of two truly great players enjoying the sort of friendship only sport can bring.

At the end of the day the pair of them were in the car park heading for their transport. Compo, struggling on his sticks and probably not helped by the hospitality, waved across at me. Seeing me, Keith Miller broke away and came over. He shook my hand. 'You were very good last night,' he said. It's a treasured memory.

I spoke with Compo just the once, at Huddersfield. It was a pleasant evening raising money for a hospital scanner. It went on a bit, and Denis and I stayed up with the guests until about two a.m., even though he had to get an early train to attend a relaunch of Brylcreem the next morning. I said that I would not be joining him at such an hour. He went off to bed and I followed about an hour later, cancelling all alarm calls. At six a.m. he was hammering on my door. 'Come on, old boy, we've got a train to catch.' If I'd had my wits about me I'd have asked him who had reminded him. Instead, I protested that I'd only just got to sleep. 'Come on, old boy, you've got to look after me.' So I went. And I'll always be glad I did.

34. PAPERS BLOWING ACROSS THE PITCH

'I didn't like it, Sam,' rejoined Mr Weller. 'I never know'd a respectable coachman as wrote poetry, 'cept one, as made an affectin' copy o' werses the night afore he wos hung for a highway robbery; and he wos only a Camberwell man, so even that's no rule.'

from *The Pickwick Papers* by Charles Dickens

I was back at the Football Writers dinner three more times. I did it when John Barnes won in 1988 and Eric Cantona in 1996. In between I did Gary Lineker's in 1992. Feeling the need to do some new material, I decided to write one of my poems – always a risk, but fortunately it was well received. Before you read 'Goodbye Gal' (all due apologies to Neil Simon on the title), I need to remind you of a few things: Gary had decided to retire to end his career in Japan; Terry Venables was manager of Spurs (not to mention his club, Scribes West) and Alan Sugar was chairman, taking over from Irving Scholar; Sir John Quinton of Barclays had become chairman of the Premiership; there were merger rumours about the Midland Bank; the League of Wales had just started; Michael Knighton was still remembered for his rather bizarre attempt to buy Manchester United; Gazza was off to Italy; Graham Kelly, Glen Kirton and Sir Bert Millichip were still at the FA; and Ken Bates' tenure at Stamford Bridge was looking a bit shaky.

Now read on.

One day after playing West Ham,
Gal said: 'My career's in a jam.'
So he went to El Tel,
Said: 'Though you pay me quite well,
I think I'll sod off to Japan.'

Gal said: 'The last thing I want is a rift,
But my release is within your gift.'
Tel said: 'Leave it 'til later.
I'm planting a tater,
So next season we'll have something to lift.'

But Gal just would not be stopped,
Though Tel begged 'til his eyes almost popped.
He even talked of Terry Neill,
Who left Ireland for Muswell Hill,
And the IQs in both countries dropped.

As it sank El Tel looked quite ill
And searched in his purse for a pill
He said 'This is a real bugger,
I must 'phone Alan Suger,'
Then he stopped and cried in Scribes' till

Alan said, though it made him feel sick,
He would not take a decision too quick.
He said: 'Still, if he goes to Nip land,
I could bid for the Midland.'
Tel said: 'We'll offer cash – plus Terry Fen-wick!'

Tel said: 'After that I'm feeling quite merry.
Let me pour you a Scribes West dry sherry.'
He said: 'Do you think in Japan,
Their top FA man
Is some sumo they call Glayham Kerry?'

Gal said: 'I'll not miss that lot on this trip,
Though I don't wish to say things too flip.'
He said: 'One thing's for certain,
There won't be a Gren Klirton.
Nor, I hope, a Sir Berr Mirrichip.'

Tel said: 'Our parting will be without rancour,
For here at Spurs you have been our anchor.
I might sign Andy Sinton,
Or perhaps Sir John Quinton!
Now there is a wit of a banker!'

Tel said: 'Just before you get on your bike,
Are you sure it's a country you'll like?'
Gal said: 'I've thought long and well,
Told my Dad and Michelle,
And had it all blessed through David Icke.'

Then, just as their chat started to tire,
Ken Bates came on the phone breathing fire.
He said: 'Tel, I would like it much better
If you'd not sent that letter
Addressed "Stamford Bridge, the Occupier".'

Ken said: 'Of such jokes I've had my fill,
For I'm having those nightmares still.'
He said: 'You would be more caring
If you'd dreamt of ground sharing
With Noades, Sam Hammam and Jimmy Hill.'

Ken raved on 'til Tel just couldn't follow.
Then he felt a cold sweat on his collar.
As he put down the phone
He felt all alone,
And thought how much he missed Irving Scholar.

So while Gazza's off to play for some greaser,
We've lost Gal, our other crowd pleaser.
And it's not just football's loss,
For in life he's some sort of cross
Between Doug Ellis and Mother Teresa.

So before our bladders swell up like a spinnaker,
And my rhyming becomes even more finnickier,
Let me say, at the end,
We're all proud to have as our friend
A great player – more important – great man, Gary Lin-Acre.

By the time I had got to the John Barnes dinner in 1988 I was no
longer using notes. Three years earlier I had done a boxing dinner for
NABS (National Advertising Benevolent Society). This is a legendary
occasion as many of the TV companies give air time and Jimmy Hill
auctions several slots and some cars, always for six figures. Ron Miller
was the sales director of London Weekend Television, and he took me
to lunch in Langan's to thank me. 'If ever I can do anything for you,
just let me know,' he said. Ten minutes later he thought of something
himself. He told me that the TV industry ran an annual conference in
Monte Carlo to which all their advertisers were taken. 'I'd want you

to do a small dinner for us,' he said, 'and you could do twenty minutes at the ball and then introduce Elaine Paige. But you'll have to do it as a cabaret, it wouldn't look right to use notes. If you don't fancy it, it doesn't matter.' I thought back to the disaster five days after the 1980 FWA dinner but I would have to throw them away some time. I said that I would do it.

It was an unusually nervous build-up. While I was away I was going to hit 40, and I really didn't want to be 40. That, combined with the nerves, made me a pretty miserable git. Gaby, who I was with then and who had accompanied me to Monte Carlo, was not enjoying herself. All this despite the fact that my writing partner, Robbo, was unexpectedly there helping to run the conference. It's his proper job, you know.

On the night I walked out on to the floor and my voice was trembling. At least it sounded as though it was to me. Fortunately, as I've said, I don't seem to sound nervous to others. I did twenty minutes and must have gone down well because a guy approached me in the casino later. He was Todd Evans of Peugeot. In a spooky repeat of the Ranjit Anand booking in 1980, he hired me for a year hence for the Peugeot 309 launch. They would be having two shows in the Monte Carlo Sporting Club. Clearly thinking that I did cabaret and stage work all the time, he wanted me to host them.

Twelve months later, still nervous but with a notes-free year behind me, I walked out on to the stage in front of a thousand people. I did five minutes and then introduced some dancers. My next spot involved introducing a magician whose name had inexplicably failed to stick in my mind all through rehearsals. Fortunately I had given myself a safety net. As the time came for me to announce him, sure enough his name again went out of my head. On the video the join shows, and a guy on the side of the stage says, within my earshot, 'He's forgotten his name!' However, my safety net then kicked in – when the Ayatollah came, the Shah hid.

'Ladies and gentlemen, please welcome Shahid Malik!'

Sweat was pouring off me when I went off, but I'd recovered by the time Shahid had produced a live lion, and then a Peugeot 309 out of nowhere with me in the back. I then had to do twenty minutes while the band set up behind the curtain prior to introducing the surprise star, Elkie Brooks. While I was working, one of the band touched a guitar string while it was live. Fortunately, it happened at the end of a gag. Everyone in the theatre heard it, and out of nowhere came an ad lib I'd heard used by a great after-dinner act, Jan Harding, sadly no longer with us. 'I don't remember eating that,' I said. It brought the house down, and the band instantly became my mates. I spent the following day, which we had off, getting sloshed with them. By the time we got to the second show I was flying.

In 1999 I was asked again to do the PFA dinner. They don't normally have anyone back, so I played on that and said that I'd been there eighteen years earlier and gone down well . . . I only had a short spot, though, and I still had a mountain of stuff Robbo and I wrote which I didn't use. At the time Glenn Hoddle's infamous post-France 98 World Cup book, which upset the players and featured the faith healer Eileen Drewery, had only recently been published. I told the audience that the Old Wilsonians 7th XI had also now employed a faith healer – Irene Brewery. She was not as good as Eileen, but she was more fun. I also used a joke wondering if referee David Elleray was into faith healing, as he seemed to see things that no one else did. Unlike Paul Durkin, who never saw anything. It was also a time when everyone was worried about the millennium bug, so Robbo wrote a routine on how the FA might handle it. Sadly, I didn't get to do it, but here I give it its debut.

At the FA they have been most concerned about the advent of the new century. Apparently, David Davies paused from writing Kevin Keegan's diary and noticed that the rubber date stamp they use on the post had got no '2' on it.

On learning this, David and the whole of the FA swung into action and immediately called an emergency meeting of the Admin Resource Structure Executive, otherwise known as ARSE. Well, they immediately passed it on to the Personnel Resources and Training Section, otherwise known as PRATS – that's right, you're with it now, aren't you? After further deliberation, they called in Operational Standard Handbook Information Technology, otherwise known as, as you will have spotted, O SHIT. Finally, the whole matter was, as usual, swept under the carpet for future reference by the – wait for it – Finance Underwriting Committee. (*Pause.*) K Division.

LATEST SCORES
Ajax 1 Harpic 2
Hibernian 0 Lowbernian 4

35. TIME ADDED ON

'I keep a video of Tony Blair reading Corinthians at Diana's funeral and threaten to show it to anyone who is impressed by the PM's sincerity.'

Labour MP Bob Marshall-Andrews

I was just taking my father out for a curry when the phone rang. It was Seb Coe – Lord Coe these days. Incidentally, I remember a press trip to the US on Continental Airlines when I was travelling first class and he was up the back. We met in the terminal, and during the flight I got the air hostess to take a bread roll to him with a suitable note. He's never got over it. Anyway, we've been friends for twenty years, and he was calling to see if I would help Tory leader (as he was then) William Hague with his speeches. I said I would be pleased to, so long as I could bring my friend Brian Robinson along.

Hence both Robbo and I headed for the House of Commons for a meeting with William Hague. It was hard to take in the fact that the two of us, who had met on a muddy football field in Walthamstow and at some dodgy dinners in even more dodgy clubhouses, were now walking the corridors of power. The Leader of the Opposition has spacious accommodation in the House, and we spent 45 minutes with Hague and Coe sitting in big leather armchairs and laughing. We liked William immediately, even more so as we've come to know him. I believe his image problems have robbed the nation of a decent prime minister. He always appears to be smiling. Nothing ever seems to get him down.

Our first task was to provide him with some material for a dinner at a club called the Saints and Sinners. This was co-founded by Percy Hoskins, a crime reporter on the *Sunday Express* with whom I used to drink in El Vino's. That year Jimmy Tarbuck was the chairman, and Princess Anne would also be at the dinner. Robbo came up with the idea of Hague confusing Tarby with Bruce Forsyth, and he seemed to like the idea.

When we left, Seb mentioned that his secretary was convinced I was Sir Robert Bevan. It seemed he had said it as a joke, and she had taken it on board. He had done nothing to correct her. It was strange, because I had heard someone use the name Sir Robert when I walked in, and as only my close family use the name Robert it had registered with me. This seemed to amuse the other three, and I told William that he had better become Prime Minister pretty quickly so he could make it official.

Later, we sat down and wrote this stuff for him:

Ever since I became Leader of the Opposition it has been my policy to go for a ten-mile run every morning with my colleague Sebastian Coe. This morning, when I'd finished my run, I showered, got changed and sat down to wait for him to get back. After some delay, he eventually staggered through the door. I helped him to a chair and sat him down. When he'd recovered, I lit his cigarette for him and sat back down to await my instructions for the day.

He said, 'You know, I'm very worried about tonight's dinner. I'm not sure you know enough about the chairman.'

'Don't worry about that,' I said. 'I well remember his appearances on *Sunday Night at the London Palladium*.'

Of course, I didn't actually see them myself; I wasn't allowed to stay up that late. But my grandmother – one of his biggest fans, incidentally – used to tell me all about it. She told me of his many famous catchphrases, such as 'I'm in charge.' If I remember rightly, that was a favourite of Margaret Thatcher's as well. Then there was 'Didn't he do well?' I quite like that one myself. And, of course, there's the one you can all join in with: 'Nice to see you (*raise both hands*), to see you . . . (*audience call out 'Nice!'*).

And to think people say we politicians are out of touch.

I was also able to tell Seb that I knew that your chairman and I have a great deal in common. For example, I know that he has a big golfing friend called Parky. In fact, only recently I appeared on his TV show – if you'll forgive me for name dropping. The Duke of Edinburgh's always telling me off about it. Well, I too have a friend called Parky. Your friend is called Michael while mine is called Cecil. Do you think they could in any way be related? I think we should be told.

[. . .]

Well, on behalf of the guests, I must say it's been an honour and a privilege to be asked here this evening. Of course, as a speaker here tonight I have had the distinct advantage of not having to have my address cleared by Alastair Campbell. You probably weren't that fortunate, Tarby. I'm pretty sure I spotted his influence on one or two of your comments earlier.

Of course, I couldn't comment on your speech, Ma'am.

I am also well aware that your chairman greatly admires all that is best in the traditions of show business. So, in his honour I felt I should close with a monologue. And here I should also offer my apologies to Stanley Holloway.

There's a famous seaside place called Liverpool
What's noted for fresh air and fun,
And a couple whose surname was Tarbuck
Lived there with young Jimmy, their son.

A smart little lad was young Jimmy,
A bright-eyed and neat little bloke,
With a gap in his front teeth
Through which he could tell you a joke.

His family looked on with great pride
As young Tarby grew to be a big star.
He's come a long way has young Jimmy,
To be chairman of this shows how far.

I hear you ask – and is he to be chairman next year?
I have to tell you he ain't.
Next year, a new man steps in.
Next year it's the turn of a Saint!

Apparently it all went well, except that he ducked out of delivering the Bruce Forsyth lines. Seb liked it and thought it was very funny. We knew it would be all right because the audience was more our age than William's. Still, at that time William had surrounded himself with some very young advisers and I can only guess that they talked him out of it. Even so, we became part of his team of writers, and he put in no small measure of good stuff himself. He has a natural comic talent and sense of timing.

THROW-IN

They couldn't get me a ticket for the Saints and Sinners, largely because they decided they wanted to keep me under wraps. I therefore had a spare evening at home until I got called out for the pub darts team. I reflected, as I stood there, that I should have been with Jimmy Tarbuck, William Hague and Princess Anne at that moment. But I couldn't tell anyone.

Just before the Tory Party Conference that year, we were due to have lunch with Seb. William spotted our name in his diary and said he would come too. As usual, we spent a lot of time telling each other jokes he couldn't possibly use. When Robbo asked where Blair would be during the conference, and was told he was in China, we told another gag he couldn't use: 'Tony Blair is rather like Mao Tse-tung. After a hard day's work he can always murder a Chinese.'

CORNER

During the time when Labour were tearing themselves apart over the first elections for the London mayor, William said to Tony Blair during Prime Minister's Questions, 'Why don't you have Frank Dobson as your day mayor and Ken Livingstone as your night mayor?' Even Blair laughed.

Robbo also came up with a good idea. Paddy Ashdown (then the Lib Dem leader and MP for Yeovil) had been hoping to join some Cabinet committees but then Blair had got his landslide and no longer needed the Lib Dems. Nice business, politics. Robbo suggested a lonely hearts letter for the conference, and I went home and wrote this in just a couple of hours:

I've come across this very sad letter only recently which I thought I would read out to you, in confidence. It's from Heartbroken of Yeovil, and it reads as follows:

Dear Clare,

In May last year I became involved with a married man called Tony. He said he was very keen to form a relationship, and although all my friends warned me against him I was blinded by all the power he said he now had. He said personal relationships (or PR, as I call it) were high on his life's agenda, although looking back, he always winked at his friends when he said it.

I didn't like some of his friends. There was a brooding, dark Scotsman who was always playing with his calculator and kept trying to pull Tony's chair away. Then there was a little ginger Scotsman who was always looking at a lady's picture and smiling. And a rather portly northern gentleman who often told Tony that I was a waste of space and that he couldn't understand what I was doing there.

But recently he hasn't written, he hasn't telephoned. No flowers. No chocolates. Even worse, he's been horrible about me in public when he had a big meeting with all his friends.

Now I'm terribly confused – not a new experience for me, Clare – and I wonder if I should trust this man? Are we really going to have a relationship, or were my friends right all along?

Clare replies to Heartbroken of Yeovil, again in complete confidence:

Dear Paddy,

I'm sorry to have to tell you that you have been taken in by this man. But take heart. You're not alone. Many others have suffered similarly. One day people like him will find out they are a bit too smooth for their own good.

I think your friends were right all along. It's time to go away and get a life. You'll be much happier hanging out with little groups of chums. Just like you've always done.

And one day, I promise, lots more people will be let down by this man and he will have to go away as well.

I didn't see it go out live, but I watched it later and noted that of our stuff the best reaction was from the agony aunt letter. It was even re-run on Chris Evans' breakfast show the following morning. Yet I don't think William made the best of it. He moved 'Heartbroken of Yeovil' to the back of the letter when it really needed to be flagged up at the start. I don't think the audience got it until halfway through, and he could have taken the roof off with it. The speech was good, but still a bit long and a bit repetitive. But William's delivery and timing are unequalled by any politician. Afterwards everyone – the press, Kenneth Clarke, John Redwood – said that the jokes were good.

Perhaps the line that pleased me most came at a time when Tony Blair was frequently saying that the only good thing about William was his jokes. We gave him an ad lib to use if it was repeated during Prime Minister's Questions. He bided his time, and when the opportunity came he pounced. 'At least my jokes are proper ones,' William retorted. 'All your jokes are in the Cabinet.'

LATEST SCORES
Hull 2 Fo'c's'le 2 (winners to meet Crewe)
Fulham 6 Emptyem 0

OUR LIPS ARE ALWAYS MOVING

'Friendship is like money – easier made than kept.'

Samuel Butler

The Grand Order of Water Rats may not be as well known now as it was in the days of music hall and variety, but it's still an honour to be part of it. It is an indication that you have been accepted as being part of show business. Since 1889 there have been fewer than 850 Water Rats, and every one was or is an entertainer. Chesney Allen, Arthur Askey, Charlie Chaplin, Tommy Cooper, Lonnie Donegan, Bud Flanagan, Laurel and Hardy, Dan Leno, Ted Ray, Tommy Trinder – they were all Water Rats. Today there are some top names, too: Max Bygraves, Frank Carson, Michael Crawford, Johnnie Dankworth, Bruce Forsyth, Sir Bob Hope, Engelbert Humperdinck, Roy Hudd, Brian May, Sir John Mills, Joe Pasquale, Jimmy Tarbuck, Rick Wakeman, Sir Norman Wisdom . . . the list goes on. We raise money for people in our business who need help, and we make charitable donations too.

Our meetings can be hilarious, and there are always plenty of gags and stories flying around about the old days. About a year ago a top ventriloquist called Arthur Worsley died. After respects had been paid, the stories started. Arthur had a dummy which he operated while keeping a deadpan face and saying virtually nothing himself. Eric Morecambe openly admitted that he stole from Arthur the dummy's line, 'Look at me when I'm talking to you, son.'

You may just remember a singing double act called Bob and Alf Pearson. They were very famous in their day; they had a hit with 'Tears' about 25 years before Ken Dodd did. Alf is still going strong at 94, and he talked about appearing with Arthur Worsley. He said that while Arthur was technically the best 'vent' he had seen, there was another called David Pool who was funnier. 'Unfortunately,' he added, 'you could see David's lips move.'

In those days, when Sunday performances were banned, actors and entertainers used the day to travel and were often changing trains at

Crewe. The famous comic Rob Wilton met David Pool on one of these occasions.

'Where you working this week, David?' he asked.

David said he was at the Lyceum, Sheffield.

'You should go down very well there,' said Rob.

'Do you really think so?' said David.

'Certainly. It's very dark.'

36. FINAL WHISTLE

'It won't be kiss and tell. Or even kiss and El Tel. But I have worked with nearly everyone once so there should be some interesting stories to tell.'

Willie Rushton

When he died just before Christmas 1996, the *Daily Mail* described Willie Rushton as 'the jack of all trades who was master of all'. He was one of the first famous people I got to know well, and I was flattered that he was impressed with my style of comedy and delivery.

'You should try a bit of acting, Cat,' he said to me once in Swansea, after I'd had a particularly good evening.

'Do you really think so?'

'Delivering a funny line is only acting,' he said.

On another occasion he brought his son Toby with him to a Lord's Taverners cricket match. 'I've told him to watch you tonight in the cabaret,' Willie commented. 'I want him to see someone who can do it and someone who can't.' I won't reveal the name of my fellow artist that night, but it was the first time I'd ever heard Willie say anything negative about anyone. The second and last time came when he resigned as a trustee of the Taverners. I phoned him. 'I've done my time, Cat,' he said. He added that he didn't have too much respect for a new staff member. He didn't get into details, but he apparently knew one of his ex-colleagues and as a result was less than impressed. Later, in a colour supplement article on after-dinner speakers' favourite after-dinner speakers, Willie named Barry Cryer and myself as his joint choice.

At the end of November 1996 I was standing outside the church near Lord's as a steward at Leslie Crowther's memorial service when my mobile phone rang. Relieved that it had reminded me to turn it off during the service, I took the call. It was from Willie's agent. She told me that he hadn't been well but that he was now out of hospital and was getting better. He could not, however, fulfil an engagement on 5 December and had recommended either cartoonist Bill Tidy or myself. I was working already on that date, but, amazingly, Bill was standing nearby so I called him over and told him he'd got a job. I also said I'd call Willie to see how he was.

It went completely out of my mind, though, so I was hit between the eyes a fortnight later when the TV news announced his death. I had to call his great friend and comedy partner Barry Cryer just to speak to someone. Barry was out, but his wife, Terry, told me that even Barry had not known of Willie's heart trouble.

I'm sorry he's not around to read this book because I'm sure his advice would have made it better. Still, he has been a great inspiration for this book and for its title. Here I take you back to an event that took place during a Taverners game at Sittingbourne in Kent in 1985.

The fact that I was almost never approached for autographs was a source of some amusement to Willie, but at Sittingbourne I assured him it would be different. 'I've been on the box down here, so I'm quite well known,' I said. During the afternoon we strolled together around the boundary. Then a woman came out of the crowd brandishing an autograph book. She ignored Willie and asked me to sign. I nudged him. 'Told you,' I said.

'I am right, aren't I?' the woman said. 'You are the weather man?'

Willie couldn't get back to the dressing room fast enough to tell the other lads.

There have been at least two other memorable 'nearly famous' incidents. In the late eighties I was in Dubai doing an ex-pats dinner, and the sponsor, a bluff Yorkshireman in the duty-free business, invited me to lunch. 'I'll be frank,' he said. 'I've never heard of you. But Frank Carson and Fred Trueman said you were OK so I've taken a chance. Mind you, a lot of people go home at this time of year, so if it doesn't work out it won't matter.' And only this year, when I arrived at Yorkshire TV to record some episodes of *Countdown* (we do five shows in a day), I was put in the contestants' room for a full five minutes (still going red, Paula?). I wouldn't mind, but I'd done five shows as a guest in Dictionary Corner a few months before.

Even the Amazon website, when it first advertised this book before publication got my name wrong.

But back to Willie. When I first met him he was doing this brilliant poem which was published in one of his books. He sent me a copy of it with a nice message written across the top. I have permission to share it with you here:

This song, which was written for the late, great Dame Vesta Wicket at the turn of the century, could well have been one of the

most popular songs ever written. Alas, not one copy of it was ever
to be sold, nor was it ever to be sung in public. Scotland Yard
seized every copy and sold them at a discount to the MCC, who
destroyed them all in a massive fire in the Tennis Courts. The
composer, Eric Low-Grubber, robbed of fame, slit his wrists. The
adorable Vesta Wicket was offered a damehood and a rich old
Conservative in the country.

Here are the lyrics, whispered hoarsely into the ear of Sir Rambo
during 'a night of passion in Eaton Square between the wars'. The
tune was stolen by several composers and used for songs as
different as 'Burlington Bertie' and the Peruvian national anthem.

I bowl maiden overs,
I'm never no-balled,
And yet all the members
At Lord's are appalled;
They accuse me of constantly lowering the tone.
I'm Maurice from Marylebone.

The girls say my googlies
Exude loads of charm;
Then I give 'em the one
That goes through with the arm –
Behaviour that no decent club would condone.
I'm Maurice from Marylebone.

I'm Maurice, I'm Maurice,
I've made ducks and Doris
And Delilah and Deirdre, and Deirdre's best friend.
I've had girls by the million
Behind the pavilion,
And many wound up at the Nursery End.

I've relished their bouncers,
I've pounced on their lobs;
I leave them in no doubt
I'm one of the snobs.
I undoubtedly stand in a class of my own.
I'm Maurice from Marylebone.

I'll meet you, m'dear,
Under Old Father Time,
Then you'll witness an inning
By a man in his prime.
If they don't move the sightscreen we'll be wholly alone.
I'm Maurice from Marylebone.

My box is enormous,
Jam-packed with delights;
It seats seven ladies
With vast appetites,
Huge black women, none under 23 stone.
I'm Maurice from Marylebone.

I'm Maurice, I'm Maurice [with French accent here],
W.G.'s at the crease.
I don't care, I have strawberries and ample champagne.
Come, my dear, let's be lovers,
Let's get under the covers,
We shan't be disturbed unless play stops for rain.

The girls all adore me,
I'm such a gay fellow,
Entirely bedecked
In the old red and yellow.
If they ever black-ball me, I'll be cut to the bone;
Where would I go, if from Lord's I was thrown?
Perhaps to the Oval, and be just as well known.
As Maurice from Kennington.

LATEST SCORES
St Mirren 1 Helen Mirren 2
Hamilton Academicals 0 Hamilton Idiots 9

---

37. BACK IN THE DRESSING ROOM

'You would think if any team could put up a decent wall it would be China.'

Terry Venables, during the 2002 World Cup

Among all the famous people I've met there are two I regard as really good friends – Terry Venables and Jimmy Hill. Both have had their ups and downs, but they have always bounced back and managed to see the funny side of life.

I first saw Jimmy on Good Friday morning, 27 March 1959 – yes, got the programme – when he scored a hat-trick. (He will be pleased to have it mentioned twice.) I saw Terry play for the first time on 5 March 1960 at Dulwich Hamlet. He secured his one amateur international cap that day against Germany and will forever be the only man to hold a cap at every level. No amateurs now, you see?

I have always liked Terry a lot. We've been through some interesting times together. When he was writing the TV series *Hazel*, he and his partner Gordon Williams came up with a comedy idea involving a jobsworth type. Why they thought of me I can't imagine. I went to a small room in Oxford Street for a kind of audition, straight from my office, in a suit. At one point I was on my knees singing 'Mammy'.

When he was at Barcelona, Terry Neill and I went out for a game against Real Madrid, which was some experience. We had one problem, though: all weekend, whenever someone shouted 'Tel?' they would both turn round. Venables was already El Tel, but from that time on Terry Neill became known as O Tel.

One person who doesn't seem to like Venables is Patrick Collins of the *Mail on Sunday*. Everyone's entitled to their opinion, but it's hard to view Collins as a trusted opinion-former when he does seem to have a severe case of Vennerphobia. Here is an entry from my 1998 diary, at the time of Venables' most publicised court battles:

Laura has been asked to book George Best, but his number has changed so I spoke to Rodney Marsh. George is already working that night so we talked about El Tel. Rodney said he was very down and bemoaned the fact that he had been dropped from a promotional opportunity. I'm not sure Rodney realises the commercial difficulties of associating with El Tel until the heat dies down. With nineteen charges admitted he clearly cannot be used as a role model in business terms. All of this reminded me of the clearly delighted journalist Patrick Collins. He has been a serial critic of Tel, and in his latest article he suggested that Tel had let down all his friends and that we should abandon him. It doesn't say much for Patrick Collins' idea of friendship. A lot of El Tel's problems have stemmed from his strong loyalty to friends who have let him down. I have always had a great relationship with Tel. He has made me welcome from Tottenham to Barcelona and I have appeared for nothing for him a few times. Friendship is surely about sticking together through thick and thin. Thus enthused, I left a cheery message on Tel's answerphone and I'll take him to lunch.

When El Tel was sacked by Leeds early in 2003, Collins had another go at him without mentioning at any point that he had had his best six players sold from under him. I was disappointed such a fine journalist could write such a lop-sided piece.

Unlike Collins, I was delighted a couple of years ago when another good friend, David Willis, asked me to do the turn at the National Sporting Club launching of El Tel's new book – published, of course, by Virgin. Terry had written about all his football heroes, some of whom were at the lunch. Jimmy Hill was one of them.

Jimmy has become a bit of a figure of fun to people who know no better. It's partly his own fault because he is always so ready to laugh at himself. Yet he is one of the great innovators in the game of football, maybe the greatest. Aside from full international honours (he did get a B international cap), he played at the highest level. He led the campaign to scrap football's maximum wage – something Beckham should send him a fiver for every morning – and he took Coventry City from the Fourth Division to the old First Division, now the Premiership. Until they were relegated two years ago they were the fourth longest-serving side in the top level, behind Arsenal, Everton and Liverpool. Perhaps most significantly, he also introduced three points for a win – a system copied now around the world.

Yet some people still think he's a bit of a prat.

Tel, a funny speaker in his own right, does a very good Jimmy Hill impersonation. To be fair, it's more Bruce Forsyth than Jimmy, but it's funny anyway. Venables told two stories on the day of the launch. One was from the time when Jim was playing football for Fulham. During one match Jimmy came off the pitch at half-time and said to skipper Johnny Haynes (who was also at the launch lunch), 'Johnny? The crowd are booing one of our players and I don't think it's very nice.' Remarked Tel, 'Jim, the most confident man I know, didn't think for one minute that they were booing him – which they were!' His second story was about the time when the two of them, long since retired, were walking out together on to the pitch at Goodison Park, Everton, to make a presentation. It didn't take long for the crowd to spot Jim, and they immediately started on him. 'Jimmy Hill's a wanker! Jimmy Hill's a wanker!' Tel said, 'Jimmy leant over to me and said, without the trace of a smile, "Y'know, they love me here." '

As usual, Jimmy took all this in good part. No matter what anyone says it all seems to wash over him and he remains his usual affable self. I think he really does believe that all publicity is good publicity. When I stood up and started into a routine about how Jim had bored me to death all through lunch (totally untrue), the audience started to feel some sympathy for him. In fact, I returned to this theme on several occasions throughout my act. Near the end, when I started on a joke about reading a label on a mineral water bottle just to get away from Jim, the audience was still laughing, but they were very much in his corner.

At this point, down in front of me, I heard Jim say something to Johnny Haynes which I then interrupted my joke to repeat to the audience. I said, 'I've just heard Jim say to Johnny Haynes, "I'm not even speaking and I've had more mentions than anyone else." ' The roof went off. I couldn't continue for several minutes. When I thought I might get back into the gag, Jim, with immaculate timing, stood up and took a bow. They rose to him again, laughing and cheering. Once again, I couldn't continue. And as the noise subsided and I drew breath, he got me one more time. He leapt from his seat again and said, without the use of or the need for a microphone, 'Sunday morning, Sky Sports, nine thirty.' They cheered him again. A couple more minutes elapsed, then I managed to finish the gag and get off, unable to follow any of that. We all went to Motcombs Wine Bar afterwards and were still laughing about it at midnight. A couple of years on, El Tel and I rarely speak without mentioning this lunch and lamenting the fact that we have no recording of it.

It was after this memorable lunch that Virgin came to me and said they thought there was a book in me.

But I don't know. I'm not sure there is.

_____

FINAL SCORE
Alloa 1 Cheerioa 2

_____

INDEX